THE PRACTICE OF SOUL-CENTERED HEALING

Vol. II: Navigating the Inner World

An Instructional Manual

Thomas Zinser, Ed.D.

Paperback, ISBN 978-0-9834294-3-2

Published by
Union Street Press
2701 Union SE
Grand Rapids MI 49507

To Jane,

And to my parents, Ken and Pearl Zinser

Contents

Introduction

This book is a companion volume to *The Practice of Soul-Centered Healing, Vol. I: Protocols and Procedures*[1]. Like Vol. I, it is written for hypnotherapists who wish to practice Soul-Centered Healing, or incorporate certain elements into their own practice. In Vol. I, the focus was on the protocols for working with ego-states, external entities, and etheric devices and energies found within a client's inner world, or affecting him or her from outside the self/soul.

This book draws a clinical map of the psychic and spirit dimensions of the self and soul. It offers a deeper and expanded look into the practice of Soul-Centered Healing as a process. The aim of healing is still the same—bringing Light to all parts of the self/soul that are dissociated, and where there is terror, pain, or darkness. The focus in this book is on various phenomena, inner conditions, and practices that can come into play in a client's healing process. New protocols for identifying and dealing with these different situations are provided, along with case examples and sample dialogues. Some of these will apply to all clients, such as the necessity for notetaking, or making sure the client's higher self is aware of the *energy point* in the body. Others, like dealing with the *dark spot* or retrieving missing parts of a soul, are situations that do not present with every client. They come up frequently enough, though, that it's good to be aware of them and prepared.

1 Hereafter referred to in this book as *Vol. I.*

Part 1
Record Keeping

1

Taking Notes: Ariadne's Thread

Backtracking

In Soul-Centered Healing, taking notes as you work with a client is a necessary part of the practice. Without these notes, you will become lost in your client's inner world, get knocked off track, or twisted around. The notes will help prevent this. They serve several purposes, the most important being that they will enable you to backtrack. In working with a client, you never know when you will encounter a block, and when you do, you never know how easy or difficult it will be to resolve.

Some blocks can be quite complex, involving a network or chain of ego-states, entities, and/or devices. Often, so much is presenting that the therapist moves from one phenomenon to another, using several different protocols. Working only through *yes/no* questions and ideomotor signals, it's very easy to become confused or diverted when dealing with an inner world we cannot see. Any number of blocks might interfere with the healing process. In some cases, by the time those blocks are resolved—which may take several sessions—you won't remember where you were or who you were working with when the block first occurred.

This is when you will have to refer to your notes and retrace your steps back to the particular ego-state, spirit, or issue you were dealing with when the block presented. Whatever or whoever it was, it was left unresolved, and the therapeutic question is whether you need to return to it and resolve it. In my experience, the answer to that question most of the time is *yes*.

Occasionally, a higher self will communicate that it's better to continue on the course that has opened up and that there's no need to go back. Most of the time, though, it will be important to backtrack and resolve the situation before continuing, either on the same course or on a new track. It would be impossible for a therapist to remember in detail from one session to the next, and from one client to the next, what has occurred in previous sessions and what was left unfinished. Yet, these are the details we have to come back to once the block or detour has been resolved.

In one session, for example, you might identify an ego-state and find out that it is part of a group of seven, three of whom are being tormented by a spirit. It could take five sessions to work through that group in terms of resolving the spirit attachment, and then helping the ego-states move through the sharing and release. In the process, you might have to: 1) deal with devices that the spirit put into place before it left; 2) help a terrified ego-state share its experience in small increments; and 3) deal with an ego-state from outside the group of seven that has come forward to block the group's sharing because its own pain has been triggered.

If you decide that it's more important to continue working with the group, you may need to ask higher self to move the triggered ego-state to a safe place and come back to it in a later session. In all your work, with all your clients, it is unlikely that you are going to remember that ego-state several weeks later, or the context in which it presented. The ability to backtrack ensures that you can return to it once the present group is resolved.

Here's another scenario: the client's higher self identifies an ego-state to work with. It agrees to communicate, receives Light, but then all communication stops. Working with the higher self, and using the protocols, you determine that the source of the block is a spirit operating from outside the client's self/soul. It refuses to disengage, so you have to find its access. In the process, you find out that it has five accesses to the inner world, seemingly spanning several lifetimes. Each access may involve an ego-state(s) and/or energy device(s) that has to be identified and resolved before all connections to the spirit are severed. As you see the extent of the spirit's involvement, severing its ties to the soul becomes the focus of treatment. Once all accesses have been closed and all ties severed, you go back to the original ego-state where the block began.

In the healing process, these kinds of blocks, as we have seen, are a frequent occurrence. This means that frequent backtracking will be called for, as well.

Reviewing

Backtracking serves a second important purpose. It enables the therapist, when necessary, to recount to the client details of what occurred at different points in the session. There are a number of reasons why a client might not remember clearly what happened. It may be that the inner work moved so quickly from one ego-state or entity to another that the conscious mind does not keep track. Clients may also have difficulty remembering because of the nature of trance itself. Much of the time, the conscious mind does not need to pay attention or be actively involved, and so the client's conscious awareness can phase in and out. Another major reason a client may not be able to recall details of a session is because the presenting material triggers an abreaction in which the intense emotion clouds out details of who and what are involved in the sharing. An abreaction, for example, may involve both present- and past-life ego-states, all of whom experienced a similar kind of trauma. It is also possible that a client may be amnesic for certain parts of the session due to internal blocks meant to protect the self or to stop the Light from entering. We know that therapy in general, and hypnotherapy in particular, can open up very frightening and painful areas for a client. Memories and revelations can come at any time triggering intense emotions, or psychological shock.

Like with blocks, we cannot predict what will present, how a client will react to it, and how much he or she will need to process it after coming out of trance. The only thing we can do is be ready to provide the details as the client consciously and emotionally begins to integrate what occurred in the session. Without notes, there will be times you won't be able to recall the twists and turns of a session, the interweaving of past- and present-life ego-states, or the particular vulnerability that a spirit used to create different accesses. Without notes, there are times you won't be able to recount for your client the sequence of events, or entities involved, leading up to his or her experience.

At the same time, we usually cannot explain to the client all that presented in the session or what it all means. We're never in a position to do this. We can offer insights, observations, or point out connections, but it is the client who needs to find where the pieces fit. We cannot offer clients the meaning of their own experience. The notes allow us to reflect back to a client, when necessary, what presented in the session. The more accurate and detailed the reflection, the more likely the client will reconnect with it cognitively and emotionally.

This kind of review, where a client needs to go over what happened in a session, can extend into past sessions as well. Clients sometimes ask to review previous sessions as new material comes forward that brings a new understanding or perspective to what presented in those past sessions. You, or your client, might make connections to earlier sessions and recognize a significant pattern that points to the root of a client's pain. For example, you might find that a spirit entity that is interfering is one you thought had been taken care of. Without your notes, you won't be able to go back and recount for yourself, or your client, the details of what happened in those sessions and how they relate to the present recurrence.

Continuity

Finally, notes accumulate from session to session. The ability to backtrack over several sessions means, over time, the ability to backtrack and review all of a client's sessions. If necessary, a therapist could sit down with a client's notes and retrace his or her healing process from the beginning. I seldom have to do a full review. When I do, it's usually in order for me to get an overview and take stock of a client's treatment. Occasionally, a client may also ask to do a partial review.

Shorthand Notes

Taking notes at each step in a client's healing process may sound daunting. However, the repetitive nature of the protocols, each with a repeating sequence of steps, lends itself to the development of a shorthand code. For example, whenever I read in my notes the sentence, "HS sends light," I know that whatever ego-state or entity I was working with had agreed to receive light, and that I asked the higher self or a spirit guide to send Light. If the next line reads, "Received," it means I have asked the ego-state or entity whether it has received the Light, whether it feels good and comfortable with it, and whether it wishes to keep the Light for itself. I do not need to write all of that out. It's what I always do with ego-states, spirits, and other entities I encounter. I ask them to receive the Light and then confirm that it was received.

This same thing is true for most of the inner work. If I read, "HS reviews," I know that I was asking the client's higher self at that time to review inside for the source of a problem, an answer to a question, or the cause of a block. I know the next line will tell me what it found or didn't find. If I see "PLMA," I would know that higher self had identified a past-life, male, adult ego-state. Its name, if it has given one, will be on the next line. This kind of shorthand applies to most of the steps in the healing process. In part, it's like keeping a checklist.

Most of the time, I don't need to write the details of how each step was accomplished; I just need to know that it was. I don't need to know in what form the higher self appeared to an ego-state. I just need to know that the contact was made. When higher self communicates that a separate entity is present, I don't need to know the details about that entity if the higher self also communicates that it can be removed immediately. During a session, a few words or a sentence is usually all it takes to summarize each step.

The one step where I frequently write in greater detail is when an ego-state is sharing its experience to the conscious self. In hypnotherapy, these are called critical experiences. Whether from present life or past life, it's an experience where self/soul consciousness fragmented or dissociated, usually because of overwhelming pain, terror, or confusion. We could say that healing these critical experiences is what the healing process is all about. Understandably enough, these are also the experiences a client will usually come back to when he or she needs to talk about what happened in the session. This is where the value of the notes and details come into play.

I will write as much detail as I can at these points, but I also try not to disrupt the momentum and flow of the session. It's a balancing act. I do the best I can to get the gist of what is being shared, but from my point of view, the priority is the client's experience of the process. If necessary, I will go back after the session and fill in more details that I did not have time to write during the process.

The second thing about these critical experiences is that they are also the points where we most often encounter resistance or blocking.

It may be an ego-state that stops its sharing in order to stop feeling the pain. It may be an ego-state blocking another because its own pain has been triggered. It may be the conscious self or the protective part that stops the sharing because it is threatening to overwhelm the person. It may be a spirit that blocks the sharing because it is information that will reveal its presence. These are examples where we can run into complex blocks and will later need to backtrack.

Sample Notations

The following are examples of standard phrases I use in my practice. Again, these are my abbreviations and phrases. Someone else could develop a different system of phrases and abbreviations. The point is that some shorthand method will be necessary for taking notes while remaining focused on the client and the healing process. These are examples of repeating phrases I use. They give you some idea of how I abbreviate as I move through each step of a protocol. I cannot put these phrases in a particular order because they are all used at differ-ent times and in different contexts throughout a session. If you have read Vol. I, then you will already have seen many of these phrases and abbreviations.

1) *HS identifies someone*
2) *Sep from s/s –* (Where *Sep* means *separate* and *s/s* means *self/soul.*)
3) *HS identifies something*
4) *an energy, part of s/s*
5) *a sep energy*
6) *a device/object, part of s/s*
7) *a device/object, sep*
8) *HS sends Light*
9) *Received*
10) *Stopped*
11) *Blocked*
12) *refuses Light*
13) *willing to look inside*
14) *afraid to look inside*
15) *willing for guide to come forward*
16) *receives comm (communication)*
17) *comm stopped*
18) *HS reviews inside*

19) HS shows place of Int. – (Where *Int.* means *Integration.*)
20) HS helps them have CE – (Where *CE* refers to a *conscious experience.*)
21) *willing to share*
22) *now sharing*
23) *sharing again*
24) *HS comm about healing* – (Meaning that the higher self has communicated to the ego-state or ego-states information and knowledge about the healing process and how it/they can be free of pain and distress.)
25) *Received. In agreement* – (Meaning the ego-state(s) has received the information about healing and, when asked, communicated that it is in agreement and wished to have healing for itself.)

This type of shorthand notation makes it possible to record what is happening in a session without getting caught up in extraneous detail and description. This keeps the focus on the client and what is happening.

Part 2
The Diamond

2

The Energy Point/
Soul Connection

The Energy Point

An essential step in Soul-Centered Healing is to determine whether a client's higher self is aware of and in good connection with the energy point. Gerod first suggested this step when discussing ways in which the higher self might be helpful in a person's healing process.

According to Gerod, when a soul incarnates, an energy point is created in the heart center where the soul first touches and enters the body. He said the energy point is part of the body, and it is the vital link between the body and soul. He described it as an umbilicus, through which Light energy flows to the person, and personal experience flows to the soul. Without the energy point, he said, the body would die. Once created, the energy point acts as the central conduit for the soul's Light. Using one of Gerod's analogies, the energy point 'steps down' the Light energy to a physical level compatible with the body.

Here is an excerpt from a session where he described the energy point.

There is a spark of energy within each person that is most certainly the divine point within them. It is the place where the soul, upon entering the body, slips into place, so to say, and there is an engagement that creates life. Without both parts there will not be a physical and spiritual body to move a person through the existence that they have chosen for themselves. …And when that piece leaves, there will be most certainly death because the soul cannot remain without that part. (Session #99—July 15, 1989)

As a vital link, I think of the energy point as the soul's anchor in the body and central reference in physical reality. It is the one point in the body that always has direct connection to the Light.

Many people who have an out-of-body experience see a silver cord that they know leads back to their physical body. Many of these same people report an initial anxiety about whether they would be able to return to their body should the cord break or be severed. If one were able to follow that cord back to the body, I wouldn't be surprised if it led to the energy point and the self/soul connection. I don't know, but it might be the last point the soul touches as it vacates the body at death. It's a speculation.

Gerod's suggestion was to ask the higher self whether it was aware of this energy point. This caught my attention because it contradicted something I thought would be obvious, i.e., that a higher self would always be aware of the self/soul connection. Gerod talked about it, though, as if it could be veiled, hidden, or blocked from the higher self, or the higher self could be somewhat dormant, or idling in place. Whatever the case, it implied a level of disconnect or diminishment within the person. And when this is the case with a client, Gerod's suggestion was to facilitate the higher self's awareness and reconnection to its source, the soul.

He said many people already have a good connection with their higher self. However, he said others had a higher self that was not fully awakened to what it is, i.e., a direct conduit to the soul's Light. He said a higher self may not be functioning highly because it was suppressed or blocked in the person's early childhood, or it may have been hidden because of the approach, or even intrusion, by dark spirits or entities. I asked Gerod if he could suggest a way to assess a person's higher self or help it to become awake and active.

The following excerpt is from the session when Gerod first identified the energy point and said that it would be helpful to make sure the higher self was aware of it.

G.   One important question is to ask the higher self to go within and discover that point that it is. To go inside and discover where it exists. To find that energy point within the physical being. A higher self that is aware and active and growing and doing well will be able to respond that it can find that energy point and that it does feel it and it can connect to it. If it cannot find it, then you will know that you have a higher self that is unsure, not well connected, and in need of direction, and you can suggest to it what to look for.

T.   Let me first ask you to talk a little bit about this energy point. I think we've already been talking about it, but this energy point sounds like that link to the Light.

G.   That is, and it is the soul. It is the point of the soul, it is the energy of the soul, and it is that point where the light comes in. Each body has the light within it in the form of the soul. If you picture this body and you picture the soul as a mass of matter, it would be as a lump, but it is a lump of energy. And the higher self who cannot find that lump of energy is not in good connection with the soul which it is part of; and if it is not in good connection with the soul which it is part of, then it is also not in good connection with the incoming energy and Light. And in order to move along, it needs to have that connection. And if you ask it if it can find that energy within the body and feel it, then you know you have directed it and grounded it well to the body, and you know that you have a higher self that is ready to move along and to understand. It will more readily respond, "Of course I know where that energy is, I am part of it and I can feel it and I see it and I am it."

T.   Would it be accurate or appropriate, Gerod, to say that this linking up would be a primary first step in helping at this level?

G.   I think it would be a very important step. Because what will happen, especially if you are working with someone who is not open to working consciously, your question will be quite non-offensive. They must know that there is a spark of something in them that keeps this heart beating and this body moving, and that is one way of describing it. They may consciously understand what you are saying in a way that they wish to, but the inner self and the higher self will most definitely understand it in the way that is important for you to assist them. And if you are not able to continue working with these persons, to continue truly being of assistance to them because of their inability to work at this level, or their fear or their lack of acceptance, what you have done by making this first assessment and asking this first question and suggesting to the higher self about finding this point, is that if you never see this person again, you have done them one service most definitely and you have opened up a door for them.

T.　Yes, I believe that from what I've seen.

G.　It is a provoking question to ask.

T.　A second question, Gerod—a next step—could you give some framework or picture of what a second step might involve as far as how a higher self might be best assisted to accomplish its aims in line with the body, the personality?

G.　Well, the second step is not too far removed from the first step in that it is just a strong connection with that energy point. That in itself will accomplish much. And if you find a higher self that cannot seem to find this energy point, then you will have to describe to it what it will feel like. That it will be a strong vibration, that it will be almost a hum, it will be almost a tingle. To describe it almost in that physical sense because the higher self is then relating more to the physical body than to the spirit body. And once that higher self can find it and experience it, it will draw more energy to itself, more strength, more confidence, and more confidence in you. Just as when in the past you have gone in looking for spirits and you go armed with names, you go armed with information, there is a greater respect, a greater trust, and a greater alliance with you. Thus the same with the higher self—once you are able to offer it something that is concrete, that is usable, it will be able to gain the confidence and the strength and energy to communicate and to help you.

T.　And when that link is there and the higher self has come to that awareness, how might I help from that point? Does the higher self know then exactly what to do or are there some things...

G.　Now, it will not know exactly what to do. You will have to continue its education process somewhat, except that it will be able to trust you better and will be better able to understand because of the higher level of energy and the renewedness that it will feel. The higher self will then be able to better take in information from the universe. It will be able to engage the intuitive process in a greater strength, which then, of course, will link it to the consciousness and that is what you need to do, because that causes an empowering of the conscious mind. (Session #58—November 18, 1988)

After this session, a higher self's awareness or not of the energy point became another focus in my dialogues with Gerod. I began testing his information with many clients. It appeared to be a simple procedure: check whether a client's higher self is aware of the energy point, and if it wasn't, help the higher self to find it.

The results confirmed what Gerod had said. In most cases, the higher self seemed to readily understand what I was describing and signaled that it was aware of the energy point. In those cases where the higher self wasn't aware, it was usually able to find it when directed to look for "that hum or vibration," as Gerod suggested.

It didn't take long, however, to discover that the situation with the energy point could be more complex than initially thought. There were cases where the higher self had trouble finding the energy point, or if it did, there was a problem with the energy point/soul connection itself. Before discussing this further, though, I need to talk about the body and the language of energetics.

Energetics

In the context of healing, subtle energies refer to levels of energy not able to be perceived through our physical senses. Much of what we know about these energies comes from the eastern and indigenous cultures. The *chakras*, the *meridians*, the *energy bodies*, the *aura* are all terms referring to different energetic dynamics or levels of a person. These energies themselves are generally held to be manifestations of, and sustained by, the universal energy called Chi (from Chinese), Prana (Indian), or Ki (Japanese), and what I call the Light.

In our Western culture, we are coming to these energetics lately. Einstein demonstrated a hundred years ago that mass equals energy— $E = mc^2$. Everything is energy. If we could view our bodies at subatomic levels, what would we see? We know in the back of our minds that we are energy beings. Other cultures have recognized this for a long time and have identified subtle and distinct levels of energy comprising the body, and some extending to mental, psychic, and spiritual levels, as well. They also recognized that there could be damage, injury, or interference at these energetic levels just as there can be at the physical.

In our own culture, we lack a scientific paradigm and language by which to talk about and deal with these subtle energies. Empirical science does not even acknowledge that they exist. It's the source of resistance in the medical field, for example, to treatments such as acupuncture that uses needles to affect the flow of an invisible energy through invisible meridians running throughout the body. What is "evidence-based" medicine to do with this? It is an example of the dichotomy that science has created by declaring matter to be the ground of all reality.

In the context of healing, this means whole dimensions of the self and soul are excluded from having any relevance or importance in a person's health and wellbeing. This stance also shuts down the debate about mind over matter. The potential of a person's mind and consciousness to affect his or her own energy levels is dismissed as "placebo effect" or "spontaneous remission," as if that explains it.

Before I met Gerod, I also was aware of the popular energy terms, but I had no real knowledge and understanding of what they were about, or how they might be relevant to one's mental and emotional health. This changed almost immediately after I began the collaboration with Gerod. So much of what he talked about concerning clients, and reality in general, was couched in a language of energy. Just as he talked matter-of-factly about the soul, the existence of spirits, and reincarnation, he also talked matter-of-factly about energy dynamics occurring within a person and between people. His point of view, as I gradually came to understand, was absolute Einstein: everything is energy (at all levels).

It is far beyond the scope of this book to give an exposition on subtle energies or energy healing. There are so many different ways to classify and understand these energies, depending on different cultures and traditions, that I cannot offer an integrated model. I'm also aware that there are myriad healers around the world practicing different forms of energy healing. In essence, Soul-Centered Healing, too, is a form of energy healing. Its central aim for a person is to clear blockages and impediments to the Light. SCH is in basic agreement that these energetic levels do exist and that they can be an important factor in a person's healing process. This includes not only the subtle energies comprising the body, but the mental, psychic, and spiritual levels of energy and consciousness as well.

This point of view is implied in everything I've written. I want to be more explicit about it here because much of what I will be writing about in this book needs to be understood from this energetic point of view. Even ego-states, higher selves, spirits, and the soul itself could be viewed as different levels and forms of energy/consciousness. The integration of an ego-state, in my mind, can just as easily be viewed as one energy coming into attunement with another.

In the healing process, there can be problems within the client's own energy levels. The energy flow in one or more chakras, for example, might be blocked, damaged, or out of balance as a result of physical injury, emotional trauma, or psychic or spiritual pain. Emotional energy may be somaticized and stored in a particular area of the body. The higher self might identify a dark energy located in a specific area of the client's aura that needs to be reintegrated or expelled.

Sometimes there can be interference or disruption in a client's energy field due to external causes. It might involve a psychic attack by another person. It may be a spirit or other kind of entity that has accessed a person at an unconscious level and whose activities are affecting the person energetically. Sometimes there is external energy that has impacted or even entered a client's energy field that needs to be found and cleared.

I believe we are on the brink of a paradigm shift in which consciousness, not matter, will be accepted as the ground of all reality. I also believe this shift will bring with it a revaluation of material causality. The recognition of consciousness, as a force in itself, will change the debate about mind over matter from *whether* consciousness affects matter to *how* it affects matter. What are its limitations and what is its potential? In the context of healing, the power of the mind to heal the body may very well become a science of the placebo.

The Energy Point/Soul Connection

Returning now to the energy point, it is one of those phenomena that must be understood energetically. Its linkage with the soul is an energy link. It exists at a subtle level, as does the soul. I said earlier that in most cases a client's higher self was aware of the energy point, and if it wasn't, it could usually find it readily once given direction. The bigger problem was finding the energy point and then learning there was a problem with the energy point/soul connection itself.

I found that this connection could be impaired or damaged in a number of ways. Usually, the impairment was the result of present-life trauma. However, past-life trauma, if significant enough, can also break through to affect the soul's present incarnation and the self/soul connection. In addition, attacks or intrusions by spirits or outside entities can also affect the connection. I learned about these different problems on a case-by-case basis, and it took a number of years to reach a general understanding and develop an approach for healing the energy point/soul connection when necessary.

Going back to Gerod's view, the soul first touches the body in the heart-center creating the energy point, allowing the soul to join the body. From that point, as I picture it, the soul's Light emanates instantaneously throughout the body. If the connection remains undisturbed, then the energy point and soul usually remain joined in the heart-center. However, as a response to trauma, pain, or threat, the energy point/soul can be moved out of the heart center to another area of the body. You might look at it as the soul's version of the shell game. In my experience, when this has happened with a client, it was almost always as a protective move. It makes sense that this vital link would be especially protected. At the time, though, I didn't understand how this connection could move around the body, and how such a move affected a person, consciously or unconsciously. I also did not understand why one area of the body was chosen over another as the best place to lodge.

There is little more I can say beyond this in a general way. Each time I find this displacement with a client, it's a unique situation involving many individual factors. From a clinical point of view, it's not always necessary to understand why it happened, or at what specific moment in the client's past it occurred. Sometimes this information comes through very clearly, and other times not. The aim, in any case, is to heal the trauma or remove the threat so the energy point/soul can return to its natural seat in the heart-center.

Besides moving the connection to another area of the body, there is a second layer of defense used by the self/soul to protect the connection at this level. The energy point/soul connection can be encapsulated. It can be wrapped in an energy, or sealed in a container, or carried within an ego-state. When this is the case, the aim of treatment is to free the energy point/soul connection from the encapsulation using the basic protocols, and return it to the heart-center, if it has been moved.

In terms of treatment, these two defenses lead to four configurations. The energy point/soul connection is:

- in the heart-center, free (optimal, no treatment needed)
- in the heart-center, encapsulated
- outside the heart-center, free
- outside the heart-center, encapsulated.

The Energy Point and Soul Separated

There is a third level of defense that complicates the assessment of the energy point/soul connection. This defense is the ability for the soul and energy point to be separated. It's not a severing, but an alteration in the energy connection. Sometimes the separation seems for the benefit of the soul—like when under attack by dark spirits, abuse by a perpetrator, or oppressed by darkness. Sometimes, it seems for the benefit of the body, where the separation acts as a buffer, bringing a level of numbness in physical sensation, or suppression of intense emotions. Again, the soul's emanation continues, but it's as though it flows through a set of filters or switches in some combination of separation, encapsulation, and or displacement.

The downside of this defense is that once the energy point and soul separate, they do not appear to rejoin on their own. It's not out of resistance necessarily, as much as there being no need to move again, even after the trauma or threat has passed. It's also very possible that whatever precipitated the separation may involve someone, something, or some energy that is still in place and would block any rejoining of the energy point and soul.

What complicates the separation even more is that the defenses for the energy point/soul connection—displacement and encapsulation—are possible for each. Once the soul and energy point separate, each is free to move to another area of the body. One can remain in the heart center and the other move to another location, or they can both move out of the heart-center. Also, if the energy point and soul have separated, one or both can be encapsulated within someone or something. I view it as the self/soul creating layers of protection for this vital connection.

From a clinical point of view, the separation of the energy point and soul increases significantly the possible conditions you will find with a client's energy point/soul connection. The number of possibilities increases from four, when the two are joined, to sixteen configurations if the two are separated. From a therapeutic point of view, it means peeling back those layers of defense until both energy point and soul are free to return to the heart-center and rejoin.

The following is the list of the possible conditions you might find when the energy point and soul have been separated. It's not important that you remember these possibilities right now. It's a list that can be referred to when needed.

If the Energy Point and Soul are Separated

1) Both in the heart-center; both free. (Just need to be rejoined. No further treatment needed.)
2) Both in the heart-center; the energy point encapsulated, the soul free.
3) Both in the heart-center; the soul encapsulated, the energy point free.
4) Both in the heart-center, both encapsulated.

5) Energy point in the heart-center, free. The soul outside the heart-center, free.
6) Energy point in the heart-center, free. The soul outside the heart-center, encapsulated.
7) Energy point in the heart-center, encapsulated. The soul outside the heart-center, free.
8) Energy point in the heart-center, encapsulated. The soul outside the heart-center, encapsulated.

9) Soul in the heart-center, free. The energy point outside the heart-center, free.
10) Soul in the heart-center, free. The energy point outside the heart-center, encapsulated.
11) Soul in the heart-center, encapsulated. The energy point outside the heart-center, free.
12) Soul in the heart-center, encapsulated. The energy point outside the heart-center, encapsulated.

13) Energy point outside the heart-center, free. The soul outside the heart-center, free.

14) Energy point outside the heart-center, free. The soul outside the heart-center, encapsulated.

15) Energy point outside the heart-center, encapsulated. The soul outside the heart-center, free.

16) Energy point outside the heart-center, encapsulated. The soul outside the heart-center, encapsulated.

If put into abbreviated form, these same possibilities can be written like this:

If the Energy Point and Soul are Separated (Abbreviated)

1) both in HC; both free to rejoin
2) both in HC; EP enc.; SO free.
3) both in HC; SO enc.; EP free
4) both in HC, each enc.

5) EP in HC, free. SO outside HC, free.
6) EP in HC, free. SO outside HC, enc.
7) EP in HC, enc. SO outside HC, free.
8) EP in HC, enc. SO outside HC, enc.

9) SO in HC, free. EP outside HC, free.
10) SO in HC, free. EP outside HC, enc.
11) SO in HC, enc. EP outside HC, free.
12) SO in HC, enc. EP outside HC, enc.

13) EP outside HC, free. SO outside HC, free.
14) EP outside HC, free. SO outside HC, enc.
15) EP outside HC, enc. SO outside HC, free.
16) EP outside HC, enc. SO outside HC, enc.

Generally speaking, the most complex condition would be number sixteen. The energy point and soul are separated; each has moved to another area of the body; and each has been encapsulated. The complexity, however, is not a predictor of difficulty. You could have one of the simplest conditions where the energy point and soul are still joined and in the heart-center, but encapsulated in a bubble of energy. When you ask higher self to dissipate the energy, you find that it is blocked from doing that because the energy is being held in place by an ego-state who created it under threat by a dark soul. On the other hand, you might find the most complex condition and find that higher self can free both and rejoin them in the heart-center all in one session. Whatever the condition, though, the process is to undo each layer of defense. I view this procedure energetically as a realigning of the body/mind/soul connection so that the conduit between self and soul is fully open and direct.

The Diamond Protocol is designed to identify which of these possible conditions applies to a particular client. Like the other protocols, it is a series of questions in the form of a decision tree that identifies a specific condition through a process of elimination.

3

The Diamond Protocol

Joined or Separate? Two Branches.

In the healing process, once it has been determined that a client's higher self is aware of the energy point, the next step is to assess the condition of the energy point/soul connection and determine whether any of the conditions listed previously apply. Over the years, I developed a protocol for carrying out this assessment using ideomotor signaling. I call it the *Diamond Protocol*, for reasons I will explain later.

Once the higher self has agreed that it's appropriate to ask about the energy point/soul connection, the first question is whether they are still joined. If they are, I take it as a good sign, even if it has moved out of the heart-center and/or has been encapsulated. I consider this union, or conjoining, to be its natural state, so when it is intact, I see it as some sign of strength and integrity of the self/soul connection. It also means there are only four possibilities to deal with, not sixteen. If there are problems with the connection, they are usually much easier to resolve when the two are still joined.

If the energy point and soul are joined in the heart-center and free of encapsulation, I consider it to be their optimal state, and there is usually nothing more that needs to be done about the self/soul connection. On the other hand, if it has moved to another part of the body and/or been encapsulated, these situations are addressed using the basic protocols depending on who or what is involved. Most of the time, if the connection is encapsulated, it is by an ego-state or a container created of soul-source energy. I have seen instances, however, where the soul is corralled or boxed-in by a spirit or outside entity. It's not encapsulated, but its freedom to move is restricted. On rare occasions, I have encountered an inhabiting spirit that encapsulates the client's energy point. From my point of view, this situation calls for immediate treatment.

So far, the protocol for assessing the energy point/soul connection (ESC) would look like the diagram in Figure 3.1.

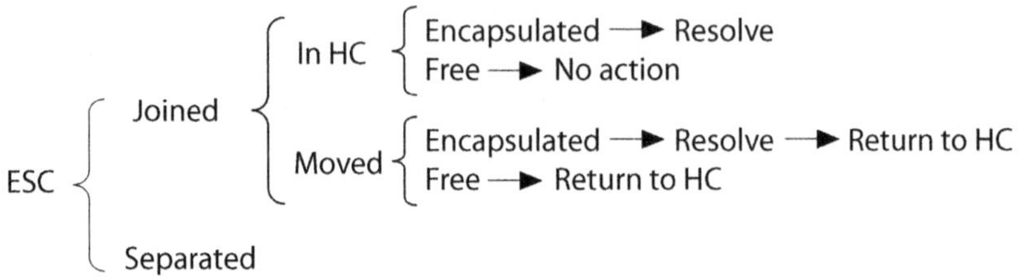

Figure 3.1

If the energy point and soul have been separated, the next step is to determine the specific configuration. Which of the sixteen possibilities are we dealing with? In a best-case scenario, the higher self can respond to questions about each one, and the specific condition can be determined fairly quickly. However, it is not unusual, that the first one identified may need to be worked with before going on to the other. The protocol does not specify which one to start with and what sequence needs to be followed, as long as the end result is that they are rejoined in the heart-center. Unless it is self-evident, I normally will ask the higher self which one is best to start with.

Once that is decided, the next step is to ask higher self to determine its location in the body. As a kind of internal check, I do not mention anything about the heart-center. Through a series of yes/no questions, I let the higher self tell me where the energy point or soul is located in the body. Once it has been located, the question is whether it is free to move or is encapsulated. If it is encapsulated, then most of the time it will be more effective to deal with that first before trying to return it to the heart-center.

Looking at all the possible configurations together, the full protocol would look like the diagram in Figure 3.2.

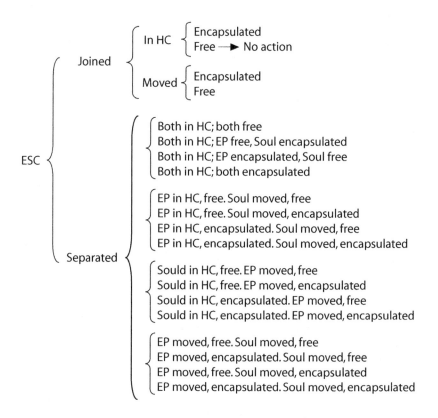

Figure 3.2

Preliminary Considerations

There is no fixed point in the healing process for when to inquire about the client's energy point or to assess the energy point/soul connection. I usually wait until good signals and reliable communication have been established with the higher self and the inner work has begun. If the higher self seems confused or hesitant in the beginning, I may ask about the energy point early in treatment. Otherwise, I rely on my intuition or wait for a natural transition. For some people, there needs to be a certain level of healing and readiness before addressing an encapsulated energy point or soul. The process may also happen in stages. When both have been encapsulated, one might be worked with early in the treatment, and the other needs to wait until later. I rely on the higher self to help determine the best sequence in which to do this.

Before starting the assessment, however, there are two things to keep in mind. The first involves a dilemma. Gerod cautioned me that sometimes it is better to wait before dealing with the energy point/soul connection. Even if there are problems with the connection, he said the healing process might require a certain sequence of steps before addressing it directly. The dilemma is how to ask about the energy point/soul connection without triggering it prematurely. Since I cannot know ahead of time the condition of the client's energy point/soul connection, there is always a risk that it carries significant trauma. At the same time, if I think it may be a significant issue for my client and I don't ask about it, then I cannot assess whether it needs to be addressed directly.

There's no sure way around this dilemma, but the Diamond Protocol tries to minimize this possibility by asking the higher self whether it is even appropriate to ask about the self/soul connection at that time. If the response is *yes*, then the protocol is designed to identify which of the conditions listed above applies to the client. As with the other protocols, it's a process by elimination in as few steps as possible. In the end, I do not overly worry about triggering the issue out of sequence. My view is that if there is a problem, it will need to be addressed at some point, and for my client, it would be better to deal with it too early than too late.

The second thing to be aware of is that addressing the energy point/ soul connection can create a break in the continuity of treatment. It can lead to a positive, but lengthy detour, and require several sessions to fully resolve. If this happens, you need to be ready to backtrack if necessary. Addressing the energy point/soul connection can also take the healing process in a new direction or to a new level. This is especially true when the energy point and soul have been separated. (This also is where backtracking will come into play later.)

Because you cannot predict where things will go once you ask about the energy point/soul connection, it's good to be ready to work with the higher self to determine the best steps to take at each point.

The Protocol

The protocol for addressing the energy point/soul connection can only be specified up to a point. The steps I list here are all part of the Diamond Protocol, but the sequence can vary a little from one client to the next depending on how it presents. The protocol is also constructed in such a way that I've tried to eliminate or minimize leading questions. The protocol begins when the client's higher self is asked whether it is aware of the energy point. This step naturally raises the question of whether the energy point and soul are joined, and if they are not, then what is their condition?

In general, these are the steps in the protocol:

1) Ask higher self if it is aware of the energy point.
2) If not, help higher self locate the energy point.
3) When higher self is aware, ask if it knows where the energy point is located in the body.
4) Use elimination process to determine from higher self the energy point's location. (I do not mention the heart-center ahead of time.)
5) Once located, ask higher self if the energy point is joined with the soul.
6) If yes, is it free or encapsulated?
7) If separated, ask for higher self's agreement about working with it at this time.
8) If yes, determine which to work with first.
9) Determine whether it has been moved or encapsulated.
10) If yes, use appropriate protocols to identify and resolve any encapsulation and return it to the heart-center.
11) Treatment concludes when energy point and soul are both free and rejoined in heart center.

The following is a sample dialogue using the Diamond Protocol.

Diamond Protocol: Example 1

Th. Higher self, are you aware of the energy point in the body, that point that is your original connection to the body?

HS Yes finger lifts.

Th. Higher self, if it would be good to ask about the energy point/soul connection now, first finger lifting. If better to wait on that, the second finger can lift.

HS First finger lifts.

Th. Do you know, higher self, where the energy point is located in the body?

HS   Yes finger lifts.

Th.   If it's above the waist, first finger lifting, if below the waist, second finger.

HS   First finger lifts.

Th.   If it's below the neck, first finger lifting. If it is in the neck or above, the second finger can lift.

HS   First finger lifts.

Th.   If it is below the heart-center, first finger lifting. If in the heart-center or above, the second finger.

HS   Second finger lifts.

Th.   If it is in the heart-center, first finger. If it is above the heart-center, the second finger.

HS   First finger lifts.

Th.   Higher self, if the energy point and soul are joined there, the first finger can lift. If they are separated, the second finger can lift.

HS   Second finger lifts.

Th.   Higher self, I know that sometimes an energy point can be encapsulated inside someone or something. If the energy point is free to move, first finger lifting. If it is encapsulated or blocked in some way, the second finger can lift.

HS   Second finger lifts.

Th.   If it is encapsulated, first finger, if it is being blocked in some way, the second finger can lift.

HS   First finger lifts.

Th.   If it is encapsulated within someone, first finger. If within something, like an object or an energy, the second finger.

HS   First finger lifts.

Th.   Higher self, are you in agreement that we work with that one now? If so, first finger. If better to wait, or work with someone or something else first, second finger.

HS   First finger lifts.

Th.   Higher self, please help that one then to come forward here with me… And to this one, do you know yourself to be part of this soul I'm working with?

Es   Yes finger lifts.

At this point, the Ego-State Protocol would be used to identify the ego-state and prepare it, or its group, for sharing and release. The presumption is that once released of its pain or distress, the ego-state will be willing and able to release the energy point. The higher self, then, can return it to the heart-center, if it's not already there. Gerod called this type of ego-state that encapsulates the energy point, the *key of life*. I'll talk about this in a later section.

Diamond Protocol: Example 2

Th. Higher self, were you able to find that energy point?
HS Yes finger lifts.
Th. Do you know where the energy point is located in the body?
HS Yes finger lifts.
Th. If it is above the waist, first finger lifting, if below the waist, the second finger can lift.
HS Second finger lifts.
Th. If it is below the knees, first finger, if it is in a knee or above, the second finger can lift.
HS Second finger lifts.
Th. If it is in the knee, first finger, if above the knee, second finger.
HS Second finger lifts.
Th. If it is in the leg, first finger, if in the hip and pelvic area, second finger.
HS Second finger lifts.
Th. Higher self, are you aware now of where the soul is located?
HS Yes finger lifts.
Th. If the soul and energy point are joined, first finger. If they have been separated, second finger can lift.
HS Second finger lifts.
Th. Higher self, do you know where the soul is located in the body?
HS Yes finger lifts.
Th. If it is above the waist, first finger lifting, if below the waist, the second finger.
HS First finger lifts.
Th. If it is in the heart-center or above, first finger lifting. If below the heart center, the second finger can lift.
HS First finger lifts.
Th. If the soul is in the heart center, first finger lifting, if it's above the heart, second finger.
HS First finger lifts.

Th. Higher self, the soul is in the heart center, is that correct?

HS Yes finger lifts.

Th. If it is free, first finger. If it is encapsulated within someone or something, second finger lifting.

HS Second finger lifts.

Th. Higher self, if it would be best to work with the soul or energy point now, the first finger can lift. If we should wait on this, second finger lifting.

HS First finger lifts.

Th. If we should work with the energy point first, the first finger lifting, if the soul, then the second finger.

HS First finger lifts.

Th. Higher self, I know that sometimes the energy point is free to move and sometimes it can be encapsulated by someone or something. If the energy point is free to move, first finger. If it is encapsulated or blocked in some way, the second finger can lift.

HS Second finger lifts.

Th. If it is encapsulated, first finger, if blocked in some way, the second finger can lift.

HS First finger lifts.

Th. If it is encapsulated within someone, the first finger lifting, if something, like a device or an energy, the second finger.

HS Second finger lifts.

Th. Higher self, whatever is encapsulating the energy point, is it part of self/soul energy?

HS Yes finger lifts.

Th. If it is something like a device or an object, first finger, if more like an energy of some kind, the second finger can lift.

HS First finger lifts.

Th. Higher self, can that object be opened or dissipated now and the energy point freed?

HS Yes finger lifts.

Th. If the device or object needs to be dissipated and removed, first finger. If it should be reintegrated within the soul energy, second finger.

HS First finger lifts.

Th. Higher self, I'm going to ask, then, that you dissipate the device, and remove it from the energy point, and from the self/soul. On three:

one, two, three… and higher self, dissipate that device now, remove it from the self/soul. First finger when complete, second finger if there's a problem.

HS First finger lifts.

Th. Higher self, were you able to remove that device all right?

HS Yes finger lifts.

Th. Is the energy point free now?

HS Yes finger lifts.

Th. Higher self, are you in agreement that the heart-center is the best place for the energy point?

HS Yes finger lifts.

Th. Can the energy point return to the heart-center now? If so, first finger lifting, if not yet, the second finger can lift?

HS Second finger lifts.

Th. Higher self, if there is someone or something blocking that, first finger lifting. If there is something we need to do first, then the second finger can lift.

HS Second finger lifts.

Th. Higher self, if we need to address the soul first, the yes finger can lift, if someone or something else needs to be addressed first, the second finger lifting.

HS First finger lifts.

Th. Higher self, is the soul still in the heart-center?

HS Yes finger lifts.

Th. Is it encapsulated or being blocked in some way?

HS Yes finger lifts.

Th. If it is encapsulated, first finger, if blocked in some way, the second finger can lift.

HS First finger lifts.

Th. If it is encapsulated within someone, first finger, if in something, second finger.

HS First finger lifts.

Th. Is that one an ego-state?

HS Yes finger lifts.

Th. Is it one we should work with now?

HS Yes finger lifts.

Th. I'm going to ask that you help that one come forward here with me… and to this one, do you know yourself to be part of this self and soul I'm working with?

HS Yes finger lifts.

At this point in the process, the Ego-State Protocol is used to work with the ego-state for its sharing and release, and for the release of the soul. It may be a simple process, but it might also be quite complex depending on the ego-state, the experience in which it was created, whether there are others with it, etc. Ultimately, though, the aim is to free the soul, and then check again whether the energy point can be returned to the heart-center and the two rejoined.

Once the energy point and soul have been rejoined in the heart-center, I will ask higher self whether to go back to where we were before dealing with the energy point/soul connection, or whether there is someone or something else that would be best to address.

Diamond Protocol: Example 3

Th. Higher self, before we move to another part, I want to ask whether you are aware of the energy point, that point that is your first connection to the body? Are you aware of that energy point, higher self?

HS No finger lifts.

Th. I'm going to ask then that you look inside and find that hum, that vibration, that you've known since the beginning of this life. First finger if you find it, second finger if you do not.

HS First finger lifts.

Th. Higher self, I'm aware that the energy point is normally joined with the soul. Higher self, is the energy-point here still joined with the soul?

HS No finger lifts.

Th. Have they been separated?

HS Yes finger lifts.

Th. Higher self, I'm also aware that the energy point or the soul can be encapsulated within a part of the self. Higher self, has the energy-point here been encapsulated?

HS Yes finger lifts.

Th. If it's encapsulated by someone, first finger. If by something or some energy, the second finger can lift.

HS First finger lifts.

Th. If the soul has also been encapsulated, first finger lifting. If it is free, second finger.

HS Second finger lifts.

Th. Higher self, is the soul still in the heart center?

HS Yes finger lifts.

Th. Is the energy point still in the heart center?

HS No finger lifts.

Th. Do you see where it is in the body?

HS Yes finger lifts.

Th. If it's below the waist, first finger. If above the waist, second finger.

HS Second finger lifts.

Th. If it's above the heart center, first finger; if it is in the heart center or below it, second finger lifting.

HS First finger lifts.

Th. Higher self, if the energy point is above the neck, first finger. If it is located in the neck or below, second finger lifting.

HS First finger lifts.

Th. Higher self, the energy point is in the head, is that correct?

HS Yes finger lifts.

Th. Higher self, would it be most appropriate at this time to work with that one who carries the energy point?

HS Yes finger lifts.

Th. Please identify that one and help it come forward here with me. (Pause) To this one, as long as it's safe, are you willing to communicate with me?

HS Yes finger lifts.

Th. Do you know yourself to be part of this self and soul that I'm working with?

Es Yes finger lifts.

(The process continues here with the Ego-State Protocol.)

4

The Key of Life

Most of the time, when the energy point is encapsulated, it is being held within an ego-state. Gerod called this type of ego-state the *key of life*. It may be an infant that is hidden deep inside the self, or it might be a strong and active adolescent ego-state that exerts significant influence on the self at different times. Gerod viewed the *key of life* as having a special relationship to the self and the soul. It's as though by encapsulating this part of the soul/body connection, the key gains a more direct access to the soul than other ego-states do. According to Gerod, the key can be aware to some extent of past lives and gain a soul perspective. In the process, the key's expanded awareness and understanding then also becomes available to the self, whether consciously or unconsciously.

Sometimes the key knows it carries something special or has a special job, but usually it isn't aware of its significance or full potential. One of the aims of healing is to help the key come to this awareness. If the key is not aware of this potential, the higher self can help it to review and awaken to this knowledge.

The treatment of the key is the same as for other ego-states. There is an additional step, though. The key will need to release the energy point before it moves to its place of integration. I will usually ask higher self whether it's better to do this before or after the key's own sharing and release. Sometimes the key is not willing to surrender the energy point in the beginning, and it's only after its own healing and release that it understands and is willing to let it go. Once released, the higher self is asked to return the energy point to the heart-center and the key is moved to integration.

If a person's energy point is encapsulated by an ego-state, I assume that it affects him or her energetically. I also assume that it is a negative effect in that it's encapsulated within the ego-state's limited consciousness and perception. Finally, I assume that releasing the energy point and integrating the key enhances or attunes the energetic connections between the self and soul. Since I cannot observe these energetic conditions directly, I rely on the higher self or the key to confirm that a release of the energy point is the most appropriate step to take. This always gets a yes from the higher self. I can't think of an exception.

Because of the difficulty in conceptualizing the key of life, I want to use Gerod's own words. The following is an excerpt from the session in which Gerod introduced the terms energy point, key of life, and the perimeter. Gerod also talked about the separation of the energy point and the soul and about their ability to move. We were discussing a client session where I had encountered a strong and unusual ego-state named Selemica who shared her experience to the conscious level.

Before you read the excerpt, I'll provide a brief summary. Selemica was a present-life ego-state created partly from a past life experience. The client had been abused as a young child in her present life, and Selemica was created during the first instance. Once created, based on the past-life experience, Selemica's response to the trauma was to leave the body and return to the Light. Since she carried the energy point, if Selemica had left, the body would have died. To prevent this, Gerod said a perimeter was created to keep Selemica and the soul separated. The impression is that Selemica got a safe place to be—away from the trauma—and the soul remained incarnate, where it could continue its lessons and its journey.

In the discussion about Selemica and the soul, Gerod gave a great deal of information that could apply to many people, especially those who had suffered trauma or abuse. The thing to keep in mind is that every client where you find a key of life will have its own unique story. If I had not encountered Selemica, I'm sure that sooner or later I would have encountered one like her with another client.

T.   My understanding at this point is that Selemica was the part created and involved in what must have been the first trauma, which was so traumatic that it created the need for the splitting, and it put Selemica into a kind of in-between space, away from the memory and the feelings, but also in a place that she was aware of the Light and wanted to leave. At that time, it also seems that something happened with the soul. That either it went into a protective place, separate from the self, or went into a place with Selemica or close to Selemica. To this point is that accurate?

G.   Yes, it is.

T.   The term the key of life—you said Selemica is the "key of life"— meaning that part which is the body's spark of life or energy? Is she what you and I had talked about as the energy point?

G.   Most certainly.

T.   Is Selemica an ego-state?

G.   Yes, she is

T.   Now, Selemica did apparently continue to grow. She was created at three, but was six years old at the time I first communicated with her. How is it that Selemica continued to grow in this limited way from three to six?

G.   I will explain it to you this way. There is a spark of energy within each person that is most certainly the divine point within them. It is the place where the soul, upon entering the body, slips into place, so to say, and there is an engagement that creates life. Without both parts there will not be a physical and spiritual body to move a person through the existence that they have chosen for themselves.

The ego is there to protect, to keep the body alive, and when that energy point leaves, there will be most certainly death because the soul cannot remain without that part. And it is as if to say early on an experience of great trauma will affect that energy point, because that is the vital core of each person, and when there is an experience that goes to the very core of a person, then the ego must react in order to keep and protect, and there was an ego-state created around this core, around this divine spark and that is Selemica.

Selemica is also from the past. She is part of a memory of a past life that this person has lived, and Selemica is aware of this memory and she could share that also. So this is part of what is going on. Now continue to ask questions so I do not lose what it is you are looking for.

T.   That's all right. You may continue.

G.   So when, as if to say, this core then receives certain identity, it was almost as if the identity because of the knowledge it had of the past, of the present, and perhaps a very strong idea of the future, it is as if she chose to leave. And we could not allow that to occur and we would not remove free will from any person, but we will very strongly urge someone to something if it is important. So what Selemica has not remembered is that she chose to return. She would not want to remember that because what she has done has not been very happy for her, but she did choose to return and she knows this very much because she is in very strong communication with the soul. She is an ego-state, but she is more than an ego-state. She is the core. And she has maintained identity not only from becoming an ego-state because of the protection of the ego, but because she has drawn identity of the past, present, and future from the soul.

T. It's as if you're saying that at that moment of trauma, when protection was needed, there was in a sense this reaching into the past, somehow this moved to an identity?

G. It is almost like a desperate-measure step to try to understand what is unfolding.

T. Okay. When that happened, can you give some idea what happened to the soul?

G. Okay, the soul is there. This soul was a well protected soul, and Selemica has great knowledge of what is within the soul, the soul's purpose, and so there is great awareness of what is unfolding there. But the soul has been elusive, has moved, and has never been stationary in one place. Has moved throughout this person as needed for protection...

T. Once the trauma started. And has the soul moved about in this way because of how severely affected the core was by the things that happened?

G. Yes. And you will find that when you are working with people you will encounter the soul in various places, but it may be elusive even to you. It may move as the healing process takes place. The soul may even move about in response to that until there is some sense or trust and sureness of what is unfolding.

T. So would you say, Gerod, that for people in general... Well, let me go to the other extreme and say that if we're talking about someone who has suffered very little trauma, their life has been fairly supportive and nurturing, I would take it that the soul would in that life grow in a very integrated continuous way with the rest of it, the whole self would do that together.

G.   That's right.

T.   In people in general, what would lead to a soul needing in some way to separate or start to move, is it any time there is trauma, or is it particularly intense trauma? I know this probably cannot be pinned down exactly.

G.   It usually will have to do when there is a very strong disturbance in the self, and it does not even have to be necessarily a strong intense trauma because what for some will be extremely painful, for others it will not be because of the history of the soul, the reaction of the soul to it, so to say. The soul has to be protected because the soul is here to learn, to grow, and to go through experiences that are necessary for conscious growth and understanding, and when the choice has been for an extremely painful experience, it is stressful, it is painful to the whole being. And so there is some necessity for protection of the soul. Partly because when people are in this vulnerable position they are very vulnerable to many outside forces, to spirits, to strong influences. So it is almost like the soul is on an evasive tactic to protect itself from the side effects of the trauma, to try to keep itself intact and whole and safe until it is clear, so to say.

T.   If, in communicating in hypnosis with anyone, would that soul personality know itself to be that at all times and able to identify itself to me if it chooses to?

G.   Yes.

T.   Is there an optimal relationship between the self and soul we should be working toward?

G.   That is not extremely important. It is and it isn't. It is important that you know the soul is there, and that the soul has some awareness that there is some type of a cooperation that is going on and that you only need to know that it is there. It is not necessarily important to find the soul or to engage it, because as in this incident, there are other parts that have great awareness and are able to be the key players, so to say.

T.   So in some sense you're saying that to do the healing work and work with the ego states as we've been doing, that to do that, the soul will in a sense take care of itself in the process?

G.   Yes, it will.

T.   Okay. Yesterday at the beginning of the session, Gerod, when I asked Selemica to move into the wall and through it, there appeared to be a block. I asked about that block and a forty-one year old identified herself. I kind of had hints before that I was dealing with the soul. She identified herself as the soul and I asked her to join, well, let me ask first, is that accurate that the soul was blocking Selemica?

G.   No, the soul was not blocking her.

T.   Can you say what happened there?

G.   This forty-one year old is not actually the soul, but is past life experience from the soul, so in some way is part of the soul because of no great… how do I explain this, no great involvement with this life experience, although it has been part of it. A state re-created in this particular lifetime, almost like a phantom from the past that has come forward, has aged because of the age of the particular body, a very strong identification with that, but still not the soul. The soul is there, elusive, orbiting, moving. But this one, this forty-one year-old one, is not the soul.

T.   And she was not blocking Selemica?

G.   No.

T.   Was it basically just Selemica's fear that I was kind of running into at first?

G.   Yes. Selemica knows about the past and that this one is one more from the past.

T.   Was it important that this forty-one year old join with J.A.?

G.   I think that it is very fine that it has.

T.   Okay, my question would be, would there be difficulty if she had not joined her, if I had not identified her?

G.   I don't think great difficulty. It is like there is a perimeter and Selemica and this one have been outside the perimeter. So certainly for a fully functioning intact person to have everyone within (end of tape).

T.   Well, that's a good question maybe to throw out right now. The perimeter—it was clear that Selemica and this one were outside, wherever outside is. Can you talk to me about what the outside is?

G.   Certainly. It is as if all beings emanate from the center of themselves, the core. Ideally at the center is the diamond, created by the soul and created by this core. And everything emanates from this point. But when there is an imbalance, when there is something that is wrong, a perimeter is often times created. In a perfect example of one who is centered, the perimeter, you might say, exists, but the perimeter is all that is. One is unlimited, one is boundless. But when there is a separation of the soul and the core, there is a perimeter that is created. And in this instance Selemica was confined, so to say, to help her, to keep her safe, to keep her from feeling. That was her way of coping when she returned, and so she went outside the perimeter. And the perimeter was to keep some feeling, some functioning, some awareness there with the soul, which was inside the perimeter, so that this person could come through life functioning very well and coming to some understanding of what she is and what she is here to do. If Selemica had been on the other side of the perimeter, within, so to say, there would have a been a certain conflict. And because the core is so strong and the one that is the greatest influence, then there would have been a greater degree of unfeelingness, paralysis, so to say, and it could have taken much longer to come to this point of healing.

T.   If she had been inside.

G.   If she had been inside. The trauma effects would have been experienced in a greater way.

T.   Yes, right.

G.   So she was confined outside of this perimeter.

T.   I guess another question is how common might this be with people in general who have suffered some trauma in life, that the core would move outside of that perimeter?

G.   Not too uncommon.

T.   Based on what you're saying, the way things proceeded with J.A. in dealing with memories and other ego states, in a sense saving Selemica for last, was the most appropriate route to take in order to reduce as much as possible the feeling, the intensity, and reliving. Is that accurate?

G.   That is accurate.

T.   The core moving outside the perimeter. But it's as if you're saying there is almost a reflection of the core that is left in the perimeter to in some way function as a normal person, the body/soul connection.

G.   It might be called a reflection as long as the core is still within the body, then functioning can take place very well because life still exists, the energy is still there.

T.   So as long as she is in the body. Is there a particular part of the body that Selemica has resided in?

G.   No, not in particular because it is as if there is still movement, but there is a perimeter. There is a place that she has been physically more than another and that is over in the left side of the body, not too far away from the heart.

T.   When you and I talked about the energy point and you said to direct the higher self to find the energy point and that energy point can move within a person—be in different places—so there is no set place. The energy point…, it seems like from what you are saying that the energy point does not necessarily reside in an ego state. If that energy point has not needed to be protected, then would it remain in a "normal place" within a person?

G.   It probably would, in that it would find a place of comfort and stay there. There would not be as great of a need to move. Again, it's like speaking of the ideal, the unique, the perfect, where there is no trauma, there is a very high level unfolding and awareness, then it is as if there is no ego state at all. There is only one perfect whole state, and all parts then function without identity except as a part of the whole. (Session #99—July 15, 1989)

In Soul-Centered Healing, I think it's important to determine whether a key of life exists within the client's inner world, and if so, determine whether it needs to be addressed. When a key is present, I rely on the higher self to help make this determination. Having said that, I've always found it an important issue to address at some point. In these cases, release of the energy point is the primary aim, and healing of the key of life should occur whenever possible.

5

The Diamond

The Neutral Zone

The concept of the *key of life* added a new dimension to my understanding of the energy point/soul connection. The same is true for what Gerod called, "the diamond." He introduced the term while discussing a case in which the client had been so traumatized that her protective part appeared to be stuck within an ego-state's perception, and so was constantly in a state of alarm. Gerod suggested that the protective part could be moved to a "neutral zone" where it would perceive more clearly and be able to consciously refocus in the present. He described this neutral zone as a diamond-shaped area in the heart-center and that the higher self could help find it or create it. I wasn't quite sure which.

In the following dialogue, I am asking Gerod about the client and the protective part.

T.   Another question about B.R. that pertains to the ego. I believe that I have communicated with the ego and identified that part. And when I did, it seems to be a young child who is still in one of the abusive situations. My concern, of course, is that the ego will still employ those protective mechanisms from that child's point of view. I guess first of all I would ask if you could confirm or not whether that ego is *in* that child state.

G.   It would appear that it is, however, that is not permanent. The ego is somewhat ageless and free from that limit. It is, so to say, locked into it, but if removed, it will definitely become more adult-like, and that isn't even correct for me to say because the ego actually does not have any type of an age identity. It becomes locked into a particular memory place perhaps and then would seem to have the identity and the age of that particular memory, but in actuality the ego does not have that. Even present within a child, the ego is as it will be as an adult, but can in severe situations certainly become locked into one place as the mind becomes so fragmented that there seems to be no neutral zones or no safe territory.

Working with that particular memory, and continuing to address the ego very pointedly, would probably be a very good path to pursue—to remove it, to extricate the ego from the memory and to set it free, so to say, even to the point of imagining a neutral zone, a territory where it may be separated from the memories, where they may be on their own without actual ego functioning there within that particular ego state.

T.	If I could free the ego from that memory into a neutral place, would that neutral place then be described as a place where the ego would be in the present and have, then, some perspective on what has happened?

G.	I would suspect that it would. And it's like a piece of machinery and perhaps an assembly line piece of machinery, as something gets caught and clogged, it stays in one place and it needs to be extricated, allowing it to move on, and that seems to be the case here. And I don't perceive that you would have great difficulty helping the ego to remove itself from there. I don't think it will be too difficult to you. You have had experience addressing the ego, and I believe that you could do it, not necessarily to have it become greatly aware of the higher self or the soul or any of these states at this point in time, as it can make the choice to move into a neutral zone on its own.

T.	Okay, I will certainly give that a try.

G.	The neutral zone, too, I will tell you is diamond shaped.

T.	For everyone, or for her?

G.	Well, let's say that within everyone there is a diamond shape that is sometimes a neutral territory, that is a good place to work from. And for some people it will be there and it is necessary, but to visualize it, to help it create it, it is a diamond shape, not necessarily with any depth or great dimension, but just visualizing that shape is to create that neutral place, to visualize it and to have the ego recognize it and move into it.

T.   And for people in general, is the neutral place—a place for the ego—diamond shaped?

G.   Yes. Let's say this can be a tool you can use. Let me describe it in this way: that it does not always exist within each person, but the potential for existence is possible with thought, with that created thought, and it… how do I describe it… it is not something that pre-exists, but is something that can be created and fit well in that there is room for it, almost as if to say, when we have room for new ideas within our mind we have room to create new spaces, new concepts that can work within the mind, and if we can believe that we can create them, then we know that they already exist.

T.   And so for many people this diamond-shaped place would develop naturally or not?

G.   Not usually. For some it would seem that it would, but what it would be is that for these individuals the ego is already functioning in a more neutral way, and by neutral of course we mean not taking a strong stand, being more aware, being cooperative, functioning more in a higher level way. So for this woman to create that neutral zone, that diamond shape, is to move it into a place where perhaps the ego won't respond exactly like this, but it has that neutralizing effect, more able to be objective, cooperative with you, and then engaging the other parts of being—the soul, the higher self—to help it have greater awareness.

T.   And when you refer to this diamond-shaped, neutral place, are you referring specifically to a place specific for the ego or other parts of the mind?

G.   More reserved for the ego, although other parts of the being can come into it. It's almost as if you picture the universe divided into half with the buffer zone or the connecting zone or the middle point. And when the ego is at the middle point the diamond shape with all of the rest attached to and revolving off of it, not that it's necessarily the central point but it just happens to be there, then that ego has the ability to perceive from many directions and to receive information and to begin to make choices and considerations from a most definite higher level.

T.   Conceptually, Gerod, would it be better to conceptualize this as a three-dimensional place, kind of like a diamond stone in the sense that it is three-dimensional and has its facets or more like a two-dimensional? Neither one of these probably apply in terms of the dimension we're talking about.

G.   Well, just so you have the four points. So in that respect it can be three-dimensional as long as it will have its points. Often times people will confuse that diamond shape because of the traditional stone faceting that removes that upper most point, but it needs to have that sharp apex at the top as well as the sides and the bottom. (Session #83—April 8, 1989)

A little later in that same session, I came back to the diamond:

T.   In trying to help the ego move to that diamond shape, would the higher self or the inner mind—either or both—be able to help in that?

G.   Well, they can, but once again, it is often times a position that the ego can do on its own, because it is almost like that place, that zone, is an attractive place to be. It is like a position of power when each person finds their point of power from which they address life, the feeling is there, and the ego is quite amenable to that feeling. It is different somewhat from that feeling of power it has when it is employing all of its defenses, but it is rather a superb point to be in, and quite often if it can sense it, it can be drawn to it.

T.   So finding it is it's own reward.

G.   Yes.

T.   That should make it easier. (Session #83—April 8, 1989)

A few days later, I had another session with Gerod. I came back to the diamond and the main focus was on its clinical implications. Would such a neutral zone, as described by Gerod, be beneficial for my clients, or some clients, and something I might incorporate into the healing process?

T.   Gerod, when we talked about the diamond, and just for me to re-peat to you and see if I'm understanding this correctly. You, I think, have told me that this diamond shape is a place that can be created for the ego, which is a more neutral place, and that this really can be created by each person. The suggestion may have to be given at times, but it can be created then by all persons, and when it's there, that place is always beneficial or a place of strength for the ego. Does that sound like it fits?

G.   I like the way that sounds.

T.   Okay. And it would seem to me that that diamond shape would be a fairly routine thing to do then with clients, if such a place would give anyone further strength or perspective, that it would be good for anyone to develop that.

G.   I would agree with that. There will come times when there are certain people with whom you are working that it will become more appropriate to work with it more directly and in an out-spoken way, and that will become obvious to you.

T.   I'm not sure why there would be a case where it wouldn't be good to work with it in a direct way.

G.   Well, perhaps I would say that there are times when there are other areas that you would wish to concentrate upon, where the ego is not necessarily impeding or causing difficulty, and to have too many situations unfolding at once can become confusing. Almost as if to say, anything done too routinely can remove the individuality away from what is taking place. So perhaps I am only speaking to it in that sense. I would not want you to do anything too routinely, as you would well want not yourself to do either.

T.   Okay. Are you saying, then, it may be more distracting or might in a sense clutter the work?

G.   Well, not necessarily distracting or cluttering, but sometimes if you use it too routinely, I would be concerned that it might cause you to miss something, to not pick up on something that perhaps you might have if the ego had given itself away. Say if it is in a very defended position, sometimes those positions of defense are your clues as to what might be unfolding or what may be taking place, or what areas are more sensitive than the others.

And if you move the ego into too neutral of a position before certain work is done, then you might not find all that you need to. So that is why I would always put some type of an intuitive judgment to work here, as to what point the ego needs to be. It is a beneficial place many times, but not always at the beginning at the process of therapy, maybe at a certain point, but not always at the beginning. So if you were to do it too routinely, you might lose a thread that you need to be aware of.

G.   …I'm hoping that you do understand because this is a very valuable tool and it's almost like disarming some type of a defensive weapon. There is a time to disarm and there is a time not to disarm. And sometimes the time to not disarm is when you are looking for something. It's almost like you look for that defense and it will take you somewhere, point you in a direction. And once you have a strong feel for what is going on, then you will know, perhaps, when it is time to make that suggestion.

T.   …Just out of curiosity, if the ego moved into this place too early, could you describe how I might, or it might, lose or reduce its ability to identify or stay in touch with a part that needs to be identified but somehow the ego has shifted too quickly.

G.   It would probably manifest itself in a very, I would almost describe it as a very indeterminant way, not able to respond as well to you, to your questions, to your directions, and as if to say, that process of identification, as you call it, of all of the players, also gives the ego some understanding, some view of what has been going on and to move away from that too early leaves it in somewhat of a muddled state and not as well able to perform.

It's almost like when it moves into that neutral zone, into the diamond shape, it needs to be at that point in time where it has gone through that first phase of helping to identify and lay the ground work and have some understanding of what is going on. And then it is able to have that more neutral view that is more comfortable because it has already gone through this initial process, if that's any kind of an explanation to you of what would be happening. It's clarification somewhat not only for you but for the ego.

T.   And I could see that the ego in terms of, in a sense, almost reviewing the situation, coming to understand it again, or understanding the broader picture of it.

G.   Because as we have discussed, the ego is usually capable of being cooperative, has concern, is valuable.

T   Well, I think this fits for me in terms enough to bring that to the work, so that's helpful. (Session #84—April 11, 1989)

Gerod and I continued to talk about the diamond in regard to the treatment of specific clients. We also talked about it in general as I tried to grasp it conceptually. A year after the session just cited Gerod discussed the diamond in a way that gave me a glimpse of its spiritual implications for a person.

T. When we have an ego-state move into the diamond in order to perceive, is that part of what we're suggesting happen, that kind of perception not only of this present life but a perspective also from that past and the soul?

G. Yes, it is. The diamond is a neutral zone. It is almost as if it is not the present, not the past, nor the future, but all of them together. It's a place where everything is, so it becomes a place in which there can be a relinquishment of influence and an understanding of certain situations. It is as if stepping out of the rain for just a moment to dry off, or to step into a silent room for just a moment to stop all auditory, verbal influence.

T. And when one does that, would they undergo change then because they've had some new perception and understanding when they step back out of it?

G. Yes, to a degree. It's not so much that they undergo change as they undergo reconnection. It's like a recharging, a connection with ALL THAT IS, a removal from all the illusion of physical reality for just a brief moment, enough to clear the surface, so to say, for a period of time so that the perspective then, upon stepping back into the situation, may be clearer, may be then viewed from that point of nothingness and yet from that point of everything, of allness, where everything is condensed back down into... here I go looking for words. Condensed back down into ALL THAT IS in its most infinite and minuscule form, removing everything else. And then when you come back, expand back out of that, you come from that perspective which then gives you a different perspective of where you have been. Now, for some it may be more profound and for some others it is fleeting, but is usually enough to be helpful at least.

T. Well, would repeated times in the diamond help to strengthen that perception?

G. To some degree, yes it can. (Session #142—April 25, 1990)

Looking back, my underlying confusion about the diamond and the energy point/soul connection was that Gerod described them both as in the heart-center (ideally), and both integrally involved with the self/soul connection, but they weren't the same thing. Gerod made a distinction between what I've termed here the energy point/soul connection, which seemed like a body/soul connection, and the diamond area that seemed more like a mind/soul connection.

Gerod and I had the following discussion five years later. The term "self/soul connection" in the excerpt is being used to mean what I've talked about in this chapter as the "energy point/soul connection."

T.   In the energy point/soul connection that we've talked about, is that in any way strongly linked to this (diamond) area?

G.   It is seated in the heart, but it is linked to it, yes.

T.   The energy point/soul connection is seated in the heart. Is it connected with the diamond?

G.   Yes.

T.   Is it inside the diamond?

G.   Simply put you could say that, yes, but it is not dependent upon it.

T.   It is not dependent upon the diamond?

G.   No.

T.   The diamond can be separated and encapsulated?

G.   Yes.

T.   Is it more like a copy of the diamond or an image of the diamond?

G.   No, not necessarily.

T.   But it is independent of the diamond?

G.   Yes.

T.   If the diamond is brought back together and cleared and set, is that any strengthening to the energy point/soul connection?

G.   (Pause) It could but it's not necessary.

T.   Are they almost two separate things?

G.   Yes.

T.   The diamond is that more associated ... well...

G.   The diamond is more associated with the fact of existence in the physical. It is created so that that physical experience can take place. It must be there... but it does not have to stay engaged or intact in order for life to continue. But the energy point/soul connection is not dependent upon the diamond, or the diamond being intact, or the diamond being engaged, to have that good connection.

T.   Yet it is a connection that brings both the physical and the soul together?

G. Yes. But the diamond in a sense is more related to the experience of the physical. It is that ignition as we've compared it to an auto ignition—you have to have that to make the car move but once it is moving it doesn't't have to be there and have to be functioning. Once it is started, it is started, but the soul/self connection, it must stay connected in order for that to be strong. And therefore, it cannot be dependent upon that diamond because the diamond does not have to be connected and it usually in many cases, as you are aware, is not.

T. Yes. Is the energy point/soul connection then more etheric?

G. I'm not certain that's the right word, but that would be somewhat descriptive. It's more etheric than physical. It is something that in a sense exists before incarnation into the physical body. It will be or it won't be. It's an attribute that is carried at the soul level.

T. (Pause) Its quality, even before incarnation, is that quality or character of it a result of a history of incarnations?

G. Not always, no. There can be the intervention of the Light to assure that it is there for our purposes as well as the purpose of that soul. If we have a need and there is an agreement at the soul level for that soul to do specific work that would require a strong soul and self-connection, then we will do all that we are able to do to ensure that happens. So it is not something that always occurs randomly or by result of that soul's experience, but it can occur because the Light supports it and it is a necessary element for an unfolding plan that that particular soul and that particular physical incarnation is to be a part of. If that is not a requirement or an element in that soul's incarnation, then the soul/self connection will be more influenced, shaped, by the soul's history.

T. Okay. Would you say generally speaking that would be the more common situation?

G. Yes.

T. It would also seem that we're saying that a strong energy point/soul connection for the soul is highly desirable.

G. Yes.

T. It is a goal?

G. Yes, because it aids in the development and expansion of that soul. It enlists or it ensures that the physical experience will be one quite likely that will be directing itself toward supporting the goals and needs of the soul.

T   (Pause) Well, it is difficult for me to conceptualize this. I'll be patient about that. Who knows, maybe it won't even come to a conceptualization, but I'm still trying to get a clear sense of it. You're saying that this energy point/soul connection is carried with the soul?

G.   Yes. (Session #429—July 8, 1995)

Once Gerod began talking about the diamond, the focus of treatment began to shift away from the energy point/soul connection. As you can see from the transcripts, my understanding of the energy point/soul connection and the diamond developed over many years. Today, I view the diamond as a higher-level connection between the self and soul. It seems multi-leveled like the chakras. Where the energy point/soul connection is the conduit between the body and soul (without it, the body dies), the diamond is about the connection between mind and soul. Gerod called it a neutral zone. It's a place that opens onto the past, present, and future all at once. It is a consciousness beyond the ego. It's a knowing of one's connection to Source.

In working with clients, joining the energy point and soul in the heart center is to put the pieces into place so the diamond can be activated. At some point in a client's healing process, I usually will communicate to the higher self about the diamond-shaped area. I consider this beneficial for all my clients, but for some it is more critical than for others. The quality and clarity of this consciousness, according to Gerod, helps determine the soul's experience in the physical. This is also the level at which trauma, abuse, or shock can be such a threat to a person that it affects the diamond (or its potential) through splitting, displacement, and/or encapsulation. This is the level at which I work with a client's higher self to assess the self/soul connection and determine its condition.

Part 3
Ego-States in Depth

6

The Science of Ego-states

The science in Soul-Centered Healing is not in predicting what ego-states will present in a person's healing process. That will never happen. The science is in knowing how to help any ego-state that does present move through its sharing, release, and integration. That process starts in Soul-Centered Healing by facilitating an ego-state's contact with the higher self and the Light. This step is based on the knowledge that once an ego-state experiences the Light, ninety-eight percent of the time it will say *yes* to the healing process. This positive response by ego-states is so predictable, that if an ego-state rejects the Light, you know something is wrong; someone or something (including the ego-state itself) is blocking.

Over many years, working with thousands of ego-states, I encountered blocking of all kinds. I learned a great deal from those situations where particular ego-states refused the Light or became stuck or blocked in their healing process. Blocking occurred even with ego-states who had contact with the higher self, received the Light, and were saying *yes* to the healing process.

In pursuing the source of these blocks, I observed the same or similar situations, dynamics, and phenomena present with different clients. Sometimes it was simple. It could be an earthbound spirit interfering, or the ego-state itself was afraid to remember. I also discovered, however, that the blocking could be quite complex, involving more than one ego-state, and often, outside interference. It was in working through the many different blocks and forms of resistance with individual ego-states that I began to see the depth and intricacy of this inner world of protection. I came to recognize several types of ego-states, internal groupings, structures, and obstacles that present frequently enough that I keep them in mind as possibilities when I am dealing with a strong block.

Anytime communication with an ego-state is blocked, the next step in the Ego-State Protocol is to identify the source of the block and resolve it, so the ego-state can receive the Light or continue in its healing process. In Vol. I, I listed the four primary sources of blocking that I have found. For convenience, I list them here again with slight modification.

1) Contact with the Light can begin to draw up an ego-state's own pain and, perceiving it as the Light causing its pain, the ego-state shuts down the Light to stop the pain.

2) The second reason an ego-state might refuse contact with the Light is because someone or something is threatening it in present time to stay away from the Light. It may be a spirit who is threatening it, or it might be threatened by another ego-state.

3) The third reason is that an ego-state has been given the message in the past to stay away from the Light because the Light will harm or destroy it.

4) Finally, there may be a device or energy of some kind that has been programmed and placed on, inside of, or close to an ego-state. Any approaching Light will trigger the device and deliver the negative reinforcement. The ego-state then stops the Light in order to stop the effects of the device.

I have written about these complexities to a certain extent in my earlier books. In the next two chapters, I will expand on these and introduce some new ones in the next three chapters. There are certain dynamics that can occur among ego-states that exist in a group, as well as dynamics between groups. There is what I call *special* ego-states. They can present a serious stumbling block or even end in a shutdown if the therapist doesn't't know to look for them. They don't come up with every client, and with some clients, there may be more than one type present.

This information, from my point of view, is interesting in and of itself. I offer it here, though, as a set of diagnostic tools that might help unlock a puzzling block, or save you some time and trouble. Knowing about group dynamics and special types of ego-states might help you diagnose a block more quickly and take the appropriate steps needed to resolve it.

7

Ego-State Groups

Like Attracts Like

One of the major complications in working with ego-states involves their ability and propensity to form groups. When you first identify and communicate with an ego-state, it is probably not alone, but part of a group. When this is the case, it automatically introduces group dynamics as an important consideration in communicating with the identified ego-state. The number one dynamic is the ability of one or more ego-states in the group to block the one with whom you are working. They can override or block the identified ego-state from receiving the Light, sharing its experience, or even communicating to the therapist. It can occur at any point in the process. This kind of blocking happened so frequently in my early work that I soon added a new step to the developing Ego-State Protocol and learned to preempt it by identifying and working with the entire group.

At its most basic level, I view each group of ego-states as a constellation of energy. There's a reason they are together, a kind of magnetic pull. Most of the time, all members of a group share a common element that acts as a bond. That common element might be an emotion, a specific type of experience, a chronological age, or a particular area of conflict or pain. For example, all the ego-states in a group may have feelings of rejection. Even though each one was created in a different experience, it is the feeling of rejection that binds them together. For another group, each ego-state may have suffered a bodily injury. Usually, the therapist can infer a group's common bond after one or two ego-states have shared their memories.

From a clinical point of view, I have found it helpful to think of ego-states in a group as comprising a field of energy. It's an energy created by the resonance among all those in the group. They all *resonate*, so to speak, to the central feeling, conflict, or concern that they share in common. This energy field is not independent of the ego-states that create it, and it does not operate as an autonomous consciousness. It does appear strong enough, however, that what affects one member of the group affects the group as a whole, or the reaction of one or two can incite the entire group.

This could explain, for example, why a person can be confused and have difficulty pinning down what has triggered a certain mood shift, feeling, or reaction. By the time the conscious person is aware of being triggered, and if they begin to reflect on it, the entire group of ego-states is already resonating. In effect, they are all the cause of what the person is feeling and perceiving, though one may have triggered it. At that point, it is difficult for the person to pinpoint a specific trigger. By then, the specific ego-state that triggered the group is no longer the point anyway; the resonating force of the group is the issue. The entire group needs healing and release.

This group resonance or vibration might also explain, at least in some cases, why contacting and working with one ego-state triggers significant resistance and blocking. It may not be just one ego-state blocking another. It might be that contacting one ego-state taps into and triggers this collective energy that, in turn, triggers the entire group.

I assume that whatever holds the group together also holds the ego-state I am communicating with. If I ask it to do something that disturbs that bond, there is likely to be a defensive reaction. If, for example, you ask an ego-state to receive the Light, that Light will approach the others also, and it may trigger fear or pain in one or more in the group. If you want an ego-state to share its feelings and memories of rejection, and feelings of rejection are the common bond in the group, then the others' feelings will likely begin to resonate too.

It is interesting that other practitioners and theoreticians have also recognized this grouping effect. Stanislav Grof, a psychiatrist and founder of *the International Transpersonal Association* describes a phenomenon he observed in his therapeutic work with patients. He called them COEX systems.

Another important discovery of our research was that memories of emotional and physical experiences are stored in the psyche not as isolated bits and pieces but in the form of complex constellations, which I call *COEX systems* (for "systems of condensed experience"). Each COEX system consists of emotionally charged memories from different periods of our lives; the common denominator that brings them together is that they share the same emotional quality or physical sensation. Each COEX may have many layers, each permeated by its central theme, sensations, and emotional qualities. Many times we can identify individual layers according to the different periods of the person's life.[1]

Another example is Barbara Brennan, author of Hands of Light, who is an energy healer and has probably trained thousands in her methods of healing. She is also clairvoyant and has observed this same kind of energy grouping in her own work. She views them as groups of thoughtforms.

In the course of my years of bioenergetic practice, I have observed a phenomenon which I refer to as moving spaces of reality... In terms of psychodynamics, there exist "spaces of reality" or "belief systems" containing groups of thoughtforms which are associated with conceptions and misconceptions of reality. Each thoughtform contains its own definitions of reality, such as, all men are cruel; love is weak; being in control is safe and strong. From my observations, as people move through daily experience they also move through different "spaces" or levels of reality defined by these groups of thoughtforms. The world is experienced differently in each group or space of reality.[2]

Grof's "bits" and "COEX systems" and Brennan's "thoughtforms" and "spaces of reality" are quite similar to the ego-state groups I am describing. While there are important theoretical and clinical differ-

---

1 Grof, Stanislav. *The Holotropic Mind*. San Francisco: Harper, 1993. P. 24
2 Brennan, Barbara. *Hands of Light*. New York: Bantam Books, 1987. pp. 93-94

ences between these models, all seem to be describing the same, or similar, phenomenon.

Shared Consciousness

The ability of an ego-state group to block, i.e., its ability to act as a collective, is the same ability the therapist can use to preempt that blocking. The higher self has the ability to communicate simultaneously with each ego-state in the group. It can bring Light and information to each ego-state that is willing to receive it. Once that has happened, usually the entire group will signal its agreement to the healing process. This ability of the group to act as a collective extends to the steps of sharing, release, and integration. One client called it "batch processing." Most of the time, the sharing involves their common bond, and what needs to be shared can be done collectively or through one ego-state, whatever is called for. The same is true for the release and the integration, which, of course, are the easy steps.

Because of their potential for blocking, the identification of groups became a major step in the Ego-State Protocol. Once an ego-state has been identified and received the Light, it is asked whether it is alone or whether there is another or others there with them. If it is alone, then it is led through the steps of sharing, release, and integration. If there is more than one, then the protocol is adapted to address the entire group. In my mind, it becomes a group healing from that point on, even if working with one specific ego-state. Most of the time, all the ego-states are willing to receive the Light, and when they do, they say yes to the healing process. Often enough, however, there is resistance or refusal by one or more ego-states, or by the entire group. These situations are unpredictable. It can be as simple as one ego-state afraid the Light is going to burn. It can be as complex as several ego-states from past lives shutting down communication because they are being threatened by dark souls.

Whatever the situation, the task becomes one of using the protocols to identify and resolve the source(s) of the refusal. The higher self is usually able to do this. Often, the ego-state itself knows who or what is blocking or is in the way. The aim is always to achieve unanimous agreement of every member, so the entire group can act in concert.

The following dialogue is an example of addressing a group of ego-states. It begins with a twelve year-old, female ego-state that has received the Light and signaled its agreement with the healing process.

Ego-state Group: Example 1

Th. 12yo, were you able to receive that Light all right?

12yo Yes finger lifts.

Th. Does that feel good and comfortable to you?

12yo Yes finger lifts.

Th. And did you receive the information about healing and release?

12yo Yes finger lifts.

Th. Do you wish to have that healing for yourself?

12yo Yes finger lifts.

Th. Before we do that, I'm going to ask that you look around and see if there is another or others there where you are. (Pause) 12yo, is there another or others there with you?

12yo Yes finger lifts.

Th. Are there more than three of you there altogether?

12yo Yes finger lifts.

Th. Are there more than six?

12yo No finger lifts.

Th. Are there six of you there altogether?

12yo No finger lifts.

Th. Are there five of you ?

12yo Yes finger lifts.

Th. To the other four there: is each of you willing to receive some Light/ Love energy for yourself? If so, the yes finger can lift. If anyone is not willing, the second finger lifting.

Egs. Yes finger lifts.

Th. To all four, then: I'm asking higher self to send you that Light/love energy. Beginning, one, two, three… and higher self, please send to each of these here that Light/Love energy… communicating to them also the information about healing and release. First finger when that's complete. Second finger if it is stopped or blocked.

Egs. Yes finger lifts.

Th. Did everyone receive that Light/Love energy for yourself?

Egs. Yes finger lifts.

Th. Do each of you want to have this healing and release for yourself?

Egs. Yes finger lifts.

Th.   Higher self, if these five can do their sharing together, the first fin-
      ger lifting. If someone needs to be addressed individually, then the
      second finger.

HS   Second finger lifts.

Th.   Higher self, please identify the one best to work with first. (Pause)
      And to this one: have you and I already communicated in this
      way?

___   No finger lifts.

Th.   Are you one of the five I've just been working with?

___   Yes finger lifts.

Th.   Do you know yourself to be a part of this self and soul I'm working
      with?

___   Yes finger lifts.

Th.   Are you one first created in this present life of Carol's?

___   Yes finger lifts.

Th.   Are you younger than ten?

___   Yes finger lifts.

Th.   Are you younger than seven?

___   No finger lifts.

Th.   Are you seven years old?

7yo   Yes finger lifts.

At this point, the therapist would use the Ego-State Protocol to help
7yo through the steps from sharing to release. She might integrate at
that point, or need to wait for the others. The higher self, then, is asked
to determine whether any others in the group need to be worked with
individually, or whether they can be worked with as a group, or whether
all can have a release now that 7yo has done her sharing. The higher
self is the one that can determine this.

Ego-state Group: Example 2

Th.   7yo, were you able to have that release all right?

7yo   Yes finger lifts.

Th.   Does that feel good and comfortable for you now inside?

7yo   Yes finger lifts.

Th.   Higher self, if 7yo can move to integration at this time, first finger
      lifting. If better to wait, second finger lifting.

HS   Second finger lifts.

Th.   Higher self, if another one in the group needs to work individually, the first finger lifting. If not, the second finger can lift. If you're not sure, the hand can lift.

HS   Second finger lifting.

Th.   Does the group need to do some sharing yet?

HS   Yes finger lifts.

Th.   Can they do that sharing together?

HS   Yes finger lifts.

Th.   To the four of you: are you willing to share, or allow to be shared, what needs to come forward for healing?

Egs.   Yes finger lifts.

Th.   I'm going to ask, then, that higher self surround you with that Light and support on the count of three you can let share what needs to be shared. Beginning, one, two, three… and just share to the present now what you need to share about it. Higher self, right there with you. (Pause)

Egs.   Yes finger lifts.

Th.   Carol, is there something you received?

Ca.   Yes, I was little, in my crib. My mother was angry. She put me in the crib and then left and closed the door. I was just crying and crying.

Th.   To the group: is there more that needs to be shared?

Egs.   No finger lifts.

Th.   Higher self, is there anything you see yet that this group needs to share yet?

HS   No finger lifts.

Th.   Can they all have a release now?

HS   Yes finger lifts.

Th.   To the group, on three, let yourselves release any pain, distress, hurt or fear. Beginning, one, two, three, and just release… any hurt, pain, or distress, just let it release right through the body and out. The higher self is right there to help. First finger lifting when all has been released that's ready. Second finger if there is a problem.

Egs.   First finger lifts.

Th.   To the entire group: is anyone still feeling some distress or pain there?

Egs.   No finger lifts.

Th.   Does that feel good and comfortable inside?

Egs. Yes finger lifts.

Th. Higher self, can all five move now to their place of integration?

HS Yes finger lifts.

The next example is more complex and involves outside entities. It starts with a fourteen-year-old who has received Light and, through questioning, communicates that there are seven others there with her. Once I know that, I address the group as a whole and ask if all are willing to receive the Light for themselves.

Ego-state Group: Example 3

Th. To the entire group, is everyone willing to receive that Light/Love energy? If so first finger can lift. If anyone is not willing, the second finger can lift.

14yo Second finger lifts.

Th. Is there more than one who doesn't't want the Light.

__ Yes finger lifts.

Th. Is it more than two?

__ No finger lifts

Th. Two of you do not want the Light, is that right?

__ Yes finger lifts

Th. To this one: are you afraid of the Light?

__ No finger lifts.

Th. Are you angry at the Light?

__ Yes finger lifts.

Th. Do you blame the Light for what happened?

__ Yes finger lifts.

Th. To this one: I know that sometimes there can be misunderstandings or misperceptions about what occurred. Sometimes someone can be tricked into believing something. Would you be willing to receive further information about what happened and why? It is only information. There's nothing you have to do with it. It is only for you to consider and you can let it go if it doesn't't make sense.

__ Yes finger lifts.

Th. Higher self, I'm asking that you communicate that greater knowledge and understanding about what happened, and whether the Light was the cause of their pain. First finger when that communication is complete. Second finger, if it's stopped.

___ First finger lifts.

Th. Did both of you receive that communication?

___ Yes finger lifts.

Th. Did that make sense to you?

___ Yes finger lifts.

Th. Would you be willing then to receive that Light and judge for your-selves whether you want to keep it or not?

___ Yes finger lifts.

Th. I'm going to ask higher self, then, to send you that Light and let yourselves receive it. You can stop it if you need to, but if you like it, you can bring it inside to whatever level is comfortable. First finger when you have received it, second finger if there's a problem.

___ Second finger lifts.

Th. If one of you, or both needed to stop the Light, first finger lifting. If neither of you stopped it, the second finger can lift.

___ To the one I was communicating with: if you need to stop it because it caused pain or distress, the first finger can lift. If there's someone or something threatening you, then the second finger.

___ Second finger lifts.

Th. If it's someone, the first finger lifting. If something, or more like an energy, the second finger lifting.

___ First finger lifts.

Th. Higher self, are you aware of that one who is threatening?

HS Yes finger lifts.

Th. Is that one part of the self/soul?

No response.

Th. higher self, are you still able to communicate with me?

No response.

Th. To the one who is blocking: are you willing to communicate with me?

___ Yes finger lifts.

Th. Are you part of this self/soul I'm working with?

___ No finger lifts.

Th. If you believe you are yourself a soul, or part of a soul, the first finger can lift. If not, or you're not sure, the second finger can lift.

___ First finger lifts.

Th. To this one: did you know that if you are a soul, you have your own soul-source energy? Did you know that?

___   No finger lifts.

Th.   If you are a soul, or part of a soul, you have your own Light inside you. Are you willing to look for yourself and see if that Light is there?

___   Yes finger lifts.

Th.   On three then. One, two, three... just look inside now. Move your vision right to your center. See the Light that you have there. First finger when you have found that. Second finger if you do not.

___   Second finger lifts.

Th.   To this one: if you needed to stop that, first finger lifting. If someone or something got in the way, the second finger can lift.

___   Second finger lifts.

Th.   If it is someone, first finger. If something, the second finger.

___   First finger lifts.

Th.   Are you being threatened?

___   Yes finger lifts.

Th.   Did you know that as a soul you have the absolute free choice to end any agreement or sever any connection to that one threatening you?

___   No finger lifts.

Th.   Are you willing to receive more information about this from the higher self or a high-level teacher?

___   Yes finger lifts.

Th.   To the higher self or that high-level teacher, please communicate to this one that information and knowledge about themselves as a soul, and their absolute free choice to sever any connections with this one threatening. First finger lifting when you've received that communication, second finger if you do not.

___   First finger lifts.

Th.   Did you receive that information all right?

___   Yes finger lifts.

Th.   Do you wish to end that connection?

___   Yes finger lifts.

Th.   On three, then. One, two, three... let yourself receive that Light now and you can sever that connection. First finger when that's complete, second finger if there's a problem.

___   First finger lifts.

Th.   To this one: do you remember now about the spirit realm of Light and your own place in the Light?

___ Yes finger lifts.

Th. Would you like to return home to the Light?

___ Yes finger lifts.

Th. If you're ready to do that on your own, first finger. If you need some assistance, the second finger lifting.

___ First finger lifts.

Th. On three, then. One, two, three... and just move now right into that corridor of Light. Higher self, first finger when that one has gone, second finger if they do not leave.

HS   First finger lifts.

Th. Now, to the group of eight. Two of you were going to receive the Light. Are you still willing now to have that Light?

___ Yes finger lifts.

Th. Higher self, please send the Light to these two. First finger when you've both received that, second finger if either of you do not.

___ First finger lifts.

Th. Everyone in the group now is receiving Light, is that correct. If so, first finger. If anyone still is not, second finger.

___ First finger lifts.

Th. To the entire group, I'm asking higher self to send each of you the information about healing and release, how you can be free of any pain, hurt, or distress. First finger when you've received that information, second finger if anyone does not.

___ First finger lifts.

Th. Is everyone willing now to move through that healing process?

___ Yes finger lifts.

Identifying and addressing a group of ego-states early in the protocol is not always the best way to go. Sometimes, it will be important to stay focused on the identified ego-state because of its intense fear, or belligerence, or its confusion. If that's the case, then it may be better to work with that one until it is stabilized and cooperating. It might also be that an ego-state has come forward in reaction to the group you are working with. At that point, it may be more important to stay focused on the relationship between the ego-state and group. What was it specifically about the group that triggered this one? What's the connection?

Another strategy is to work with the identified ego-state, knowing that any others are listening and watching. In helping the identified ego-state move through the steps of healing, it demonstrates to the others that it is safe and it will be safe for them. When you do address the group, then, they will usually be receptive. Which way to go? Address the group or stay with the ego-state? It's a judgment call. Everything being equal, I lean toward addressing the entire group.

8

The Ego-State World

Psychic Space

Another factor that can be important in dealing with ego-states is their environment. Sometimes, it will be useful to check out the *place* where an ego-state or a group of ego-states exist. These are not physical places. They are created of consciousness. Even though I talk about them in spatial metaphors, I think of them, and the ego-states that inhabit them, as existing at a psychic level. There is no space/time at this level, so their creation does not have to obey the laws of physics or three-dimensional reality. In the psychic reality, an ego-state can live in a thimble, or a group may live in a cave, or still live in a room from its childhood home.

These environments seem to be created from many possible sources. Ego-states, for example, often live in some version of the place where their original trauma occurred. It might be in the backyard, in the bedroom, or in a classroom. Other times, the particular place is a reflection of the experience they carry. A group of infant ego-states, for instance, may be found in a nursery in the inner world. There are also exotic places and there are dark places. There are places read about in childhood, or from a past life, and there are imagined places as well.

As long as the healing process is moving smoothly, the therapist may not need to know much or anything about an ego-state's environment. Often that information comes through in the sharing. It can be quite interesting, but it isn't necessary for the sharing and release to occur.

In general, I find that there are primarily two clinical situations in which it becomes important to know about the ego-states' environment.

The first is when the source of a block is not found within the ego-states, but is somewhere in their environment. It might be someone—a spirit or another ego-state—that has been hiding in a corner. It might be a dark soul that just showed up, seemingly out of nowhere, and began to threaten the ego-states to stay away from the Light. It could be some sort of device or object that is scaring or threatening them in some way. It may be some sticky substance on the floor that keeps their feet stuck. It could also be something like an energy appearing as a wall, a fog, a vortex, or a dark cloud approaching. Whichever it is – someone or something – the protocols are used to identify and resolve it.

The second situation where information about the ego-states' environment can be important is when the ego-state or the group appears blocked, confused, or resistant. Information about where they are can offer clues as to their perceptions, beliefs, or feelings that are keeping them stuck. There might be something like a letter, or a box, or a closet that contains further information that the ego-states need to know in order to move forward. It might be that they are in a sealed vault, or they are outdoors but lost in the woods. The ego-state environment, just like the ego-states themselves, is unpredictable, but it is usually a reflection of what the ego-states are about.

The following is one example of how the protocol would work to identify the source of blocking in an ego-state's environment. The situation involves an eight year-old ego-state that had received Light and had begun sharing.

Th. 8yo, did you need to stop the sharing?
8yo No finger lifts.
Th. Did someone or something get in the way of that?
8yo Yes finger lifts.
Th. If it's someone, first finger lifting, if it's something, then second finger. If you're not sure, the hand can lift.
8yo Second finger lifts.
Th. If it's more like a device or object, of some kind, first finger lifting. If it's more like an energy, second finger. If neither of those fit, the hand can lift.
8yo First finger lifting.
Th. 8yo, is there more than one?
8yo Yes finger lifts.

Th. More than five?

8yo No finger lifts.

Th. Are there at least three of those devices?

8yo No finger lifts.

Th. Are there two of them.

8yo Yes finger lifts.

Th. Higher self, are you aware of these devices?

HS Yes finger lifts.

Th. Are they created of soul energy?

HS No finger lifts.

Th. Higher self, would it be best to dissipate or remove those devices now?

HS Yes finger lifts.

Th. 8yo, would you like to have those devices removed?

8yo No finger lifts.

Th. Do you like having them there?

8yo No finger lifts.

Th. Are you afraid to have them removed?

8yo Yes finger lifts.

Th. Do you believe something bad will happen if they are taken away?

8yo Yes finger lifts.

Th. Did someone tell you that?

8yo Yes finger lifts.

Th. 8yo, whoever told you that has lied to you. You are part of this self/ soul and so you have your own soul-source energy. Would you like to see that soul-source energy?

8yo Yes finger lifts.

Th. I'm going to ask higher self to help you. On three, you can look inside and see your Light energy. One, two, three… and higher self, help 8yo to look inside… 8yo, look right to your center and see that Light you have inside. First finger when you see it, second finger if you do not.

8yo First finger lifts.

Th. 8yo, knowing the connection now to your own Light, are you willing now for higher self to remove those objects?

8yo Yes finger lifts.

Th. On three then: one, two, three, and higher self, I'm asking that you dissipate and remove those objects now from the self-soul. First finger when that's done. Second finger if there's a problem.

HS   First finger lifts.

At this point, the therapist returns to 8yo and continues with the Ego-State Protocol. If there is still a block, the procedure is repeated to identify the source. It would not be unusual, for example, to find a block involving a chain of several different devices (like building in a redundancy system). A chain of devices could also lead to a spirit that controls them from outside the client's soul.

We can think of these environments as a creation of the ego-states that inhabit them. Usually, they will dissolve when the ego-states release and integrate. However, there can also be environments that are created partially, or even wholly, out of external elements and energy.

9

Rooms, Doors, and Layers

Doors: Inside and Out

A third major issue in dealing with ego-states is the existence of doors. In the practice of Soul-Centered Healing, dealing with doors is a constant part of the process. I use the term door in a generic sense. An ego-state may literally see a door. It could be a trapdoor, a castle door, or a bedroom door. It could be a door into a dollhouse where other ego-states live. The term can also refer, though, to a gate, a hole in the ground, a portal, a window, or a crack in the wall. In short, a door is anything that leads from "here" to "there." It's a connector.

According to Gerod, there are basically two kinds of doors. The first are what I call intra-psychic. These are doors or openings that lead to other ego-states or entities existing within the self/soul. They lead to places from early childhood, from other lifetimes, or into rooms created to hide something or contain it.

In the following excerpt, Gerod talks about these doors in general, while also talking about a client's specific situation. The term doorways had come up as an issue in the client's session.

> T.   Gerod, I worked with Alice J. who we have talked about. There was a group of eight that I was already aware of. A six year old in there; the little one in the plaid dress who had gone out walking. The question I asked, Gerod, is whether the higher self could see whether there were others behind any of those eight. The response I got is that each of those eight is a doorway to others. I'm wondering if you are able to see that?

G.   I see it, yes. There is a doorway. However, that does not necessarily mean that there is something behind every door.

T.   Behind the six year old she said, I think, there were twelve others. When we talked about all eight of them as being a doorway, now is this something... can you describe what that means, that they are each a doorway even though there may not be something behind each door?

G.   Well, in actuality every ego-state is a doorway, so to say, and that, should they choose to open the door, then the potential for further development is there and it is not always there in all situations. As I look at this situation, I see a doorway. I see a door behind every one of them. However, I do not necessarily see something behind every door. Some are a void. Some are a door that you open to walk through to go somewhere else...

     ...What will need to be done is, as you work with each one of them, ascertain if there is something behind them, behind the door, that needs to be worked with. If there is, you open the door and you go through and you do the work. If there is nothing there, then you seal the door up.

     ...One suggestion I would make, a general blanket statement as you begin working in this area, is to work with the higher self to put Light at each door. This will help you with this individual situation. By working with the doors at this point, what you may do as you work closer in this area and as more emotions are aroused, you may prevent a door from being opened and something from being created behind it. It is like putting the plug in the drain.

T.   So not to seal the doors, just to put the Light there?

G.   No need to seal them but to just... it is almost like sealing it, but it is more of a protection so that nothing new will take place behind the doors. You don't wish to seal them in case there is someone behind them that needs to come forward. So if you put Light at each of the doors and protect them it is as if the ones who are behind will not be sealed out if they need to come forward and that you will not know that until you come to each door to inquire. But it will keep anything more from developing or taking place until you have the opportunity to get there to check. (Session #168—September 22, 1990)

I picture this dynamic like a bubbling. When an ego-state cannot tolerate and contain the force of an experience, then a door or doors are created, along with who or what is through the door. If there is enough pressure, then more doors can be created off of them. A door may lead to another ego-state or a group, or to several containers of raw emotion. It can also lead into a hallway, or a tunnel, or another room with more doors. In this picture, the creation of doors expands outward until the force has been expended or plugged, to use Gerod's term. You might think of it as psychic coagulation. At this level, consciousness is free to react and create whatever is needed to stop the pain or terror.

The second kind of door Gerod talked about are those that lead outside the soul. I call them extra-psychic doors. Most of these doors are created by, or in reaction to, outside influences and forces. Spirit attachment, alien contact, and psychic attacks, for example, would involve these kinds of doors or openings. Some extra-psychic doors are created by ego-states whose pain, guilt, or terror has driven them to flee the soul in search of safety or relief. I do not find these kinds of doors with every client, and when I do, it is usually a limited number. With some clients, extra-psychic doors are a minor part of the healing. With others, however, it's a major focus of the work.

After describing the ego-states as doorways, Gerod talked about the two kinds of doors.

> I would describe it in this way with these doors: Some of them are two-way doors, some of them are one-way doors, meaning that what is behind the door was created behind the door and comes forward. This is usually something that comes in from somewhere else. Then there are the doors that are the doors outward, so that those who are in may begin the process of escaping outward and further away, so to say, to get further and further from what it was that created them. (Session #168—September 22, 1990)

There are also extra-psychic doors that are positive and connect to the realms of Light or the Light of other souls. These doors can present in the healing process, but I wouldn't say it is common. In some sense, they take care of themselves behind the scenes. When they do present as an issue, it's usually because these connections to the Light are being blocked, or a spirit guide is making direct contact. What is more common in Soul-Centered Healing is to enlist the aid of spirit guides and teachers, thereby creating a door or opening one that's already there. Most of the time, though, the extra-psychic doors that present in the healing process are those where there is trouble.

The Inner Labyrinth

There are two different protocols for dealing with doors, depending on whether they are intra-psychic or extra-psychic. Each kind of door calls for a different approach. Before I discuss the protocols, however, I need to address the phenomenon of doors itself. The existence of doors introduces a new level of complexity, both in understanding how the inner world is structured, and how to navigate it in the healing process. Not only can ego-states form groups, but they can also connect to other ego-states or groups or to other areas of the self/soul. In addition, they also can have connections with spirits and entities outside the soul. Theoretically, the existence of one door implies an infinite possibility of doors and interconnections. One door can lead to many, and each of those doors can lead to many more.

At a clinical level, this means we can never predict where a door leads, and who or what we will encounter. It could be one group of ego-states or a whole series of doors and groups. For convenience, I call this level the rooms, doors, and layers. It refers to the network of interconnections between and among ego-states, groups of ego-states, and outside spirits and entities. These networks can be extensive—or not—depending on a client's present life experience, past life history, and any external intrusions or attachments. A client's specific constellation of rooms and doors is unique and unpredictable. I imagine it would be like viewing the cross-section of a hundred ant colonies and never finding two the same. It is only through my work with many individual clients that I came to a general concept of networks.

The same principle of like attracts like that operates among ego-states to form a group appears to operate also at this level between groups as well. Groups connected by doors, directly or indirectly, usually share some common element. It's not always as obvious, though, as it is with an ego-state group. If there is a more extensive network, often as not it will involve past lives and/or contact with outside entities. It's not always easy to understand the connections, but usually, common threads run through a network. They resonate with each other around a central issue, conflict, or concern. In a person's day-to-day life, these networks can be triggered when one ego-state is triggered and its vibration sends ripples throughout the network. This is also what can happen in the healing process when you identify one ego-state or a group and its reaction begins to trigger others in the network. It could start a stirring, or it could set off a firestorm of reaction.

In the healing process, it's important just to know such networks exist. That way, there's no surprise when you find doors where one group leads to another, and then another. Not every client will need to work at this level, but as therapists, we cannot know ahead of time who will and who won't. In knowing these networks might exist, you can be ready to open doors if that's where the process leads.

Knowledge of these networks also gives you another place to look when you cannot locate the source of a block, or some other kind of interference. It may very well be that it is coming from the other side of a door. Since doors do not always present on their own, and some are even meant to be hidden, you may need to ask higher self or an ego-state directly to take a look.

In the healing process, when you identify an ego-state, keep in mind you may be stepping into a complex labyrinth of rooms and doors. Like in Lewis Carroll's Wonderland, you never know ahead of time where doors will lead and what kind of creature or marvel you will encounter. In the next chapter, I will talk more about these networks in conjunction with mapping the inner world.

Two Protocols

From a clinical point of view, the focus is always on one door at a time. The question is not whether it leads to a network. That's unpredictable, and it will become apparent as you encounter doors—or not. The question is: what's on the other side of a door, and does it need to be addressed directly in the healing process? The bias in Soul-Centered Healing is that if a door presents, there is probably a connection to the area being worked in. And since we cannot know ahead of time what is on the other side of any, it seems better to err on the side of caution and check out each one. Better to turn over every stone, than to miss a critical connection. In SCH, the general practice is to account for every door that is identified and determine whether it needs to be addressed. In my experience, most of the time, the answer is yes they do need to be addressed.

Step 1: Surround in Light

The higher self plays a central role in navigating these inner networks. It begins with the higher self's ability to surround a door in Light. This is the first step in dealing with a door—have higher self place Light around it. This follows Gerod's original suggestion. He said that it may "prevent a door from being opened or from something being created behind it." As he described it, the Light can act as a kind of buffer or salve, to help prevent the creation of new doors, or triggering reactions from ones already there. If the door goes outside the soul, I see the Light acting as a deterrent to spirits or separate entities that may be on the other side and who would wish to interfere with or stop the healing process. Quite often, they react as the healing process brings Light into an area and they will try to block it. They seem to know that once the Light reaches their own area, whatever they've got going is going to be lost. If Light is placed at a door when first identified, they are less likely to approach or try to enter the area where you are working. This step is not always applicable in every situation, but it's good to do when possible.

Step 2: Determine how many doors

Once a door is surrounded in Light, the next step is to determine if there is more than one door, and if so, how many. Often, the ego-state or entity that led to the first door also knows how many doors there are altogether. If not, the higher self almost always knows or can find out how many there are. Even when an ego-state or entity gives the number, however, I will confirm it with the higher self.

The reason for this step is so the higher self can place Light at those doors too, just as it did at the first, and for the same reason: to keep the inner situation stabilized. Given that every door is an unknown, each starts out with equal value. Logically, it doesn't make sense to secure only one door when there are four more in the same area.

Determining the number of doors is also the first step in identifying an inner network. If there is more than one door, then it's likely to be a network, and it can range from simple to convoluted. Two doors are usually easier to work with than eight. The clinical question is: if there is more than one door, and each is an unknown, how do you decide where to start? Without any idea of what is behind those doors, there's little basis for a clinical judgment on how to proceed. The doors can lead anywhere, and they may or may not be important.

Step 3: Identify doors that need to be addressed.

The higher self, again, is the one to determine whether a door needs to be addressed directly. Sometimes, the answer is obvious. Either something starts presenting that has to be dealt with on the spot, or dealing with a particular door is the only way forward. Usually, however, I rely on the higher self to determine whether an opening needs to be addressed or can be ignored. Most of the time, the higher self seems to have some knowledge of what is on the other side and where it leads. Also, when there is more than one door, the higher self usually knows the sequence in which they should be addressed. Sometimes, but not as often, the ego-state or entity also knows what is on the other side of a door or where it leads. This information can be helpful if offered, but in general, I find it more effective working with the higher self to methodically determine how many doors there are and which need to be addressed. The basic approach is that higher self make a determination on every door identified as to whether it needs to be addressed or not.

Step 4: How many doors are intra-psychic and how many extra-psychic?

Before having the higher self identify which door to start with, I have it determine how many doors go to other areas of the self/soul (intra-psychic), and how many go outside the soul (extra-psychic). This information, along with the number of doors, gives further indication of the complexity of the situation. The main reason for asking the question at this step is to prepare to deal with the first door. Depending on which kind of door it is, there are two different protocols. Intra-psychic doors are handled differently than extra-psychic ones. Each calls for a different approach.

Step 5A: Protocol for Intra-psychic Doors

When a door leads to another area of the self/soul, the higher self is asked to move through the door and determine if there is someone or something that needs to be addressed. If there is, the basic protocols are used to identify and work with whomever or whatever is there.

It could be ego-states or energy devices; it could be spirits or other separate entities. It could be any combination.

Once all has been resolved, the question is whether there are any doors present in that area. If not, then the higher self is asked to return to the original area and address the next door, if there is one. However, if there are doors, then the same protocol is used: determine how many; whether they are intra-psychic or extra-psychic; which need to be addressed; and identify the one to start with. This is where the network becomes more complex—when there are doors within doors.

Keep in mind that if there are spirits or separate entities through the door, it means there has been an intrusion. It also means that there is likely to be one or more extra-psychic doors through which the separate one(s) entered. These doors or openings may need to be addressed immediately, or they will wait until after the spirits or entities have left or been removed.

Step 5B: Protocol for Extra-psychic Doors

Unlike with intra-psychic doors, the higher self is not asked to go through an extra-psychic door. If a door goes outside the soul, then there's a different set of questions, all meant to answer the central one: what has gone out or come in through the door? There are many possibilities. An ego-state might have fled the soul, or stumbled out, to escape its pain or terror. It might have left out of anger, or in search of another soul, incarnate or discarnate, out of loss and grief. It's not uncommon to find these kinds of doors, and the ego-states that created them. I don't find them with every client, and when I do, they are usually limited in number. However, there can be clients where these kinds of doors are a major part of the healing process.

The extra-psychic doors I find most often are those created by, or in reaction to, outside entities. This includes all the usual suspects—spirits, alien or dimensional beings, and/or external ego-states. Whether it's to take something out of the self/soul, set up some activity inside, or to open up communication, depends on the entities involved. Motivations range from well intentioned, to predatory, to evil. A door might be intentionally created by outside entities or spirits, for example, to gain entry to the mind and soul, or to insert devices that can siphon soul energy.

In the end, though, when doors are discovered that go outside the soul, the basic aim is to 1) retrieve any parts of the self/soul that left or were taken (seduced, lured, tricked, or manipulated); 2) remove any separate ones that have entered (along with anything they brought in); and 3) have higher self close and seal the door(s). I'll write more about this in Chapter 14: Soul Retrieval.

Step 6: Return to original area

When working in an area where more than one door needs to be addressed, the first door is worked with to whatever level is necessary. It may include two or three tiers of doors. Once the first door, and all it has encompassed is resolved, the higher self is asked to return to the original area and address the next door—if there is one—until all doors in that original area have been addressed or accounted for.

Protocol for Doors: Example 1

The following is an example of identifying and dealing with doors. It follows the integration of a group of ego-states where two doors have been identified. It continues from where the previous example left off, i.e. two doors have been identified and the higher self has helped move the group of ego-states to integration.

Th. Higher self, were the ego-states able to move to their places of integration all right?
HS Yes finger lifts
Th. Are you aware of those two doors the ego-states identified?
HS Yes finger lifts
Th. Are they doors, higher self, that need to be addressed?
HS Yes finger lifts
Th. Do either of them go outside the soul?
HS Yes finger lifts
Th. Do they both go outside?
HS No finger lifts
Th. One goes outside and the other to another area of the soul. Is that correct?
HS Yes finger lifts

Th. If we should address the door going outside, then the first finger lifting; if the door going to another area of the soul, then the second finger.

HS   Second finger lifts

Th. Higher self, I'm asking that you move through that door and identify whether there is someone or something to address. First finger when that's been determined; second finger if there's a problem.

HS   First finger lifts.

Th. Higher self, did you find someone or something?

HS   Yes finger lifts.

Th. If it's someone, first finger lifting, if something, second finger.

HS   First finger lifts.

Th. Higher self, please identify that one, help them come forward here with me… and to this one, do you know yourself to be a part of this self/soul I'm working with?

Egs. Yes finger lifts.

Th. Are you one first created in this present life of Mary's?

Egs. Yes finger lifts.

In this example, an ego-state has been identified, and so the therapist begins the Identification Protocol. The ego-state might be alone or part of a group. It might be present-life or past-life. There may be spirits present or some other kind of entity.

There might also be doors. The clinical question is: if there are doors, will any of them be triggered while working in the present area. There's no way to know this ahead of time. There's also no one right answer. It depends on the inner situation. In my mind, it most often comes down to clinical judgment and intuition. All things being equal, my own approach, once an ego-state has been identified, is to direct higher self to surround any doors with Light, and then come back later to identify them specifically, once any ego-states and/or entities are resolved.

This is the second last step in the Ego-State Protocol. Before the ego-states integrate, they are asked to look around and see if there are any doors or openings. The following is an example of this step in the protocol.

Protocol for Doors: Example 2

Th. Higher self, should they have a conscious experience here in the present before integration?

HS Yes finger lifts.

Th. And to the group: Before moving to your place of Light, I'm asking that you look around you where you are there. Are there any doors or opening you see there?

___ Yes finger lifts.

Th. Is it more than two doors?

___ No finger lifts.

Th. Is it two doors?

___ Yes finger lifts

Th. Higher self, I'm asking that you surround those doors with Light and we will come back. First, I'm asking that you help each of the group move now to the conscious mind for that conscious experience and perception. Communicate to them any further information and understanding about this present point of view that can be helpful. When complete, help each to move to their place of Light and integration. First finger when these moves are complete. Second finger if there's a problem.

HS Yes finger lifts.

Th. Higher self, are you aware of these two doors?

HS Yes finger lifts.

Th. Do either of them go outside the soul?

HS Yes finger lifts.

Th. Do they both go outside?

HS No finger lifts.

Th. Is it just one that goes outside?

HS Yes finger lifts.

Th. Do either of these doors need to be addressed?

HS Yes finger lifts.

Th. Do both need to be addressed?

HS No finger lifts.

Th. Does that one going outside need to be addressed?

HS Yes finger lifts.

Th. Are there any parts or pieces of self/soul energy that have left or been taken out through that opening?

HS Yes finger lifts.

10

Mapping the Inner World

Worth a Thousand Words

When I am working with a client, and writing notes, I am also creating a visual map of what is happening in the session. They are simple line drawings depicting whom I am working with in the client's inner world, whether it is alone or with others, and whether the area it is in has any doors or openings. Technically, this mapping is not a necessary practice in SCH. The same information conveyed by the map could also be found in the notes. However, reviewing the notes can require a good deal more time and effort, especially when dealing with complex areas. If you need to backtrack or review, a map provides a quick visual reminder for what has been happening during a session, or occurred in previous sessions. Often, the map is enough to recall what has been happening from one session to the next, or where to look in the notes for a more specific review.

On Notes and Mapping

Over the years, I developed a format for notes and mapping that enabled me to be as succinct as possible, yet still provide a sufficient record. I'm sharing this format and mapping here, not because it's the only way to do it, but it's the only one I know. I offer it as a kind of template where you can borrow elements and pieces that you find helpful. You are likely to develop your own shorthand methods, using your own symbols, abbreviations, drawings, etc., to help you take sufficient notes. What is important is that you have an accurate record of where the healing process has been, how one step followed another, and where the process is in the present.

There isn't time while working with a client to take anything like complete or verbatim notes. There isn't time to tape every session and review it before a client's next session. This could be done in a research setting where every session is taped and able to be analyzed later. In clinical practice, though, it is not practical. As a therapist, you will need to develop a shorthand method that lets you stay focused with the client in the present, and at the same time provides a coherent record that can be referred to later.

The Basic Map

One of the most basic components in mapping the inner world is the room. Like doors, *room* is a generic term for any area or environment, as discussed in the last chapter. In my own work with clients, many ego-states described, literally, being in a room, but others claimed to be outdoors, or in a cave, or propped on a ledge somewhere.

The first time I encounter a specific ego-state, I will immediately draw an oval representing the room or environment, and I draw a smaller oval inside to represent the ego-state. If a client's higher self, for example, identifies a three-year-old ego-state, I will write that information down and then draw a picture on the right side of the page (see Figure 10.1).

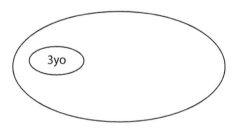

Figure 10.1

As I work with the three year-old, I will add to the diagram as I gain more information. I may find out, for example, that there are other ego-states present, along with two spirits. By the time the entire group has been identified, my diagram would look like this (see Figure 10.2).

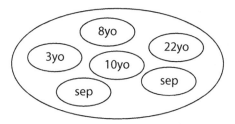

Figure 10.2

Another important distinction is whether a spirit or other non-physical entity has entered the client's energy field at some level or is operating from outside the self/soul. This information is not always relevant. A spirit presence may be resolved quickly without ever having to ask the question. Also, using the protocols, working with spirits or other entities is basically the same whether they have entered the client's energy field or not. If they allow contact from the Light, or from a spirit teacher, usually that's all it takes for them to leave or disengage from the client.

It's usually those situations where a spirit or entity refuses contact with the Light that the distinction between inside and outside can be helpful. On a basic level, it's the difference between having to remove something versus severing ties with it. This information can help us better understand the nature of the relationship between the client and the separate beings. This, in turn, can help us to narrow in on the point of access the beings use to engage or enter the client, and then determine the most effective approach for closing that access.

Going back to the example, if I was to find a spirit or other being affecting a client from outside, I would denote it like this (see Figure 10.3).

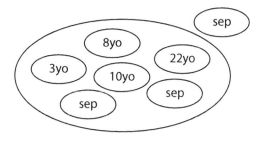

Figure 10.3

It may take several sessions to work through the entire group, so I keep the notes containing the diagram of that group on my desk and add notations as each ego-state or spirit is resolved. By the time the entire room has been resolved, the picture may look like Figure 10.4.

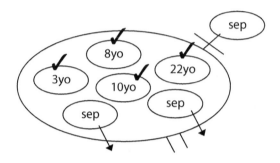

Figure 10.4

This tells me that we identified two separate spirits, and that both left or were removed. It says we worked with four ego-states, with the checkmarks indicating that all four have shared and moved to integration. A separate spirit operating from outside the self/soul also had its connection to the client severed. Finally, the two slashes represent a door or opening leading out of the ego-states' room. The diagram may be extended in subsequent sessions depending on where the door leads—outside the soul, or to another area of the soul—and whether it needs to be addressed.

Figure 5, below, is a legend of the identifiers I use in mapping the client's inner world (see Figure 10.5).

SCH Map Legend

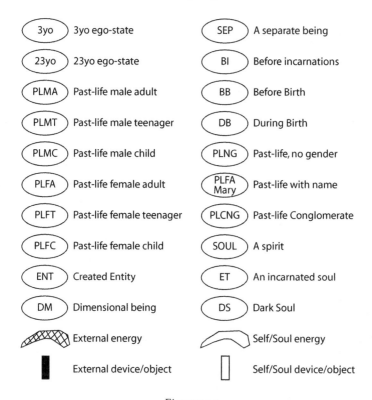

3yo   3yo ego-state

23yo   23yo ego-state

PLMA   Past-life male adult

PLMT   Past-life male teenager

PLMC   Past-life male child

PLFA   Past-life female adult

PLFT   Past-life female teenager

PLFC   Past-life female child

ENT   Created Entity

DM   Dimensional being

External energy

External device/object

SEP   A separate being

BI   Before incarnations

BB   Before Birth

DB   During Birth

PLNG   Past-life, no gender

PLFA Mary   Past-life with name

PLCNG   Past-life Conglomerate

SOUL   A spirit

ET   An incarnated soul

DS   Dark Soul

Self/Soul energy

Self/Soul device/object

Figure 10.5

Using these identifiers, it does not take much concentration to fill in a map as you go along. Some maps will consist of one group of ego-states with no doors or connections to other groups. Other maps will be extensive, showing interconnections among groups, and a variety of phenomena, both parts of the soul and separate.

Figure 10.6 depicts a complex field comprised of six groups of ego-states, separate beings, energies, and devices. This diagram is for illustrative purposes, but you could run into something like this if a client is doing deep level healing. The rooms are interconnected with one another through doors, and two of the rooms have doors going outside the soul. In one case, soul energy has been taken out through that door. In the other, four ego-states left or were taken out. All will have to be retrieved.

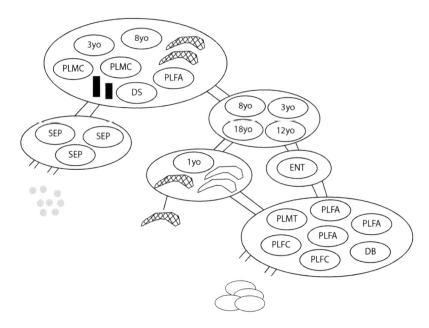

Figure 10.6

My approach is to work through any network of rooms until there are no doors, or the higher self says they don't need to be addressed. In the process, I continue to add to the map as the network reveals itself one room at a time. The map keeps me aware of the field I am working in and where it first began. In this way, the map is a powerful tool for visualizing the continuity of the healing process.

The following images were scanned from case notes. They give a good idea of what these maps look like on paper.

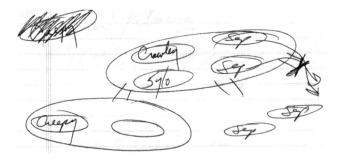

Figure 10.7

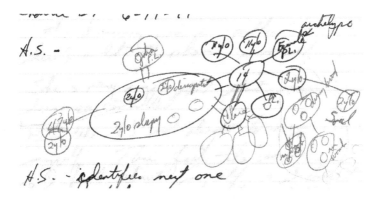

Figure 10.8

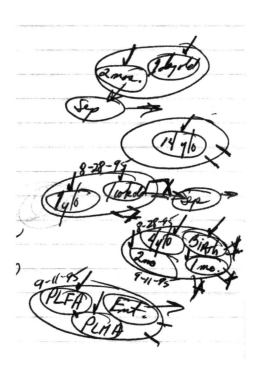

Figure 10.9

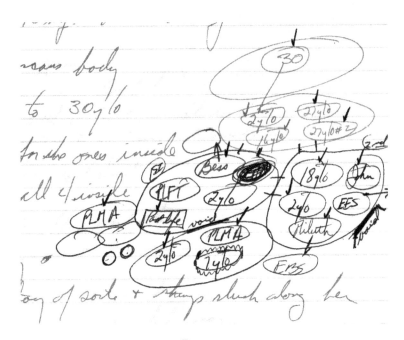

Figure 10.10

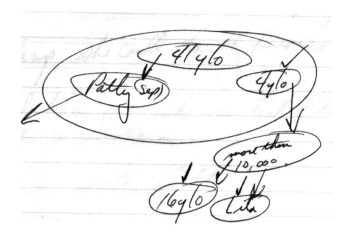

Figure 10.11

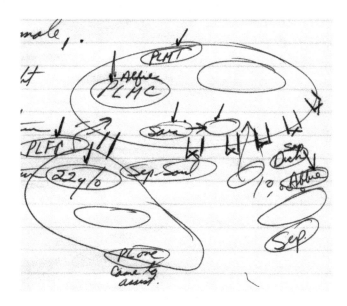

Figure 10.12

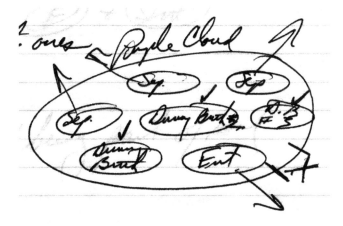

Figure 10.13

Figure 10.14

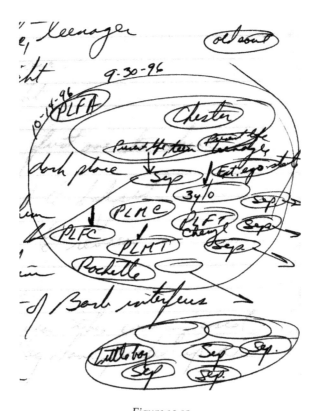

Figure 10.15

Figure 10.16

Besides keeping track of the healing process in the present, the case notes and the maps trace the client's healing journey through a labyrinth of mind and soul. Taken together, I look at it as threads of the client's soul story. It's not unusual for certain themes or issues dealt with at one point in the healing process to reappear again later. In these cases, I found it very helpful to be able to review my notes and have that segment of the treatment in mind as I address what is presenting.

Part 4

Ego-States: Split, Sliced, and Shattered

11

Multi-Experience Ego-States

Special Cases

Besides forming groups, another complication in working with ego-states is that there are certain types that are more difficult to work with than others. I look at them as special cases, extreme defenses. They are special in that each type uses a different strategy to dissociate pain from the conscious self. With these ego-states, it seems that the mind is forced to take extra steps to make sure an experience stays split off from the conscious awareness.

I have identified five types that present frequently and consistently enough that I keep them in mind as possibilities when I encounter strong blocking or confusion. They are:

- Multi-experience
- Splitting
- Serial
- Shattered
- Mirror Personality

This is not an exhaustive list. These are the ones, though, I've seen most frequently. They don't present with every client, but they present often enough that it pays to be aware of them. If you are continually blocked in your work with an ego-state, you may be dealing with one of these types. If so, the right questions can help determine this and the protocols can be modified to deal with them.

Multi-Experience

This type of ego-state, as the name implies, carries more than one experience. What appears to happen is that an already existing ego-state is triggered into consciousness when the conscious self is overwhelmed. The triggering mechanism is that the present day experience closely parallels or matches the ego-state's own experience. A child ego-state, for example, that carries an experience of being screamed at by his father, may be triggered when the boss is screaming at the person. Instead of a new ego-state being created, the one that handled this kind of experience originally is, so to speak, called back into service to perform the same function.

But it's not exactly the same. Depending on the person and the situation, a child ego-state could be triggered and respond exactly as it did when it was first created. Someone observing this reaction might describe the person as "acting like a child." More often, though, the triggered ego-state will adapt its functioning to the present reality. It will do so along the same lines as its original defense, but in a way that fits the new circumstances and demands of the more developed ego-self.

In the process, the ego-state is altered. It's as though it puts on a new skin, or takes on a new identity. Interestingly enough, what also occurs in this kind of situation is that the ego-state will advance to the current age. A four year-old ego-state, for example, that takes over consciousness during an experience at age thirteen will then become thirteen. If she comes out again when the person is twenty-four, then thirteen year old becomes twenty-four years old.

From a clinical point of view, there are primarily two problems that can arise when working with a multi-experience ego-state. The first is that the multiple experiences can be too overwhelming for the ego-state to share at one time. The sharing may need to be done in stages. In addition, an ego-state may not offer, and it may not be obvious, that it carries more than one experience. It may be afraid to feel or share the earlier experience. There may be some block or prohibition attached to it that was not present with the later experience. In these cases, if you suspect an ego-state has more than one experience, you can begin to explore it with the ego-state and the higher self.

A second problem that can occur with the multi-experience ego-state is when it does not remember its experience(s) prior to its latest one.

Its new identity, so to speak, has veiled what came before. Therefore, when asked to share, it will only share this last experience, but then be unable to have a full release. The healing can go around in circles with this type of ego-state until its earlier experience(s) is identified, shared, and then released.

A final twist on this kind of ego-state is that a past life ego-state may be triggered because it carries an experience matching what is happening in the present life. When that past-life part comes forward, it's as though it becomes a present life ego-state and subsequently identifies with the present life and forgets its previous experience(s). This doesn't't seem to happen very frequently, but it does happen and it's good to be aware of the possibility.

Shelley B.

A good example of the multi-experience ego-state is one I encountered with a client, Shelley B. Shelley was in her mid-forties, had been divorced five years, and she lived with her son, Jerry, who was now in high school.

Shelley was an excellent trance subject. The higher self and the ego-states were able to speak through her without interrupting trance. Or they shared with Shelley visually and she would relate it to me. She started our session that day by saying she was feeling a strong anxiety and had been feeling it all day. She could not identify any reason for the anxiety, except that she was in the process of buying a new house and she had talked to the woman at the mortgage company earlier in the day.

Once Shelley was in trance, the higher self did identify an ego-state involved with the anxiety. The ego-state identified itself as a twenty-six year-old female. After contact with the higher self, she was readily agreeable to the healing process. When I asked her to share, Shelley's trance was deep enough that she began to verbalize what was happening. The twenty-six-year -old shared that she was at the beach. Her son was next to her playing in the sand. She told me it is a family outing, and she is feeling happy. It's when they lived in San Diego. She looks up and sees her husband, Peter, coming over the sand hill and walking towards them. She sees just his head at first as he comes over the rise. These are my shorthand notes of what 26yo shared.

Session #5

- I'm feeling anxious now about something.
- I look at Peter's face to see if he is angry… I'm worried. I feel it in my stomach.
- He looks happy.
- I'm real nervous.
- I'm beginning to feel like I don't really love him.
- But I don't know how to get out of this… how to take care of myself and my son.
- She feels insignificant.
- If I die, nobody would care.
- I just don't matter.
- I thought about just dying. But I have a son. And he needs me because his father won't be a father to him.

At this point, the sharing stopped. For 26yo, the experience on the beach was complete, and she said there was nothing more she needed to share. At a conscious level, Shelley had been fully aware of the sharing. She could feel 26yo's anxiety and helplessness.

I worked with 26yo, then, to have her release the anxiety that she was feeling. Shelley reported feeling the release too. When I asked 26yo, however, whether she still felt any anxiety or distress, she said she did. She then began sharing a second experience. It was during her son's birthday party several months before that day on the beach.

Session #5

- I'm at a birthday party… my son's party
- Sometimes I'm worried whether he's going to be okay.
- We live in a small apartment.
- He's not very happy.
- He's been hurt.
- His dad… he's never going to love that boy.
- I want to leave
- I'm tired of the responsibility of all of it.
- He's a weak man.
- Today, I feel…
- I don't like to think about this…

- I want Peter to love us but he doesn't.
- I feel bad because Jerry wants his approval and isn't going to get it.
- I need to get a divorce.
- My husband abuses my son.
- I told Peter: Don't you ever hit my child!
- There will be no more children. I've made up my mind.

The sharing came to a stop again, and once more 26yo went through the process of release.

It became clear that 26yo had been triggered earlier that day when Shelley was arranging for the mortgage loan on her new house. Situations like this, with the commitment and finances involved, can normally arouse some anxiety for people. It's a big step. I'm sure this was true for Shelley. But for her, it triggered a much deeper anxiety. It took her to a time when she also was faced with a decision of taking on major new responsibilities, of "making it on her own" with few resources, and a young child depending on her. At that time, the anxiety about making such a move was overwhelming.

26yo was triggered during her son's birthday party when Shelley began to realize that, for Jerry's sake, and for hers, she would have to leave Peter. At a conscious level, Shelley was not able to deal with that reality at the time, and it frightened her deeply. She felt she did not have the education or job skills that she believed would be needed to support Jerry and her. She felt inadequate and insecure in many areas. She was also angry and deeply hurt by Peter's treatment of her, but even more so by his treatment of Jerry. She was trapped, and her conflict and anxiety were growing.

26yo took over at the birthday party when the truth of the relationship was forcing itself upon her. She was the one who also took over several months later at the beach when that same truth was coming to her again. 26yo protected Shelley from what, at that time, she perceived as an impossible choice. 26yo carried the anxiety and pain that was bound up in the conflicts surrounding her marriage and the need to leave. (It would be five years before Shelley finally obtained a divorce and moved with Jerry into their own apartment.)

After her second release, 26yo reported that she still felt some anxiety and distress. I asked the higher self to help her to review inside to see if there was anything else that needed to be shared. When the review was complete, 26yo began to share more. She said she had first come at ten years old and then she began to share. Again, these are my clinical notes.

Session #5

- My father's dead
- I don't want to talk about it
- He was my only loving parent.
- I'm alone
- I think I want to go with him. I feel it's not fair.
- He was my only...
- I'm trying to put a lid on it.
- He always told me to be a big girl and do what I'm told and behave.
- But I don't want to be left alone. I'm lost.
- I don't want to... I don't know anything about death, but I'm in pain
- They wouldn't even tell me
- I found out because I overheard somebody on the phone.
- He was in a bad accident at work.
- I'm at my mother's; she is making some arrangement over the phone.
- We went to see him. He was in an oxygen tent. He told me to be a good girl and mind my mother.
- My mother said she'd slap me if I cried.
- When we walked out of there I never saw him again.
- They wouldn't even let me attend the funeral. When I would go to the graveyard I always talked to him.
- I loved my daddy so... and I hate my stepfather.
- I don't want to go there but I have to. My stepmother died and there's nobody else to take care of me.
- She loved me. My sister hated her, but I didn't. I really liked her. She used to make special dinners just for me. She told me special stories and now she's gone too.

This time, 26yo was finally able to have a full release. When I asked, she reported no feelings of distress, fear, or anxiety. She said yes when I asked whether she felt good and comfortable inside. Shelley, at a conscious level, also reported again that she felt the release and no longer felt the anxiety that she had been feeling when she arrived. Following the release, 26yo was able to move to her place of integration.

The change in age that I discussed earlier also occurred in Shelley's case. The ten-year-old jumped to twenty-five years-old when she took over at the birthday party. Then she became twenty-six that day on the beach. So when an ego-state says that it is twenty, thirty or fifty years-old, that doesn't necessarily mean that that is when the ego-state was first created. This also is why an older ego-state may share a memory from an earlier time and one not commensurate with its present age.

It had been a very difficult and painful session for Shelley. Afterwards, though, she understood that her purchase of a new home had triggered a part of herself that had taken over at traumatic times in her life when she was confronting major moves. These situations incited intense feelings of insecurity and pain—from her father's home to her mother and stepfather's house, and from living with Peter to moving to a home of her own. At a conscious level, Shelley was excited about the new home and there were no financial problems about buying the house. Shelley's normal anxieties, though, appeared to have triggered 26yo whose moves had been traumatic.

Some multi-experience ego-states are aware of all the experiences they carry and some, like Shelley's twenty-six- year-old, are not. This is where there may be some difficulty in the healing process. Many multi-experience ego-states are aware only of their most recent experience. They do not always remember—and often don't want to remember—any earlier experiences, especially the one in which they were first created. It's as if the ego-state has repressed its experience and automatically resists opening up that earlier (and probably deeper) pain.

The problem in the healing process is that an ego-state shares the experience it does remember, but then becomes stuck and confused. Or the ego-state becomes frightened because the sharing has triggered its earlier experience(s) and these memories start to move toward consciousness. It's not unusual at that point that an ego-state might stop the sharing and step back, or become stuck and have difficulty proceeding.

Here is a sample protocol for dealing with a multi-experience ego-state. The situation involves an eighteen year-old ego-state who has just shared her experience of nearly drowning in a boating accident. She has just finished her release and the therapist wants to check that she has had a full release.

Multi-experience ego-state: Example 1

Th. 18yo, were you able to have that release all right?

18yo Yes finger lifts.

Th. Is there any pain, hurt, or distress you're still feeling there?

18yo Yes finger lifts.

Th. Is there something more you need to share yet for that full release?

18yo Hand lifts.

Th. You're not sure. Is that correct?

18yo Yes finger lifts.

Th. 18yo, do you know how old the body was when you first came?

18yo Hand lifts. (Not sure)

Th. Would you be willing to have a safe review with higher self about this, about how old the body was when you first came?

18yo Yes finger lifts.

Th. Higher self, very safely, I'm asking that you help 18yo to review inside what it is she carries? What's happened? What needs to be shared yet for her full healing and release? Very safely, higher self, help her with that review. First finger when complete; second finger, if it's stopped.

18yo First finger lifts.

Th. 18yo, were you able to have that review all right?

18yo Yes finger lifts.

Th. Is there something yet that needs to be shared?

18yo Yes finger lifts.

Th. Are you willing to share that now to the conscious mind?

18yo Yes finger lifts.

Th. On three, then, let share what needs to be shared. One, two, three... just share to the conscious mind now what you need to share. What you see, feel, or hear... Let it share right here to the present. First finger when that's complete. Second finger, if it's stopped or blocked.

18yo First finger lifts.

Th. Donna, here with me at a conscious level, Donna, did you receive something?

Do   Yes. It's when I was twelve. I was at a neighbor's pool. I had a seizure and almost drowned.

When an ego-state carries more than one experience, the same protocol is used for each experience that needs to be shared directly. The ego-state may need to share just one experience or it might need to share them all. The protocol, though, remains the same: share what needs to be shared, and then release. Repeat until the ego-state feels no pain or distress and is able to integrate.

Multi-experience ego-states are usually not difficult to work with once the therapist knows what he or she is dealing with. These ego-states still want healing and will cooperate with the review and the sharing. It can be more painful, and the ego-state may require more reassurance, but in the end, it can have a full release.

12

Splitting

A second type of ego-state is termed a *split*. These are ego-states—two or more—that are created at the same time in order to manage or deal with overwhelming pain and trauma. The splitting can happen along different lines depending on the person, what is happening, and what kind of protection is needed or will work. You might have a split, for example, where two ego-states are created. One carries the feelings and emotions, and the other one has only the cognitive memory; or one is female and the other male; or they carry the same pain, but it's been divided in order to share the load.

Even more complex, you can have splits of more than two. It may be four or seven, each of which carries its own part of the experience. After a splitting occurs, the ego-states may stay together in the same place, or they may separate and move to different places and never have contact again. One may be afraid of the other, or when one is triggered the other is triggered, or they may have no awareness of each other at all. There are all kinds of variations. For the process of healing, though, the same protocol is used, whether working with them as individuals or as a group. The goal, in the end, is to have these splits brought back together for the purpose of integration. Sometimes, the higher self says the different splits should remerge as one. Other times, it says they should form a group but remain individuals.

Another variation is where an ego-state is triggered by a present day trauma, similar to its own. Unlike the multi-experience ego-state, however, this one cannot tolerate what is happening and so it splits, like a cell dividing. The new ego-state takes over, is usually the present age, and the original one remains dissociated.

Going back to the earlier example of the eighteen year-old involved in the boating accident, if 12yo was triggered, but could not tolerate the trauma, a split could have occurred in which the new ego-state is eighteen-years-old, deals with the trauma, and the twelve-year-old remains dissociated from the experience. In this case, 18yo carries not only the present experience, but also the original experience at twelve years old in which it is rooted. Technically, 18yo is a multi-experience ego-state, but the bond between 12yo and 18yo will be a powerful factor in the healing process. It's likely that there won't be a full release for either until they both can have a release.

My work with Shelley B., whom I talked about in the previous chapter, also offers an example of splitting and the kind of complexity it can introduce into the healing process. This particular example involved two ego-states, 3yo and 11yo. Over the course of seven sessions with Shelley, I learned about 3yo and the splitting that occurred when Shelley was eleven. When the split happened, one ego-state remained three-years-old, and the other became eleven.

3yo is the one I met first. I had been talking to Shelley at the start of our session and she told me that she had been experiencing "a lot of confusion" during the week. She also reported a dream that she had earlier in the week. In the dream she said there was "a fog." She said she was "looking for something and can't find it." Shelley also said that a disturbing image came to her, and she had no idea what it was about. It was a "picture of a naked man. An old man."

I asked the higher self to look for the source of this confusion, and shortly, higher self communicated that there was more than one ego-state involved. The higher self also communicated that the ego-state who had the image of the naked man was involved in the confusion that Shelley was experiencing. The higher self brought her forward and she identified herself as three years old. I communicated with her, made sure she received the communication from the higher self about healing, and then we moved to the point where she began her sharing. Shelley, again, started saying it out loud as it came to her.

Session #11 – 3yo#1

- I see a small child with blond curly hair
- She has a dress on.
- It's very foggy

- There's… I can only see the little girl. It's a yellow dress.
- There's something coming…
- I'm in front of my house. It has a porch.
- There's something really evil about that house.
- I've liked that house. I had a teddy bear there, but today I don't want to go in there.
- I can see…

Then the 3yo was suddenly gone. It turned out she was blocked. I asked higher self to find the source of the blocking, and it identified an 11yo. I worked with 11yo and, shortly, she agreed to step back and let the 3yo continue.

Session #11 – 3yo#1

- I'm sitting in the lap of somebody
- They let me have their glasses and hat.
- Then they start taking my clothes off and touching me.
- It's not unpleasant and I don't feel like it's something I shouldn't be doing and I'm just sitting there hugging this person
- He took my shoes and socks off.
- And then…, I don't know… somebody has come in the room
- They've yanked me; they've pulled me, and taken me to another room.
- I'm being scolded.
- I can't see the person scolding me
- I don't think it's my mother.
- I'm confused, I don't know what I've done wrong
- I got slapped, then she left me in the room and locked the door
- I feel so alone
- It's in the back of the house
- It's my aunt's house; it's not my room
- I'm crying hard. I cry a lot.
- But only when I am alone
- I'm just so scared and lonesome and confused.
- I don't know what I did wrong
- The man is Uncle David and the woman is Aunt Martha
- This is Aunt Martha's house. Dad and Shelley lived there. They were poor.

The sharing stopped. The higher self communicated that there were five altogether in this room and I learned there was another three year-old. I asked higher self to bring her forward. These are my notes of what was shared.

Session #11 – 3yo#2

- Aunt Martha scrubs me, most of time in the kitchen sink
- The day Uncle David did that she scrubbed me very hard
- She really hurt me
- She likes to hurt me and then in front of everybody she says how she loves me.
- After Aunt Martha came, the house was evil
- She reads the Bible to me all the time…
- She pulls my hair and I can't get away
- She thinks I've done something wrong but I don't know what it is
- She sometimes sends me to my room without dinner
- Later, dad will bring me a sandwich
- Food is a balm. When I do things right I get food and when I don't, I don't get food.
- She's a skinny woman

Two days after this session I received a short letter from Shelley.

> Dear Tom,
>
> I wanted to relate something and was afraid I'd forget before our next meeting. I asked my Mom if I ever played with Uncle David's glasses. She said, "no, he didn't wear glasses. Your dad let you play with his glasses." I find that information disturbing. Can I still be hiding from myself?
>
> Shelley

The next week, we came back to the eleven-year-old who had blocked the three-year-old in our previous session. At eleven, Shelley's father had had a serious accident at work and died two days later in the hospital. Shelley was forced to move in with her mother and stepfather.

Session #13 – 11yo

- Fear is a large part of what I do
- It came – the fear – a long time ago but it stays
- The fear cripples
- It doesn't allow for good growth
- The fear is always there
- It's a fear of being alone, not being good enough
- Sometimes the fear makes bad judgments
- It isolates
- I have a vision of being in a room and just being terrified of the dark
- I do things so people don't know I'm afraid
- It sometimes makes me sick
- I'm having a hard time; I don't like the feeling and I try to overcome it and…
- People don't know that I'm scared
- I think it started here
- I'm at my mother's house
- My father died
- And it has just sunk in that I'm alone
- And when I pretend, people look up to me. They think I don't have any fear
- …but I have a lot of fear
- It hurts in my stomach and chest
- When things happen, I feel these hurts
- But it started here – the not sharing it, trying to squeeze it in

At that point in the session I had the higher self communicate to 11yo more support and reassurance. Then she continued:

Session #13 – 11yo

- The fear has affected a lot of things
- When you tell people you're scared, they get upset
- She (referring to Shelley) still feels it's important to pretend in 1991
- It hurts to be seen as someone who's not afraid.

I ask 11yo what she means by that. Why would it hurt to have someone see her as afraid?

Session #13 – 11yo

- That's private
- It's close to the core
- 11yo says she has spent a lot of energy keeping these feelings away

At that point, it was the end of the session and the higher self came forward and communicated to me directly.

Session #13 – Higher Self

- Understand please that so many things have never been shared with Shelley. This has been a guarded area. The emotions that are stirring around here have brought a lot of fear to the front. This has never been done before.

In the next session, higher self identified another three-year-old. She was willing to communicate with me. At first, though, she had difficulty getting oriented.

Session #14 – 3yo#2

- She is aware of 11yo
- She moves around
- She's having difficulty but then sees the Light
- She's confused
- Doesn't know why she's here
- She travels between groups, it causes confusion for them
- "I feel drawn to go to another area but when I get there, they get scared and confused."
- This one carries the pain
- She has done some sharing from two of the groups
- She still takes on pain
- She also causes pain when she gets close to consciousness
- 3yo is trying to prepare for the healing

The three-year-old needed to stop at this point. She needed some time to prepare for what she would have to share. All we knew was that she carried some very deep pain. I went back to 11yo from the previous session and she continued her sharing.

Session #14 - 11yo

- It's hard for her (11yo) to believe there's a way out
- "there has been some pull"
- can't think of the word
- "In the sleep stage, there has been some activity to move me but it has not gone to a conscious level. I have stopped that."
- The higher self has been the pull
- Higher self is willing to show 11yo the new place of integration
- Says there are others there she knows
- There was an invitation.
- "3yo is moving towards me; she often does."
- 11yo knows what happened, but was afraid to feel it.
- "I don't allow those feelings."
- There are so many wounds in here
- 3yo is coming closer again

In the next session, we started with 11yo again. This time 11yo described her connection to 3yo.

Session #15 - 11yo

- I was a companion. I was trying to help but I couldn't take on any more. I didn't want the pain. It was a decision. It was decided because it was too dangerous not to.

What 11yo was describing was her split from 3yo, and in that, a split from the feelings. The problem was that the healing process was bringing her back to her connection to 3yo and this meant reconnecting with the feelings as well. 11yo continued.

Session #15 - 11yo

- She has been in the dream state
- "I'm letting the 3yo get closer to me. But there is still some whirling when she gets close. Even now.
- "Maybe you should fix 3yo"

I ask 11yo if she has any ideas about how to do that and she comes right back.

Session #15 – 11yo

- "That cloud… it's like a gas that surrounds her and it creates anxiety."

The impression was that this was a toxic cloud of emotion, but I still did not know what experience it was shrouding. It brought us back to 3yo, however, and higher self suggested it would be appropriate at that point for 3yo to share.

Session #15 – 3yo#2

- I really trusted him
- I went to my dad's room because I was scared and my dad told me to lay down with him and I did.
- It was in the little room in the front of the house. I really, really loved my dad…
- He started touching my hair, patting it, and he told me how pretty I was. My dad always thought I was pretty.
- Needs to stop.

I asked the higher self to communicate to her and give her whatever support it could. Shortly, 3yo's sharing continued.

Session #15 – 3yo#2

- I knew something was wrong. I knew it. There was something telling me. My daddy said it was okay. That little girls do that with their dads
- Where was my mom?
  (Shelley/3yo was crying now.)
- He asked me to take my nightgown off and I did
- And then he just told me to touch him and I did

The higher self said it was okay to stop at this point and that 3yo could have some release.

Shelley had no conscious memory of this sexual relationship with her father before these sessions. It was extremely painful for her as these memories came forward. The sharing took place over several sessions as Shelley and 3yo brought these two realities together. In the next two sessions, 3yo shared the rest that she needed to about the start of the sexual abuse.

3yo was created when Shelley could not reconcile the contradiction of what was happening with her father. "He loves me/he betrays me." She loved her daddy, and trusted his love. She said it felt so good to be touched and pleasured and loved. And she was so alone and isolated.

But she sensed too that something was wrong. She even asked. But her daddy, by his words and actions, was saying "no," that she was wrong, that this kind of loving really is good. He would not deceive her, would he? But somewhere inside she knew he was lying.

At three years old, Shelley could not tolerate the pain of this betrayal and the profound psychological and emotional confusion it created for her. The three-year-old ego-state took this contradiction and, along with it, the pain, confusion, and fear. She dissociated the feelings from Shelley, and the truth of what was happening.

At eleven-years-old, after her father died, Shelley was living with her mother and stepfather. It was a time, she says, that it was beginning to sink in—the deep grief and pain of losing her father, and the profound rejection she felt from her mother and her stepfather. This rejection by mother was not new, but it was back in her life now full force. The hurt, pain, and grief were too much.

3yo was triggered at that time, and before coming all the way forward to consciousness, she split. One remained three-years-old, the other was eleven. 11yo tells us she came to stop the feelings and that this is the time where she became so good at closing out others, and closing out the hurt that comes with them.

Session #19 – 11yo

- It was much easier to put people out. I could close off someone to me after that. It was much easier. I don't know why.

The creation of 11yo also kept 3yo (and her feelings) closed out as well. It kept her wandering the inner world like a ship unable to find port. 11yo says she starts to "whirl" when 3yo gets too close, and she can see the energy of pain that enshrouds her. 11yo had to remember that she was also once three-years-old and when she did, the two were able to merge and move to integration as one. Not all split ego-states will merge before or at integration. Sometimes they do, but other times they remain as individuals and will move to integration together. The higher self can determine whether a merging is necessary or not.

13

Serial Ego-States

A third type of ego-state is the *serial ego-state*. In this case, at least several ego-states – and usually many – are created in chronological succession, one after another, to deal with an ongoing trauma. In these cases, it appears that an ego-state itself becomes overwhelmed by an experience, is unable to remain in consciousness, and so another is created to step in and take over. This process can continue, creating one ego-state after another, until the experience ends. It's like the protective part keeps slicing the experience into pieces as it is happening.

In the healing process, when you find a series of ego-states like this, they are all the same age, but each living a different moment of the same event. (It is possible that one of these ego-states could be triggered later in the person's life and therefore be a multi-experience ego-state.) Barbara T. was a client I worked with where I first recognized this serial creation of ego-states. Barbara was thirty-two when I worked with her. She was a woman in deep psychological and emotional trouble. She was married, with four children, and was barely coping in her day-to-day life. She was clinically depressed; feeling terror and panic every day; and becoming lost in delusions about Jesus and Satan and sex and love. She was tormented by voices, at once seductive and terrorizing.

In taking Barbara's history, it was clear that she had been the victim of severe abuse by her step-father, Frank, whose need to dominate and control were intense. Barbara was a year old when her mother married Frank, and they had three more children of their own. Barbara said the abuse had gone on since she was little, but it was the later years that she remembered. She knew, for example, how much she and her sister both hated Saturdays, when mom was working, because they would be alone with him all day. "The whole day was a torture." What Barbara described was the ongoing emotional and physical abuse by this man, and that abuse became extreme when circumstances gave Frank the opportunity.

It was an indication of Barbara's depth of pain in this area that she never referred to Frank by name. She always referred to him as "stepfather," and she visibly cringed if I said his name. I wasn't sure if this was a sign of her hatred for the man or whether it was a way of keeping the pain at bay. By not personalizing him, she did not have to personalize her own experience.

Most significantly, in one of our early sessions, Barbara told me she had been sexually abused by her stepfather, but had no memory of it. I was struck at the time by the dissociation between her certainty of what she knew, and the complete absence of any memory. It did not take long, though, after she began her inner work that ego-states came forward who carried these experiences. Unlike with Shelley, Barbara's ego-states did not each come forward and share a complete experience. With Barbara, it was as though many of her ego-states were just outside awareness and one would come forward, share a feeling or a glimpse, and then retreat. Then another would come forward who was a different age and that one would share a piece.

In the first ten sessions, we had identified ego-states who were eleven, eight, seven, five, and four years old. During this time, these ego-states shared a great many feelings, but only gradually did the specific memories begin to emerge, beginning with the more recent at eleven-years-old and working her way back in time. This was not unusual. It was like an archaeologist uncovering the deeper layers last. These memories included being forced to perform oral sex, being fondled and touched as if he owned her, and an experience at six where he raped her while giving her a bath.

Over the course of forty sessions, we had worked with numerous ego-states. During that time, there had been several four-year-olds who had shared feelings, but not memories. We had finally worked to a point, though, where a four-year-old came forward who began to share her memory.

Session #43

- House was dark.
- Kitchen light was on
- Barbara slept downstairs
- She was being led to kitchen
- Wanted to scream but knew nobody would help me
- Reviewing rest of memory from very far away.

Session #44

- 4yo
- afraid to share
- Barbara sees blood
- 2 people
- stepfather and uncle Rick (Frank's brother)

Session #48

- Panic – fear of Terry (Barbara's husband) leaving town
- Fear of not being safe
- Fear of anybody finding out. "You can't tell!"
- Somebody yelling at me is what triggers the little girl who doesn't want to be touched
- The terror of two adults around.

Session #50

- There's still something that's inside & it's frightening; just awful
- Involved the act of intercourse by the uncle during the 4yo experience

Session #54

- "There's still something that has to come out."
- It may have to do with fear of death

At this point, I worked with four very distinct four-year-olds. They shared feelings and emotions, but no visual memory. The same thing happened in the next session when I worked with several more four-year-olds. But some memory fragments began to come.

Session #55

- Can't breathe. "memory part"
- Losing consciousness
- another 4yo pops in. "It's torture!"

Session #56

- "Flash of light"
- another 4yo ready to share
- Now sharing – He was torturing me to keep quiet
- Fingers being put in electrical socket
- Foot was being burned

Session #57

- Next 4yo willing to share
- "lying on the table"
- Next 4yo part—willing to share
- (crying very hard, screaming, "Please don't hurt me daddy, please don't hurt me."
- Another 4yo part
- He's taking my fingers… he's telling me "this is electric shock. He's scaring me. I don't want to die! "Then you won't tell."
- Another 4yo
- I fainted or something
- I seem to be drugged
- "Feeling drugged"
- Another 4yo
- "I'm scared." There's more than one.
- My uncle
- Left hand clenches into fist
- Another shock from the electricity. It tingles.
- Another 4yo
- I'm crying that I want my mommy
- Another 4yo
- "I keep telling him to get out"
- sexual intercourse
- another 4yo
- my arms and wrists hurt real bad.

Session #58

- 4yo part willing to share
- "pain and hurt of intercourse"
- next 4yo
- he was kissing me and it made me sick
- he was stimulating me and I didn't want him to
- 4th 4yo
- very sore in vaginal area and I'm bleeding
- 5th
- I just don't want them to touch me
- 6th
- the smell of them down there makes me sick
- 7th
- He's masturbating me
- 8th
- He was hurting me, my heart was breaking
- 9th
- Being placed in bath and douched. Hurt me inside
- 10th
- coping with feelings after experience
- 11th
- being whipped with belt on bare skin
- 12th
- feelings of not wanting to live
- 13th
- great grief

The next several sessions alternated between helping Barbara and the ego-states integrate what had happened, and having new 4yo's come forward to share more about the experience. During the integration, it was as though the ego-states needed to go over things again and again. There were four-year-olds that shared about the mother's failure to protect her, and the deeper feelings that mother did not love her. There were also other 4yo's sharing additional pieces about the experience.

Session #61

- Thinking how mother didn't protect me.
- Barbara feels the hate and rage at not being loved
- Very hurt in vaginal area
- The whole body aches (part of memory)
- Laying on the table, I was all tensed up & feeling everything hurt, feeling like a broken person.
- My heart was broken
- Something inside seems very black
- 4yo parts involved in darkness; not more than 3 parts
- 1st – it's just hard to believe
- uncle knew he was coming over and he brought a gun

Session #63

- During all of this, there's a lot of confusion because the body was feeling pleasure and I didn't want to feel that way.
- "The gun…, he pointed it at me & pulled the trigger. The chamber was empty. I think I passed out."
- All the things he was saying as he was raping me
- "The great grief I am feeling about all of this."
- Remembering having feelings all my life of not wanting intercourse.
- "There's been so much unhappiness in my life – all the hurts with Terry, as well as before.

There was no way to determine how long the abuse by Frank and his brother continued that night. It may have been between an hour and a half and two hours, but that's a guess. The four-year-olds, however, could not provide any outside reference for time. I think they were basically lost within the experience.

If two or three ego-states of the same age share different aspects of the same experience, it is a strong indicator that you are dealing with serial ego-states. In that case, the higher self is asked to review and determine whether there are any other ego-states that were created in that same experience. The purpose is to gather all of them together so they can be treated as a group. This isn't always possible. Some ego-states need to be worked with individually, or there may be a deeper layer of ego-states that only emerge as the first group moves towards release and integration. Usually, though, because they are part of the same experience, they have an even tighter bond than most groups, and can move through the sharing and release together.

When all the ego-states have had a full release, the question is whether they need to merge into one before integrating, or to integrate as a group of individuals. I rely on the higher self to know which is most appropriate.

14

Shattered

In Pieces

The third type of special ego-state is the *shattered*. A shattering refers to an experience that is so overwhelming or painful to a person that the consciousness shatters into many ego-states simultaneously. The experience is such a core trauma that it's hard to know whether an ego-state was created and then shattered, like an explosion of clones, or whether they had all burst into creation at once, each carrying its own piece of the trauma. Maybe it can happen either way; I don't know.

When you first engage this type of ego-state, you won't know it is part of a shattering. (The ego-state itself may not even know it is part of a shattering.) First indications are usually when you start identifying more than a handful of ego-states, all of the same age and connected to the same experience. Another way to find out is when the ego-state you're working with becomes blocked during its sharing, or it does share, but cannot have a full release. In working with the higher self to identify the problem, you might discover more ego-states connected to the same experience.

Sometimes in a shattering, the ego-states will remain together in a group. It could be five, or ten, or twenty. It all depends on the person and the experience. More often, the ego-states seem to fly in all directions as if repelled by each other's pain, a kind of double dissociation. It's also possible that one or more of these ego-states could be triggered in a later trauma and become a multi-experience ego-state that has also advanced in age. You could work with a twelve-year-old ego-state, for example, and find that she was first created in a shattering.

Barbara T.

The case of Barbara T., whom I talked about in the last chapter, offers an example of a shattering. It is brutal, but as with the other special ego-states, it's an extreme defense for an extreme assault. This experience occurred when Barbara was three years old, a year before the brutal rape and torture by her stepfather, Frank, and his brother, Rick. This experience, too, involved Frank, only this time he was alone with her.

The use of threats is common in child abuse. Frank's intentional use of electrical shock to ensure Barbara's silence gave clear evidence of Frank's depravity and evil. What happened at three showed how deep it went.

After the four-year-olds had integrated, Barbara said she was still feeling the panic, and she thought somehow the fear of death was involved. In this particular session, once we started the inner work, I asked about the panic. A three-year-old came forward.

Session #66

- He put me in the oven, shut the door and put a chair in front and turned it on
- Panic!

Barbara was visibly beginning to panic and I immediately asked the higher self to communicate to 3yo and help calm her in whatever way it could help. When Barbara relaxed again, 3yo was also able to have a partial release. When she was ready to continue, I asked higher self to communicate to her about safe ways to share. Shortly, the sharing continued.

Session #66

- It was so hot, I couldn't catch my breath… I thought I was dying.
- Why did he do this?

I have in my notes that I discussed evil with Barbara at that point, but I have no record of what was said.

In the next session, our work with 3yo resumed. As more feelings were shared, Barbara told me she understood now about her claustrophobia. These kinds of comments were common with Barbara, as she came to new understandings. 3yo communicated that she still had feelings that were too frightening to share. She was finally able, though, to share more.

Session #67

- Continues sharing
- Understands now her claustrophobia
- Continues sharing
- Still has feelings too scary to share
- Finally able to
- She was laying over in oven, coughing
- The heat also was oppressive
- & then out of body experience

At this point the sharing stopped and the higher self communicated that enough had been shared for now and a rest was needed.

In subsequent sessions, we began to find more three-year-olds and they too shared about the oven. Many times, it was difficult to know which three-year-old was sharing. Barbara was visibly reacting with intense feelings and emotion. Unlike Shelley B., though, Barbara did not give a running account of the sharing. Every so often she would make a statement about what was happening, or comment on some new understandings she had reached. This made it difficult to keep track of who was involved in the sharing. Finally, the material being shared was so terrifying and so intense that Barbara needed to receive the sharing in very limited doses. So there was what higher self referred to as the "roller coaster" effect. Share a little, and rest; share a little, then rest. The following excerpts are from these sessions and are intended to give you a sense of the progression.

Session #68

- Understands now the panic attack
- When panic starts, the need to get out in the fresh air

Session #69

- 3yo reviews to find the "trigger"
- 3yo sharing
- "being trapped"
- feeling life is in danger

- HS says there is more
- Terry leaving town would also trigger
- Just can't breathe
- just doesn't believe there can be relief

Session #70

- Sharing that feeling of being trapped
- I believe I passed out and step-father tried to revive me
- There's so much hurt and grief
- 3yo still sharing the fear of death
- panic attacks are related to feeling trapped
- "I just can't feel safe"

Session #71

- Barbara hates the darkness to come
- This past week she would wake in the morning and be in terrible grief
- The reason he stuck me in the oven
- 3yo is willing to share about that
- "There's a link"—to pregnancies, especially Carley
- There was a struggle trying to get me in the oven and I wet my pants on the floor
- I was screaming when he was putting me in oven.
- The oven was used as a threat from then on to force Barbara to be submissive.

There was a break in the work with the three-year-olds during which time we worked with several older ego-states concerning a different issue. There were also a couple sessions focused on a crisis in the marriage. The work with the three-year-olds then continued.

Session #78

- 3yo sharing
- Angry! A lot of fear at doing anything wrong and showing any feeling.
- 2nd 3yo
- HS says there are four 3yo's
- HS communicates to all 4

- 1st 3yo sharing
- sharing seemed to be a separate personality
- felt like a child abused, she's in deep pain
- 2nd 3yo sharing
- strange pushing inside to have it all come out
- 3rd 3yo sharing
- being spanked very hard on bare bottom so hard I was screaming.
- 4th 3yo
- fingers were burned, I think on the stove

Session #79

- back to 4th 3yo
- Out of body experience
- It was so scary I thought I was going to die

We identified eight three-year-olds over the course of these sessions and worked to a point where higher self could find no others who were still caught in this experience. All had been released and integrated.

The shattering, it appears, occurred at the moment when the child perceived the death of the body as imminent and she lost consciousness ("passed out"). It is not unusual, I have found, for a child or an adult to have an out-of-body experience during experiences of abuse or trauma. I have had many ego-states report leaving the body as a means of protection or distancing from the trauma. These ego-states seem to hover far enough away and then will return to the body when it is safe. Many of these out-of-body experiences do not involve a shattering, though some do. What was shattering about Barbara's experience, I believe, was that the conscious mind was facing the absolute certainty of her own death. This experience forced her to that ultimate boundary and shattered her consciousness against it.

Andy F.

Another example of a shattering involved Andy F., a fifty-two year old male, married with two grown children. We had worked extensively on the early abuse by his mother. I had been working with several ego-states that were all terrified of their feelings. When I asked Gerod about it, this is how he described it:

G.   Well, I will tell you this and you may decide then. There was at one
     time such an extreme amount of rage and anger towards the mother
     that there were very frightening feelings of death... of uh... wishing
     to kill her, wishing to murder her and they were feelings and emo-
     tions that were so overpowering that the feelings were fragmented
     so small that feelings and memory were obliterated, and so there is
     still a very strong control there to prevent the emotions from reas-
     sembling themselves because that rage was very overpowering, very
     frightening. So it would be an area where it would be very difficult
     to try to... they would resist coming back together, to form a whole
     picture or form a whole feeling out of that fear. So what I feel is
     the need is to educate and reassure about emotions. The child can
     interpret emotions that strong as something that could destroy it as
     well as destroy the object of its anger. So there is a very protective
     action being taken to prevent any reassembling.

T.   Is it more like all the fragments themselves are participating in the
     resistance?

G.   Yes. Yes. There's a consciousness there, so there's some awareness.
     It's as if to say educating them, dispelling the fear, offering reassur-
     ance because I feel it is important to go ahead with this and to get
     the emotions back in there. (Session #210—December 21, 1991)

Protocol for a Shattering

Once a shattering has been identified, the therapeutic aim is to bring
all parts of the shattering back together for sharing and release. The
method is basically the same as working with a group of ego-states. The
difficulty, as Gerod described with Andy F., is the inherent resistance
to bringing back together such powerful and destructive emotions.
For ego-states created in a shattering, to remember means returning
to the chaos from out of which they were created. They don't know
that the "reassembling" can be done safely and that a place of Light
and integration is waiting for them.

   So, the next step is to have the higher self send Light and information to them about healing and release. Just as with other ego-states,
this usually brings relief and cooperation. It also means being able to
work with them collectively. However, because of the high degree of

resistance, the bringing back together often involves special handling. It can be like working with volatile chemicals.

The approach I have found most helpful, once a shattering has been identified, is to be prepared to bring them back together in stages. Each situation will be different, but the basic idea is to do it in gradual, incremental steps. The specific steps will depend on what the ego-states can tolerate. It might mean higher self doing several reviews until they all can tolerate the memory. It could mean gathering them all in the same room, one or two at a time. It could mean having one ego-state share and the others observing from a distance. Even when they are in the same place together, sharing the emotion may need to be done in stages.

Once the sharing is complete, the higher self can determine whether the ego-states need to merge as one or remain as individuals and integrate as a group.

15

Mirror Personalities

All-or-Nothing

The *mirror personality* is another kind of special ego-state. Not every client has one, and with those who do, there is usually not more than one. If you encounter a mirror personality, most likely you won't know it at the start. They present just as other ego-states do. They are usually male or female, of a certain age, and many of them have names. Most mirror personalities I have worked with were created in a client's present life, but not all. I have worked with some that were created in a previous lifetime. Then, at some point, were triggered and became active in the client's present life.

The first indicator that you may be working with a mirror personality is its adamant refusal to receive the Light despite all assurances. Or, if it does begin to receive it, it stops it immediately and refuses any further contact with the Light. If I reach this impasse with an ego-state and suspect I'm dealing with a mirror personality, there are two basic questions I ask. The first is: *Have you ever experienced the Light?* The answer will usually be no. The second question is: *Are you afraid that the Light will destroy you?* The answer will be yes. From the mirror personality's point of view, the Light will obliterate it and it will cease to exist.

In one sense, this is true. If a mirror personality steps into the Light, it will never be what it was. It will not be destroyed, but it will be radically transformed. It will undergo a conversion and, in effect, see with new eyes. Just like with other ego-states, knowing this ahead of time gives the healer leverage in treating the mirror personality. We are offering it something we know it will want, once it does experience it.

The problem for the mirror personality is that it cannot know this state of being and consciousness ahead of time. It cannot have any proof or guarantee that what the therapist is saying is true. Unlike other ego-states, it cannot receive the Light in degrees or rely on its own experience. For the mirror personality, stepping into the Light is always an all-or-none proposition. It will mean a total surrender of control, the exact opposite for which the mirror personality was created. This is the source of its resistance. It can only see this step as an endpoint. Taking this step is wholly a matter of trust, and mirror personalities are never long on trust, whether in the conscious self, the outside world, or the therapist. Building this trust is one of the main aims in working with this type of ego-state.

Treating the Mirror Personality

The protocol for working with a mirror personality is really a general approach rather than a set of prescribed steps. As with other ego-states, the ultimate aim is for the mirror personality to step into the Light and integrate with the self. However, because of its refusal, the reinforcing experience of the Light cannot be used in obtaining the mirror personality's cooperation. Instead, the protocol must appeal to its intelligence and capacity for logical thought. The aim is to give the mirror personality knowledge about the Light, the self as soul incarnate, and the mirror personality's integral connection to the self, soul, and Light. It is basically reframing the Light as a good unknown. The message is that there is a place for it in the Light, and that it is the one, in fact, that has been stuck unnecessarily in a fearful and guarded life. The central message is: "You are living with anxiety and guardedness, fear or anger, and that cannot be a nice way to live. There is a way you can live that feels good, comfortable, and safe."

The mirror personality can grasp the logical truth behind these ideas: it's better to feel good than to feel bad. The challenge lies in convincing the mirror personality that it can feel good and secure in the Light. To help persuade it, there are several major ideas I communicate, directly and indirectly, throughout our dialogue. These are:

1) You are a part of the self/soul.
2) Therefore, you do have a connection to the Light, even if it's not apparent at this moment.
3) The Light will not destroy you. It will give you a new life.

4) Being in the Light may change the way you feel and think, you may have a different point of view, but you will still be you.
5) You were created to protect the self. You did well, but that protection has become outdated, to the detriment of yourself and this conscious person
6) There is a place of Light and integration waiting for you. The higher self cannot show you that place without taking you into the Light, but it may be able to send a picture. (Sometimes higher self can do this, sometimes not.)
7) Higher self can also communicate to you further information about any of these things I've just talked about.

All of these ideas reinforce the central message: you can have a better life. The implied message, though, is that it's decision time. The person is in a healing process to resolve conflicts and fears that are blocking his or her way forward—and that includes those created by the mirror personality. Most of the mirror personalities I've worked with have chosen, in the end, to step into the Light and undergo the transformation. For some, the choice came quickly. With others, it required some talking and processing over time. At least a few times, a mirror personality chose dissipation rather than the Light.

Whether a mirror personality needs to share its experience to the conscious self and have a release—either before or after stepping into the Light—will depend on the particular mirror personality. Sometimes the sharing and/or release needs to be done and sometimes it seems to be taken care of when the mirror steps into the Light. Once it does [share?], the transformation will often be instantaneous. However, it can also take time, anywhere from a day to several days. I will go back to a mirror personality in the next session and assess whether the transformation has occurred, and whether anything more is needed before its integration.

A Point of View

The mirror personality's all-or-none point of view regarding the Light goes back to the nature of its creation. Gerod said that the mirror personality is an ego-state created as an "opposite reflection" of the conscious self (or another ego-state). Unlike most ego-states that are created within an experience of the self and then dissociate, the mirror personality is created within a wholly opposite reality as a not-self.

Before discussing the implications of this definition, I want to quote Gerod. The following excerpts are taken from different sessions. The first one is quite lengthy. It is the first time Gerod talked about the mirror personality in depth. We were discussing a client case in which an ego-state, named Natalie, was creating significant blocks in the healing process.

T.   Is Natalie some kind of energy point or soul point?

G.   Natalie is an ego-state, but she is a very strong one. She has awareness. She is a mirror, so to say. She has in her existence gathered enough energy to herself even in that sleeping state that she is a mirror of the self, of the physical self, but she is different. Do you understand what I say?

T.   Not yet.

G.   Well, then I will look for the words. J.A. is one way and Natalie is very much the same way. However, as the healing process takes place there is a separation that is occurring and Natalie is working to keep it from occurring so that she is still the reflection of the whole self.

T.   Well, J.A. said she felt like in a sense two different people and I think that is what you are describing right now.

G.   It is two different people. The same but two, and it is as if one is feeling itself in the process of being threatened – and its existence – as the whole self heals and changes. How would I describe it... when you have a body, a personality, and many parts that are one way and if the healing process takes place and ego-states are healed and the self becomes more healed there is a changing away so that the whole self is becoming less and less like the mirror that is on the inside. The mirror one, which is Natalie, becomes very frightened and threatened and will do all it can to reverse the action because it is that perceived belief of nonexistence, so to say. Natalie knows that she is not a whole. She knows that she is a fragment, but up to this point it is as if she has been a whole.

T.   Yes.

G.   So she is going to do what she needs to do to protect herself and she will use the children. It is not that she dislikes them – she is one of them – but she is the stronger one. So she cooperates with you so long as it serves her purpose.

T. Any suggestions for…

G. Recognize the difference. Recognize the two separations and diligently address it.

T. With Natalie?

G. Yes. And J.A. can do this consciously also. Almost as if instead of accepting what is, confront what is consciously and in that way confront Natalie and that will, as we talked about previously, maybe set the fire under her to move, to change.

T. So it sounds like you are saying almost confront Natalie with the reality that she is a fragment, that J.A. has changed, that there is a broader perspective to things. Maybe have the higher self as well give her information and knowledge and help receive some things?

G. Yes. It is almost as if consciously challenging every thought. Because, as I say, she is very strong and she is very close to the surface now. She is not hidden. She is much more mobile than the rest and she moves around. So I would consciously confront most thoughts to test them out.

T. Is that a suggestion for J.A.?

G. Yes.

T. Okay. This mirror—at the time Natalie was created, the mirror was being created?

G. Yes.

T. And as J.A. developed, Natalie developed and as Natalie saw things, J.A. saw things?

G. Yes.

T. Is there a particular – this is hard to put into words, but is there some kind of way of defining this point of division, this dichotomy between them? What is it based on? Where is the separation? Is it the experience or is it something deeper?

G. I would describe it more as the point of perception.

T. Okay.

G. A created fragment is created at different levels, at different points. So its point of perception is limited, is defined by where it is. Just as when J.A. was growing, her external definition of herself was fairly well dictated by what was observable in the physical reality. Influenced, of course, by the situations internally, but always taking that internal message and attempting to externalize it. To take the message of unworthiness, for example, and attempting to frame it within the physical experience.

T.   Okay.

G.   Whereas Natalie would take her experiences, her messages, and frame it within the internal place where she is.

T.   Even though she was sleeping or is this just since she is awake?

G.   It has gone on while she was sleeping. It is as if she is asleep just as when you sleep, you sleep but much goes on, and even though Natalie is a fragment, she dreams, she grows.

T.   Okay. One last question before we have to stop, Gerod. Is this issue of the mirror a common occurrence within people?

G.   Fairly common. (Session #166—September 7, 1990)

I talked to Gerod two months later about another client when the issue of mirror personalities came up again. I talked to him about an ego-state named Martie who was not being very cooperative.

G.   She will be an important one to work with over time and sharing may not always be the point as much as helping her to understand. Her perception is certainly limited to experience and not just her experience but to the general tone of past experience for this person. So that certainly colors her view of the world, her perception, her tone, emotion, regarding the world.

T.   Is this a different kind of ego-state than we have worked with before?

G.   Not necessarily. She is like Natalie.

T.   But you are saying she may not have a lot of sharing to do.

G.   It is as if to say she has experienced, she has memories, but it is not so much those memories that hold her back as it is her perception of the world. I don't know if I am explaining it quite properly. It is not so much the experience that holds her back, but her fear that holds her back. So, in that respect, it is almost as if sharing experience will not always necessarily bring about the release and healing that is needed because it may be understanding, and a perception of what fear is, and a perception of what consciousness is, that may need to be dealt with first, and then in that way sharing becomes secondary and almost natural.

T. That makes sense to me. Martie and I talked a lot about perception and perspective and the whole issue of fear. Fear and risk is quite prevalent.

G. These kinds of ego-states do very well when nothing changes. They have no quarrel with the person going through life hindered, so to say. But when a person moves into the healing state and begins to challenge the status quo, begins to challenge the way of life that has become usual and customary, then one such as this one, Martie, becomes very uneasy. They become quite angry. They become quite cynical. They are impatient with being disturbed. Healing is not necessarily their goal. Being left alone is more their goal—to remain within the state with which they have become comfortable—whatever their comfort level is. (Session #180—November 18, 1990)

There were many sessions in which Gerod and I talked about mirror personalities. The following are brief excerpts taken from some of these discussions. I hope to give the reader more of a sense and feeling for the mirror personality than a theoretical definition.

G. It is as if their perception is from a different point of view because they are created after all with the darkness which means an absence of hope, an absence of connection to the soul, an absence of connection to All That Is. So they are usually very simply described as the very negative aspect of one. If you meet a person who is a negative person, that I will tell you will be a clue that they are very strongly influenced by a mirror personality. (Session #18—November 29, 1990)

G. It does not mean necessarily that the mirror personalities are dark or evil or anything, it only means that they come from a different point of view and that they are, so to say, the balance. Because when a person becomes involved in experiences where there is a positive charge set up, so to say, then there is a creation of the negative counterpart. So the mirror is the image that focuses back to that main part what it sees as reality. (Session #181—November 29, 1990)

G.   Mirror people are strong. If they have made their way to conscious influence, they are usually powerful. They are usually quite strong. So therefore, you need to work somewhat diligently with them, and for them. Their resistance can be quite strong. (Session #181—November 29, 1990)

G.   They are created in darkness, so therefore they have a lack of understanding and an inability to change and therefore they are very adamant about change. It is perhaps one of the more threatening influences in their existence so they become a protective device, a warning against changing.

T.   Change meaning that if there is change, it in some way challenges them in a very fundamental way?

G.   It certainly does because change is a step into the unknown. Change is a process whereby one goes from one state of existence to another state of existence in the conscious reality. A certain set of givens will help one to determine what the probable outcome may be, but when one is so to say born in darkness and exists within darkness, there is not that element of hopeful deduction. So there is a very strong need to hang onto and to maintain a status quo situation. So for these, it is very threatening to have a change occur and whether this change is a physical change or a healing change, each one will set off the alarm to a different degree. (Session #182—December 9, 1990)

G.   Just because a mirror is created in the darkness does not necessarily mean it is evil. Natalie is not evil, E.S. is not evil. This one with I.G. certainly was not evil, but a certain despair that is overpowering at times. Despair can create bad situations. With Natalie and the others there is perhaps an inability, I would say, to trust in the Light, but there is not an inability to trust—and I say trust in a very reserved way—to trust that there is the possibility for adjustment. (Session #182—December 9, 1990)

T.   And is that mirror's creation often a reaction to a specific kind of experience or perception or is it more often an accumulation?

G. More often I would say it is an accumulation. It is like the situation that builds up where information piles up to create a certain thesis and then there may be an incident that would occur that would certainly precipitate the finalization of that creation. (Session #183— December 16, 1990)

T. Do you believe a mirror will recognize itself in general when I ask for the one who is the opposite?

G. Usually I would say yes. The mirror knows its position fairly well as an opposing position to ... well, I will say it this way. If the mirror is the strong opposition—the reflection back of the main presenting personality—then it usually will have quite good awareness of itself. If it is a mirror of a particular ego-state, then it may not necessarily recognize itself in such a strong way. (Session #185—January 14, 1991) **Note:** A mirror personality, according to Gerod, can be created as a reflection of the conscious self or a reflection of an ego-state. We discussed both kinds over the months as I encountered other mirror personalities. In general, what applies to one, applies to the other. The treatment approach is the same for both.

G. It is as if when you discover the mirror, oftentimes there is an acknowledgement that takes place and it is like being introduced to someone and there needs to be a period of understanding and a period of trust that needs to evolve and to develop. So, oftentimes that first encounter or confrontation with a mirror does not necessarily mean there needs to be continued and ongoing work with the mirror at that particular point in time, but more a way to touch and to establish some awareness and to say it can wait, the work that you would do with that one. (Session#187, February 3, 1991)

G. Mirrors can become, as you are well aware, very powerful and very strong and depending upon their needs and wishes and desires, they most certainly can become the assertive one if the core withdraws. It is merely like flipping the mirror. The mirror on a hinge. It is just there to the backside and in most cases usually quite aware of what is taking place consciously but not necessarily having the desire to become involved with it. Can be an observer and certainly have an awareness of it. When it is presented to consciousness, can sometimes, depending upon the situation, either be quite apathetic and quite passive or quite adamant in its responses to what may be taking place. (Session #189—March 14, 1991)

G.   It is an ego-state but it is a mirrored ego-state, and because it is a mirror, it is a reflection, and it does not necessarily need the protective part to create it. It would be as if you had the ability to hold a mirror up to someone, capture their image, take that image, and shape it. It's like creating a piece of art or viewing someone painting a picture, creating a sculpture of them and imbuing it with energy. (Session #375—October 6, 1994)

An Opposite Reflection

Gerod is describing an enigmatic figure. He said the mirror personality is an ego-state created as an "opposite reflection" of the conscious self. Most ego-states are created within a specific experience, as part of the self, and then dissociate that experience from the self. It's as though the ego-state always retains a connection to the self/soul, even if remote. It's what allows most ego-states to receive the Light so easily. Not so with the mirror personality. Its defense is not through dissociation of experience, but opposition. It is created, by definition, as a not-self. Its defense against the conscious person's feelings of terror, pain, or anxiety is to not be that person. It is a version of the self, but one that is turned inside out.

Just as with the concept of self, we cannot think about the mirror personality without becoming lost in paradox. Not just one paradox, but three. It is beyond the scope of this book to address all the philosophical and metaphysical questions raised by the mirror personality. Before offering my clinical view, though, I want to list the three paradoxes that make it such an enigma. Here they are:

1)   The subject/object dilemma. *One cannot be the perceiver and perceived at the same time.* This is the paradox that bedevils science, philosophy, and psychology when they come to focus

on the "self/mind" as an object of study. As the reflection of a self, the study of the mirror personality is always, in the end, a case of the self studying the self.

2) The second paradox is duality/oneness. The mirror reality, as an opposite reflection, is defined by the absence of light. Behind the mirror surface is darkness. The mirror is what it is because it reflects all light, not absorbs it. This is the darkness in which the mirror personality is created, and from which point of view—as Gerod emphasized—it perceives reality. To understand this point of view, one would have to be willing to step into that darkness and that perception. Even if one could do that—and I'm not sure any of us can—it would necessarily mean becoming it.

3) The third paradox involves self-reflection and the problem of infinite regress. If you have one self that is reflecting upon itself, then the question is: who is reflecting on that self who is doing the reflecting, and so on, and so on. As an opposite reflection of the self, defining the mirror personality becomes quickly lost in the paradox of self-reflection.

Mirror Personalities: Clinical Thoughts and Impressions

Given these theoretical difficulties, and my limited database on mirror personalities, there are few general conclusions I can offer about this enigmatic figure. They are tentative. I see them more as an operational definition, with some speculation as well.

1) I believe that this distinct type of ego-state does exist within some people.

2) I believe that we all have the potential for the creation of a mirror personality. This potential is rooted in the duality in which all of us live. In/out, up/down, good/bad, hot/cold, *ad infinitum*—duality is part of the very fabric of our language, our thinking, and our perception. For certain people, given certain conditions, this opposite potential appears to crystallize and form a coherent identity.

3) The mirror personality appears to serve a regressive function. Staying safe, avoiding pain, resisting change, and exercising control appear to be its primary concerns. From its point of view in darkness, the mirror personality does not relate to the

conscious self's creativity, imagination, exploration, hopes, and dreams. The mirror personality depends on the familiar and status quo. Its reflexive response to the conscious self's choices appears to be "no."

4) I'm not sure at what stage in a child's development the potential for a mirror personality is created. My speculation is either when the child becomes self-aware, or develops the capacity for self-reflection. I would place it somewhere between the ages of seven and eleven, depending on the individual. Theoretically, a mirror personality could be created anytime after this potential appears.

5) The mirror personality is imbued with self-awareness and knowledge of the self's life experience. Unlike most ego-states, however, the mirror personality is aware of the conscious self and present reality. As self-aware, it is also aware of its capacity to choose and act.

6) Once created, the mirror personality can age. With its awareness of the conscious self and present reality, it is usually aware of aging and the passage of time. Sometimes the mirror personality reaches an age where it remains, even though it is aware that the conscious self continues aging. At other times, the mirror personality stays concurrent with the person's present age. When asked, it will give the same age as the client and signal it is aware of the present reality.

7) It's possible that a mirror personality could, as Gerod said, gather enough energy to itself to become a dominant influence in a person's life. It doesn't actually take over consciousness as can happen in cases of DID where an alter-personality assumes consciousness and executive power over the body. I picture the mirror personality more as an overlay. Its feelings, moods, and perceptions can overlay the conscious self and wield a strong influence in significant areas.

8) Integration for the mirror personality is different than with other ego-states. Gerod said to picture the self and the mirror personality as back to back. He said that what needs to happen is for the mirror personality to turn around and face forward, standing side by side with the conscious self. For the mirror personality, this would involve the transformation discussed earlier. From

this new perspective, the mirror personality becomes aware of the interplay of Light and dark and the possibility of balance.

9) In my work with clients, I do not usually go looking for a mirror personality. I don't often ask a higher self to look and see if there is an ego-state "created as an opposite of the client's conscious self." I assume, first of all, that if a mirror personality is present and needs to be addressed, it will present at an appropriate time as the healing progresses. Second, because we exist in duality, I do not want to risk suggesting something that could be easily and innocently conjured up to fit my description. Unless I have a very strong intuition that a mirror personality is operating behind the scenes, I'll wait to see if one presents.

10) What triggers the creation of a mirror personality, and why for some people and not others? Beyond what I have said here, I don't know.

My own attitude toward mirror personalities is not to get stuck on a label. Identifying an ego-state as a mirror personality can be helpful, however, in knowing how to approach it. What issues will get its attention, or strike a chord. How to establish trust, and persuade it to take the all-or-none step into the Light. Unlike most ego-states that involve a separation from the Light, the mirror personality involves opposition to the Light. It never knew the experience of Light in the first place. In the healing process, the message to the mirror personality is that it doesn't need to continue in such opposition or struggle. There is a door it can walk through to a better existence.

If the mirror personality is a distinct type of ego-state, it could play a significant role in a person's social, emotional, psychological health. At this point, verification of the mirror personality awaits the findings of other practitioners.

Part 5
Special Protocols

16

Memory Protocol

The Fear of Remembering

In working with ego-states, the crucial step in the protocol, and often the most difficult, is when it comes time for the ego-state to share its experience to the conscious mind. This is where clients open themselves to an experience—from present life or a past life—that was too painful or overwhelming for the conscious self to tolerate at the time. Freud described it as "making the unconscious conscious." It's crucial, because it's in the ego-state's sharing of its experience that the dissociation is resolved. At the same time, the sharing nullifies the defensive drive that has always operated to keep the experience split off from conscious awareness. Once the experience becomes conscious, there's no longer anything to defend against.

While an ego-state's sharing is the crucial step in the Ego-State Protocol, it is also the step where the therapist is more likely to encounter blocking or resistance by the ego-state itself. This is because within the dissociative experience is the pain, fear, or threat that caused it, and in sharing it to the conscious mind, an ego-state must, to some extent, re-live or feel the pain.

The first steps in the Ego-State Protocol—making contact with the higher self and receiving Light and information about healing—are often sufficient to prepare an ego-state for this crucial step. Also, what an ego-state needs to share by this time, in order to have a release, is often minimal. It may be feelings, body sensations, or a visual snapshot of the traumatic experience. Most ego-states don't have to share their experience in depth. It usually doesn't require a full re-living of the experience. For others, however, the sharing can be painful and intense.

In Vol. I, I talked about some ways that an ego-state's sharing can be made tolerable. Most of those techniques involved assistance from the higher self that could, for example, help the ego-state have a safe review, or help it break the sharing into tolerable pieces, or review the experience from a great distance away. There are times, however, when an ego-state is still unable or unwilling to share its experience. It's as though the ego-state has its own defenses by which its pain is numbed or suppressed.

The three situations I see most frequently are, first, the ego-state that remembers what happened, but refuses to share it. It's not because it is being threatened or is opposed to the healing, but it is afraid of re-experiencing its pain or terror. The second situation is the ego-state that does not remember what happened, but also refuses to have a safe review with the higher self. It is afraid that, in the remembering, it will re-experience the pain, or maybe feel it for the first time. Finally, there are situations where the ego-state remembers what happened, begins its sharing, and stops it almost immediately.

In all of these situations, using the Ego-State Protocol, the higher self will be asked to create a bridge that will allow the ego-state to share what it needs to in the safest and least painful way. This may require a series of sharings, breaking it into pieces. It may mean a review of the experience, but from a great distance away. The higher self may help the ego-state to modulate its feelings during the sharing itself.

When these techniques do not work, I use a protocol that I developed and found effective in helping an ego-state to safely remember and share its experience. For the purposes of this book, I call it the Memory Protocol. It's based on the principle of desensitization. In some ways, it's an extension of the Identification Protocol only it takes the identification right down to the ego-state's experience itself. In those cases where an ego-state can't remember or can't share its experience, I will engage the ego-state with a series of yes/no questions that allows the ego-state to reveal its experience in small, incremental steps.

The Protocol

The protocol begins at the point where an ego-state refuses to share, or communicates that it doesn't remember what happened. Either way, it is assumed that the ego-state is afraid of re-experiencing its pain or trauma. The therapeutic goal is to facilitate the sharing in a way that is safe and tolerable for the ego-state(s). The protocol is designed to elicit information about the experience in incremental steps beginning with the least threatening or painful and moving to the painful experience itself. The steps also move from the facts of the situation—who, what, when, where—to the emotional and psychological levels of the experience.

Each step of the protocol is listed below, accompanied by a brief commentary.

Step 1: Where are you?

Generally speaking, the first step in the protocol is to locate the ego-state in time and space using the broad categories of home and not home. (It's presumed here that the ego-state has already been identified as to present-life/past-life, gender, and age. If not, that may need to be done first, if possible.) Almost everyone has a place they call home, so in asking about it, we are asking about something that is very, very familiar. It is also a place that is likely to hold myriad memories and experiences other than the traumatic ones. This is the first question: To this one: are you in your own home or house?

As soon as the question is asked, the ego-state knows the answer. If it signals that it is in its own home, the next series of questions will be to identify which room it is in.

If the ego-state is not at home, then the questions are designed to find out where it is using the categories of being inside a building/ structure or outside. This too is something everyone knows instinctually, and ego-states usually know it as well.

In practice, if an ego-state signals *no*, that its experience did not happen in the home, then I will often ask: are you in someone else's home or house? I have found that the answer to this question is frequently *yes*. This is especially true when working with a present life ego-state. By asking this question first, I am trying to minimize questions whenever possible. If the response is a *no*, then I'll phrase a question using the more generic term, *building*.

The questions of the protocol diverge at this point depending on whether the ego-state is in a building or outside. If it is in a building, then I will ask questions like these:

- Have you been in this place before?
- Is this place close to your home?
- In this place, are there other rooms?
- Is this place a school of some kind?
- Is this building used as a store or have offices inside?
- Are there other buildings close by?

If the ego-state is outside, then I ask a slightly different set of questions:

- Have you been to this place before?
- Where you are, is it close to your home?
- If you are outside in your yard, first finger, if you are in your neighborhood or even further away, the second finger.
- If you walked to this place, first finger, if you came in a car, or bus, or some other way, second finger.
- If it's daytime, first finger, if it's dark outside or getting late, second finger.
- If it's warm outside, first finger, if it's cold or winter, second finger.
- Are there buildings nearby where you are?

Which questions to ask in what sequence depends on what you know about the ego-state up to that point, your own intuitions, and how afraid the ego-state is at each step. With some experience, you will also develop a feel for it. It comes with practice.

Step 2: Is anyone with you?

Once the questions of *where* and *when* have been answered, the next step is to determine whether the ego-state is alone in that place or whether there are any others, and if so, how many. These are the kinds of questions I ask:

- In this experience, is there at least one other person present?
- Where you are there, is anyone else there with you?
- As you look around, is there anyone else there where you are?
- Is there more than one other person there?
- Do you know all the people there? If so, first finger. If any are a stranger to you, the second finger can lift.

- Are any of those people members of your family?
- If it's parents or grandparents, first finger, if not second finger.
- Are they all members of your family?

The process of identifying who is present with the ego-state in its painful experience can be touchy. We have to keep in mind that in focusing on who is present, we are likely identifying a perpetrator or perpetrators. This focus can be intense for some ego-states, and we need to be ready to back off or give reassurance as needed. Most of the time, I find ego-states can identify who is present without being triggered. By this time, you will also be getting ideas about what might have happened, and this will guide your questions as well.

Step 3: Who or what caused the pain?

Once you have identified who is present, the next step is to identify the cause or source of the ego-state's pain or terror. This is still one step removed from the pain itself, but you can expect that some ego-states will start reacting. Asking about causes implies effects, and the ego-state may begin to focus on the effects, i.e., the pain. Alternatively, our questions about causes may necessarily lead into questions about the effects. Again we have to be ready to step back or provide reassurance, whatever is needed to help the ego-state re-stabilize.

After I identify who is there, I will ask questions like these:

- Did something happen there that caused you pain and distress?
- Did someone say or do something that caused you pain or distress?
- If it was something the person did, first finger, if something they said, second finger, if both, the hand can lift.
- If it was just one person who said or did this, first finger, if more than one, second finger.
- Did the person do this (or say this) to intentionally hurt you or cause you pain? If so, first finger, if it was more an accident or they didn't realize, then second finger.

After determining the cause of the pain or distress, it's time to move to the pain or trauma itself.

Step 4: Have you been hurt physically or emotionally?

Often by this time, there is some sharing of the experience and the client may show visible signs of it or will begin to report what is coming to the conscious mind. However, if the sharing has not started yet, then I will ask further questions and get more specific. The next series of questions starts with the facts of the injury or trauma itself. The basic categories used are *physical* and *emotional*.

In order to judge the severity of the trauma I'm dealing with, one of the first things I want to know is whether it involved physical injury and pain. Depending on the injury, the threat of re-experiencing the physical pain can be extremely frightening to the ego-state involved. If I learn that physical trauma is involved, then I am prepared to break the process into smaller steps if needed. I'm also prepared to have higher self work more directly with the body for healing and release when necessary. I believe this is naturally part of the healing process, but sometimes it needs special attention.

I assume that every physical trauma involves emotional pain or distress, but not all emotional trauma or distress involves physical injury. If an ego-state says it was not physically hurt or injured, my questions will begin to focus instead on specific emotions, especially in relationship to those people present in the experience.

These are the kinds of questions I ask to identify the pain itself.

- In this experience, were you hurt physically or emotionally? If so, first finger, if not, the second finger can lift.
- If you were hurt physically, first finger lifting, if emotionally, the second finger can lift. If both, the hand can lift.
- If this was done to you intentionally, first finger; if it was an accident or they didn't mean to hurt you, second finger; if you don't know, the hand can lift.
- Were you hit in any way?
- (If so) was it more than once? Twice? Etc.
- When this happened, did it hurt you, or make you angry?
- Did this ever happen before?
- Are you willing to share a piece of that to the conscious self?

When I focus on physical and emotional pain, I also assume that a client's trauma may have significantly affected him or her at energetic or spiritual levels as well. It is not unusual to have information come forward which points to problems at these levels. If so, I adapt the questions using the appropriate protocol. There may be an energy shield around the heart, for example, or an energy blockage in the throat chakra. The client's trauma may have triggered a past-life ego-state whose hatred of God has been triggered in many lifetimes where serious physical injury has occurred. A client's trauma may have involved soul-wounding at the hands of a genuinely evil and abusive parent. If this has happened, there are likely to be parts of the self closed up in dark places.

Step 5: More specifics if needed.

At this point in the protocol, there can still be ego-states who have not fully shared what they need to for release, and then the questions need to get even more specific. These are ego-states that remember or know what happened, but are still emotionally detached or dissociated from the affect and feelings. It's as though they have their own defense by which to remain unconscious of, or numb to, the pain, terror, or hurt that they carry. If deeper sharing is called for, this next step will take them closer to that level.

When bodily injury is involved, the questions become specific about the injury itself: its location, whether it caused bleeding, the instrument used (including someone's hand). These specifics about the injury lead naturally into questions about the ego-state's emotional reactions in the experience. The goal throughout the process is to help the ego-state emotionally re-connect to the body.

The same is true for those ego-states who were not physically injured. They need to reconnect emotionally to an experience that was terrifying and overwhelming in the moment. What is important is the connection, not the intensity. Most of the time, ego-states make this reconnection without the intense emotion. Usually, it's their fear that it will be intense that is the hang-up. Sometimes, though, the reconnection is intense and apparently needs to be experienced as part of the healing. The questions at that point will focus on the specific emotions and the context. Based on what I know to that point, I'll ask about those emotions that I believe are most likely to apply.

- Do you remember now what was said?
- Do you know what he did that made you so angry?

- Do you remember now what you saw that scared you so bad?
- Do you remember what it felt like when she slapped you?
- When grandma died, did it make you want to cry?
- Do you remember how it felt when he yelled at you like that?

In my own mind, I picture the protocol as reassembling pieces of an ego-state's experience. In the process, the ego-state begins to resonate and at some point, opens to the experience and it is shared to the conscious mind. I never know at what point this will happen. Usually, I do not get all the way through the protocol before it does. The client begins to report what is being shared, or begins to abreact.

Here are two sample dialogues illustrating the protocol.

Memory Protocol: Example 1

Th. 4yo, if you needed to stop the sharing, the first finger can lift. If it seems that someone or something got in your way, then the second finger.

4yo Yes finger lifts.

Th. You needed to stop the sharing, is that correct?

4yo Yes finger lifts.

Th. 4yo, do you remember what happened?

4yo No finger lifts.

Th. Are you willing for higher self to help you have a safe review about that?

4yo No finger lifts.

Th. Is there some scare for you about remembering?

4yo Yes finger lifts.

Th. 4yo, is it all right if I ask some questions?

4yo Yes finger lifts.

Th. In this experience, were you in your own home or house?

4yo Yes finger lifts.

Th. Were you in the living room?

4yo No finger lifts.

Th. In the kitchen?

4yo Yes finger lifts.

Th. Was there at least one other person present with you?

4yo Yes finger lifts.

Th. Was there more than one other person there?

4yo Yes finger lifts.

Th. More than two other people?

4yo No finger lifts.

Th. There were two other people present, is that correct?

4yo Yes finger lifts.

Th. If both people were members of your family, first finger lifting. If not, the second finger can lift.

4yo Yes finger lifts.

Th. If they were parents or grandparents, the yes finger can lift. If not, the no finger.

4yo Yes finger lifts.

Th. Were these both your parents?

4yo Yes finger lifts.

Th. In this experience 4yo, did something happen that hurt you or harmed you physically?

4yo No finger lifts.

Th. Did it hurt you or scare you emotionally?

4yo Yes finger lifts.

Th. Did someone do something or say something that hurt you?

4yo Yes finger lifts.

Th. If it was something they did, the yes finger can lift. If something they said, the second finger. If it was both, both fingers can lift. If none of those fit, the hand can lift.

4yo Second finger lifts.

Th. If it was being said to you, first finger, if it was being said to someone else, the second finger.

4yo Yes finger lifts.

Th. If it was your father that said it, then first finger lifting. If it was your mother, the second finger can lift.

4yo Yes finger lifts.

Th. Do you remember now, 4yo, what he said?

4yo Yes finger lifts.

Th. Are you willing now to share what you need to about it?

4yo Yes finger lifts.

Th. On three, then, one, two, three…and just share here to the present what you feel, see, hear that needs to be shared. It's safe to share it now. First finger when complete. Second finger if there's a problem.

At this point, I would continue with the Ego-State Protocol.

Memory Protocol: Example 2

(Working with an eight year-old ego-state who has received Light but is unwilling to share.)

Th. 8yo, are you afraid about sharing?

8yo Yes finger lifts.

Th. Do you remember what happened?

8yo No finger lifts.

Th. Are you afraid to remember?

8yo Yes finger lifts.

Th. 8yo, what happened is in the past. It's not happening here in the present where we are. Did you know that?

8yo No finger lifts.

Th. Would you be willing to come forward here and have a conscious experience in the present, just to reassure yourself that you can have healing and release from your pain?

8yo Yes finger lifts.

Th. Higher self, are you in agreement that it would be helpful for 8yo to have this conscious experience? If so, first finger. If not yet, second finger lifting.

HS Yes finger lifts.

Th. Higher self, I'm asking, then, that you help 8yo move to the conscious mind for that conscious experience and perception here in the present. Communicate to her also any further understanding about this present point of view and her ability to be released. First finger, 8yo, when you have had that conscious experience, second finger, if that's stopped or blocked.

8yo First finger lifts.

Th. Were you able to take a look here in the present?

8yo Yes finger lifts.

Th. Was that a surprise to you?

8yo Yes finger lifts.

Th. Did that give you some reassurance that you can be free of your own pain and distress?

8yo Yes finger lifts.

Th. Are you willing then to have a safe review about what happened, knowing that it's memory, it's not happening here in the present?

8yo Yes finger lifts.

Th. Higher self, I'm asking that you help 8yo very safely review inside what it is she carries, what's happened, and just what needs to be shared for release. 8yo, first finger when that review is complete, second finger if it is stopped.

8yo Second finger lifts.

Th. 8yo, did you need to stop the review?

8yo Yes finger lifts.

Th. Is there still some scare about that?

8yo Yes finger lifts.

Th. Were you able to have some review?

8yo Yes finger lifts.

Th. Would it be all right if I ask you some questions? You can stop me at any time if a question is too scary or upsetting. Would that be all right?

8yo Yes finger lifts.

Th. In your experience, were you in your own home or house?

8yo No finger lifts.

Th. Were you in someone else's home or house?

8yo Yes finger lifts.

Th. Is this a house you have been in before?

8yo No finger lifts.

Th. If the house belongs to a family member, first finger. If not, second finger.

8yo Second finger lifts.

Th. If it was a friend's house or in the neighborhood, first finger. If it was further away, second finger.

8yo First finger lifts.

Th. Is there at least one other person present with you there?

8yo Yes finger lifts.

Th. Is there more than one other person?

8yo Yes finger lifts.

Th. More than three?

8yo No finger lifts.

Th. Are there three others?

8yo Yes finger lifts.

Th. Are any of them members of your family?

8yo No finger lifts.

Th. Are any of them adults?

8yo No finger lifts.

Th. Have you seen them before?

8yo Yes finger lifts.

Th. Are all of them males?

8yo Yes finger lifts.

Cl I remember this now. It was three neighborhood boys – they were probably twelve or thirteen. Two of them were brothers. They tricked me into coming into their house, said they wanted to show me something. Once I went in they wouldn't let me out. Their parents were gone. They started touching me…

The Memory Protocol is based on the psychological principles of desensitization and de-conditioning. It allows the ego-state to step into the memory gradually rather than being pulled in all at once by the intense emotion or shutting down. The ego-state also knows it can stop the process if it needs to. The Memory Protocol offers an ego-state a safe way to remember and share what it needs to in order to release.

17

The Dark Spot Protocol

Temporary Eclipse

I'm sure you have heard clients complain about a sudden change in mood and outlook that leaves them feeling depressed, or anxious, or disconnected from others. They will say it came on suddenly, like a dark cloud came down on them. They will describe it as the 'doldrums,' 'in the dumps,' 'in a funk,' or 'feeling the blahs.' Life feels meaningless and sapped of all joy. Often, they cannot point to anything specific that would account for what they are feeling, but can usually pinpoint when it began.

These are the same clients who, after a few weeks or so, report feeling better and exhibit a brighter and more upbeat mood. It's as though the dark cloud had lifted as suddenly as it appeared. They feel motivated once more, connected to others, and able to appreciate the relationships, beauty, and purpose in their daily life. For those people who are emotionally and psychologically healthy, and who have a good social network, the passage through this dark period can be uncomfortable and confusing, but it doesn't threaten to overwhelm them or cause deep feelings of anguish. They are bolstered by their daily routines and relationships, and they have the sense that these moods have come and gone before, so 'this too shall pass.' There's no need to press the panic button.

According to Gerod, this periodic but noticeable shift in mood, affect, and outlook is normal. He said that within each person there is a dark side, and that periodically a person will enter and pass through this darkness. It is this passage into the dark spot, he said, that can trigger these shifts in mood, feeling, and perception.

The following excerpts are from the first session in which Gerod identified the *dark spot* and discussed it. The implications of what he was saying were so significant that I spent the rest of the session questioning him about it.

G. ...You see, within each person there is a dark side... It is almost as if to say that it is part of the impetus for growing, for moving into the Light...

... It's like when the planets are orbiting and an eclipse will occur and the day will become dark. It's as if to say there is an eclipse within each of us that from time to time the personality will pass through. And the crux of the matter is, is the person going to pass through that shadow, through that darkness and come into the Light again, or are they going to get stuck there and stay there? And quite often those people who stay too long in that shadow, in that darkness, are those who will attract spirits, they will attract the spirits of darkness. Because in that dark place there is despair, there is sadness, there is depression, and there is a weakening of the will to move into the Light and that is where the forces of evil move into the darkness. But it is most definitely a purposeful place because it is that impetus for growth. When in the shadow, those feelings are the feelings that propel one forward, oftentimes to finding the opposite, the Light.

... It is somewhat like the ego. The ego is there to protect you and this dark place is put there to trigger you to grow. It is oftentimes passing through this place of darkness that will, almost as if to say, trigger another mechanism, the mechanism to begin the growth, the climb, the struggle, whatever it takes to get into the Light, just as certain experiences in life trip that lever that causes the ego to begin its protective work to insure the survival of the body and the personality in order to continue that journey. (Session #74—February 24, 1989)

And finally, in the same session:

T. Is there something in this darkness or the darkness itself, that has an awareness or consciousness like the ego and would it be able to communicate?

G. I believe that that is possible also, for it is a part that is viable. It is not so much an activity, as much as it is an experience, a place where the whole self moves through from time to time. And one way to engage the darkness is to ask the ego to move into darkness, to ask the will to move into darkness, to even ask the soul to step in and speak from that point of darkness and to give the information from that perspective.

It is as if to say you have a central core that is the soul and the person and around it is this periphery. On the backside is this dark place and all the parts of the being revolve around this core which is the life force. And as they pass through the shadow, or the darkness, or the dark spot, that is when the triggering for growth begins, and as they grow and move out into greater understanding, then more Light is brought around the curve into the dark place.

Now some will come to that dark place and stay there for a very long time, and then at that point, because there is not a smooth flow and balance, all perception is from that point of darkness because everything is holding still and the darkness has a strong hold.

And it depends upon what it is holding onto, as to how the person will react. If the ego is in darkness, there are certain types of reactions. If the soul is in darkness, then we are in very deep distress indeed. If the will is in darkness, we have difficulty also. You can well see the propensity then to attract in evil when the soul and the will, one or the other, are sitting in that dark place and not moving. To be constantly moving through and around is not as great of a distressful state because each time in the movement, Light is brought into the darkness, and each time it becomes a bit lighter and lighter. (Session #74—February 24, 1989)

The idea that there was a definable region of darkness within each person, and that a person moved into and out of this darkness on a cyclical basis, was another one of Gerod's bombshells. The implications were so profound and raised questions on so many levels that I knew it would take time to explore and come to some determination and understanding about it.

Meanwhile, on a clinical level, there was an immediate concern. If Gerod's information was accurate, did it apply to any of my clients? I thought about this specifically regarding clients who were suffering with chronic depression, profound loss, lack of love and connection with others, or living with constant fear and anxiety. Was it possible that these clients were stuck in their dark spot, and if they were, was there something I could do in our sessions to help them move out of it?

The existence of the dark spot and its effect on a person seemed too important of an issue not to check out. It became another major focus in my dialogues with Gerod. Understandably, as healers, we work with people who are in pain or distress, lonely, or afraid. For many, it means they have been living in a dark place for a while, and maybe a long while. It's a place Gerod said lacks Light, Love and Knowledge.

Over the next several years, I investigated the dark spot with select clients. The results confirmed to me that such a dark spot does exist within individuals. For some people, its painful effects are significant enough that it becomes a clinical issue. Like with other phenomena, over time I developed a protocol for dealing with the dark spot when it is a problem.

The Dark Spot Cycle

According to Gerod, a child will move into its dark spot for the first time at around age seven. It is an internal event, but one which can be heavily influenced by external circumstances and events. Generally speaking, this passage into the dark side affects the child's perception and creates a feeling of separation from the Light, both the child's own inner Light, and the Divine Light. Gerod said this experience of darkness triggers a natural impulse within the child to seek the Light. I believe for most children, at this human level, this means seeking the love and comfort of parents and family, cherished objects, and finding a place of safety.

This does not rule out that the child seeks and finds that Light at other levels as well. It may involve help from guides. The child might have an experience of Divine Love in that moment when he or she finds the Light again. Normally, a child will find that Light and, whether consciously or unconsciously, move toward it and out of the dark spot.

Gerod said that this first experience of the dark spot also establishes for the child a cycle for moving into and out of the dark spot as he or she grows. The cycle he said remains relatively consistent for each person, but the cycle can change depending on the person's experience, learning, and choices. The cycle may correlate with natural or planetary cycles, but can vary widely depending on individual and cultural factors. A person, for example, may enter his or her dark spot once a year for two weeks, or once every two years and move through it in a week, or someone might go into their dark spot every six months. A person can also, as Gerod said, become stuck there and live in the dark spot for years.

T. In terms of what you're describing as a cycle, is there some kind of standard cycle for human beings in the physical?

G. Most definitely. Your planets have their orbit and it is as if to say within the human is its own cycle and orbiting way. You've heard of the seven-year cycle, and this is very similar.

T. Would you be able to give a number on the cycle? Seven days, twenty-eight days, ten hours, what this standard cycle is comprised of in terms of earth time?

G. The first move in an earth time, in a very strong way, is the seventh year. That is the age when the child begins to depart from that more innocent state that is protected by the ego and begins that interpretation of life also from a point of darkness and if you will observe and watch and think you will realize that that is indeed the age when most children leave that time of innocence, that time of feeling connected, that time when if they have had abusive experiences, very non-loving nurturing experiences, that is the time when it may begin to interpret itself in more self-destructive, negative ways, is in that time period. Now, after that point, the cycle still continues, but it will vary somewhat from person to person. Within each person there is a natural rhythm, and that is why there is a certain importance in maintaining a smooth flow of energy through the self to keep a smooth rhythmical balance and each person will find their own type of balance and it will be more regulated.

T. And is the variation at that point just very wide about what each person's cycle will be?

G. It is and it isn't. It is somewhat dependent on those early experiences, that first cycle through the dark place, how and what the reaction is. There are those that will come to that dark place and get stuck and they may never cycle past that.

T. But if they do....

G.   Then it depends upon how much they leave there to keep proceed-
     ing from that point of view, how long they will go. There are people
     who are in three-year cycles, there are people who are in… In most
     cases the cycles are at least a minimum of a year, that is a general
     rule of thumb, almost as if the body, the human mind, the human
     universe is tracking with your physical cycle of seasons. There is a
     similarity there, and that would be the minimum, so it will depend
     so much upon the individual experiences, how the cycle is completed
     or maintained.

T.   And then whatever that cycle is for that individual, then are you
     saying also they move through that dark spot either quickly, within
     a matter of days, or may take six months or may take a year.

G.   That is most definitely the case. And it depends upon the state of
     the ego, what they are working through at that particular time, it
     depends upon their past, how well they are aligning with the Light,
     that type of situation.

T.   Well, Gerod, as you probably know, I'll start thinking about this and
     certainly come back to this.

G.   And I will be glad to work with you on it and to help you with it,
     because we are attempting to put it into terminology that is under-
     standable to you and for anyone else who may wish to consider it.
     (Session #74—February 24, 1989)

The Dark Spot as a Clinical Issue

From a clinical point of view, the dark spot is important because it
can be a significant source of a client's pain and distress. In this way,
it is like the energy point. When it's functioning normally, it probably
won't even come up in the therapy. When there is a problem, though,
it can be helpful, or even necessary, to intervene directly. I have clients where the dark spot never has to be addressed directly. He or she
moves through it without much apparent distress or difficulty. Or, it
might come up once or twice when I talk to a client about the dark
spot cycle because they are experiencing it in the present. However,
I would estimate that the dark spot is an issue, or becomes one, with
at least fifty percent of my clients. As a therapist, this isn't surprising
since we work with people who are suffering the effects of childhood

abuse or neglect, significant emotional or bodily trauma, and/or some kind of attachment or intrusion by dark entities or spirits.

In general, I have found that there are three situations where the dark spot becomes an issue in the healing process.

1) The passage into darkness has triggered intense conflict or emotional distress.
2) The self has become stuck in the dark spot.
3) Spirits or some other beings have accessed this vulnerable area and established some kind of presence.

The Protocol

When I start with a new client, I assume he or she has been through the dark spot cycle a number of times already. It can also be that the client is stuck in their dark spot and has not cycled through for quite some time. What determines whether I address the issue of the dark spot directly in the hypnosis session depends on what I hear from my client and what my intuition tells me.

If I hear descriptions like those at the start of this chapter – feelings of depression, isolation, mistrust, feeling disconnected, unable to love or feel loved – I will often at least check out whether the dark spot is involved. The intensity of these feelings and the length of time the client has felt this way are the two major factors I consider in deciding whether to ask about the dark spot directly. It may be that the client is moving through the dark spot, but is having a rough time of it, or that he or she has been stuck there for years. Either way, if the client's experience is distressing enough, I will at least check it out. After I have established reliable communication with the higher self, I'll start the protocol.

Step 1: Higher self finds the dark spot

The first step is to ask the higher self to look inside and find the dark spot or dark side within the person. In my experience, with few exceptions, a client's higher self has always been able to find this dark spot. This has been so consistent that if a higher self cannot find it, the next question is whether someone or something is blocking it. Most of the time the response from higher self is a *yes* or there is a shutdown.

Step 2: Is the self in the dark spot?

When the higher self has found the dark spot, the next step is to ask whether the self is presently in the dark spot or not. By *self*, I mean the conscious personality, the ego-self. If the self is in the dark spot, then the question is whether the client is moving through it as part of their normal cycle. If the higher self responds with a *yes*, then I don't consider it a problem as much as part of a natural ebb and flow. I can give the client support and listen to their distress and struggles with this experience of darkness, but I don't try to intervene or quicken the process. In these cases, the client may be encouraged to adjust their pace and attitude at a conscious level during this period.

How a person experiences this dark spot is unique and varies widely among individuals. For some, the passage through the dark spot might be felt hardly at all, while for others it may trigger or accentuate negative feelings and attitudes. When a person is already depressed and enters the dark spot, feelings of hopelessness, despair, or worthlessness may intensify and feel unbearable. Sometimes when a person enters the dark spot, it triggers ego-states that exist there. It's as though the self's movement into darkness has energized them, and they become like a thorn in the side. It's also possible you might come across a dark web of spirits that have entangled the self at some level and would be good to clear.

When a person is going through the dark spot, Gerod's advice is, first, not to be afraid of it and not try to fight it. Like Chinese handcuffs, this might only pull you deeper into darkness and cause more distress. Instead, he said it's a time to take extra care of yourself. Change your pace, watch movies, or escape with a novel or a video game. Take more walks in nature, or spend more time with friends. Most of all, know that it is temporary, and things will soon get back to normal. It's largely a matter of riding it out and being good to yourself while you do it. For those who experience deep distress when in the dark spot or who have become stuck in it, this advice is still good, but usually not sufficient.

Step 3: Is the self moving?

As long as the self is moving, then I assume he or she will move through their normal cycle and emerge from the dark spot in their own timing. I will come back and check in the next session that the self is still moving. The situation that is of most concern is when the client has become stuck in his or her dark spot. The prolonged experience of darkness can affect a person and be distressing in many different ways—emotionally, mentally, spiritually, and even physically. If the higher self indicates that the self is not moving, but is stuck, then almost always it needs to be addressed directly. This is where things can get complicated.

Step 4: If movement is blocked

When the self is stuck, it usually means that someone or something is blocking the self's forward movement. The therapeutic goal, then, is to work with the higher self to identify the source of the block and remove it so the self can begin moving again. One of the major sources of blocking that I have found is by ego-states that exist in the dark spot. Some of them are created there because of their particular experience. Others appear to have moved into the dark spot to escape pain or terror and to further protect the self. An ego-state, for example, might go into darkness to numb its pain, to sleep, to hide, or because it feels rejected and unlovable.

The following excerpt is from the session where Gerod and I discuss these ego-states for the first time.

T. Is it possible that an ego-state or ego-states can remain stuck in the dark spot, even when other parts of the self can cycle through it?

G. Yes, they can.

T. What you're saying then is that there are parts of the self that, because of their experience, can be thrust into the dark spot and remain in the dark spot really until death?

G. In essence that is very correct. They do not go there on their own, so to say. Usually one who has had severe trauma in life will still make those journeys through the dark spot entirely, and it is there that certain ones may find themselves unable to move out. It usually will not be profound, in that there will be many. It may be one, may be two, but it is not a place where the self is broken up. The self most definitely is made up of many parts, but they usually remain within a certain orbit, so to say, a certain radius of one another. But when passing through the dark spot, one can remain there if it seems comfortable to it.

T. So there may be some who, let's say, have a very difficult time in the dark spot, but will cycle through.

G. That is right.

T. And like you're saying, there may be one or two that remain stuck there.

G. And that is correct also. And it does not happen with everyone, but with certain ones.

T. Would the higher self be in a position to make an assessment about that, parts that have remained in the dark spot, parts that have a difficult time when it comes time to move through the dark spot?

G. It should be able to do that, yes. (Session #124—December 9, 1989)

When the self enters the dark spot, either as part of its normal cycle, or because some event precipitated it, there can be ego-states that react. It's as though when the self enters that darkness, the ego-states that exist there are energized or have a stronger connection to consciousness. They also may react to what Gerod described as the "self's impulse to look for the Light." Because of their own pain, fear, or anger, these ego-states may want to block that search for the Light, and in the process, they block the Light to the self as well. It's at that point, if the ego-state is strong enough, that the self can be stopped in the dark spot.

Contrary to Gerod's estimate, I have found in my own work with clients that there can be more than a few ego-states existing in a client's dark spot. They may not all be triggered when the self enters the dark spot, but there can be more than one or two involved in blocking the self. Sometimes it can take one session to clear the blocking and sometimes it takes many sessions. All of this is dictated by the specific client's inner world. The primary strategy with all clients, though, is to keep clearing blocks until the self is able to start moving again.

A second complication in dealing with the dark spot is its vulnerability to outside attachment or intrusion. Not surprisingly, these ego-states hold the deepest pain and terror, and so are most vulnerable to threats, false promises, and deception. At an unconscious level, ego-states that exist in the dark spot are especially vulnerable to approaches by spirits and other kinds of dimensional beings. If there has been deep intrusion or entanglement, the dark spot is a likely place to find it. What better place to keep their activities hidden from consciousness?

Finally, when working in the dark spot, there may also be openings or doors that lead into darkness itself. There may be parts of the self that have left or been taken through those openings. A part of the self may have created the opening as it fled the soul in an attempt to escape its pain or terror, or it may have left inadvertently, out of confusion. It's also possible that openings were created by ego-states reacting to the approach by dark souls or external beings, which then use that reaction to make contact and engage that part of the self. If these beings have the know-how, they may also extract ego-states or pieces of soul energy.

When the self is stuck in the dark spot, any of these complications might be involved. The treatment approach, however, remains the same. Use higher self to identify the source of the block or interference and then use the appropriate protocols to resolve them until the self is free to move.

The protocol for working with the dark spot looks like this.

1) Direct higher self to find the dark spot within.
2) Determine whether self is in the dark spot at present.
3) If the self is in the dark spot, is he or she moving?
4) If so, does anything need to be addressed directly?
5) If the self is not moving, then ask higher self to locate the source of the blocking?
6) Resolve block(s) so the self begins moving again.

The following is an example of the protocol in practice.

Dark Spot Protocol: Example 1

Th.   Higher self, I'm asking that you look inside and find that dark spot within the self. First finger, when you have found it, second finger if you do not.

HS   First finger lifts.

Th.   Higher self, I'm asking that you look inside and determine whether the self has entered that dark spot. First finger, when that review is complete; second finger, if you are stopped or blocked.

HS   First finger lifts.

Th.   Higher self, has the self entered the dark spot?

HS   Yes finger lifts.

Th.   Is the self moving through the dark spot? If so, first finger; if not, second finger

HS   Second finger lifts.

Th.   Has the self stopped or become stuck there?

HS   Yes finger lifts.

Th.   Higher self, I'm asking that you review and see if there is someone or something in the way or blocking the self from moving? First finger when the review is complete; second finger if there's a problem.

HS   First finger lifts.

Th.   Higher self, did you find someone or something in the way?

HS   Yes finger lifts.

Th.   If it's someone, first finger, if something, second finger. If neither of those fit, the hand can lift.

HS   Yes finger lifts.

Th.   Is that one part of the self/soul energy?

HS   Yes finger lifts.

Th.   Is it one that would be good to bring forward?

HS   Yes finger lifts.

Th.   I'm asking then, higher self, that you help that one come forward here with me. (Pause) To this one, do you know yourself to be part of this self and soul I'm working with?

Es.   Yes finger lifts.

At this point, the Ego-State Protocol is used to further identify the ego-state involved, and determine with higher self whether it is one to work with immediately, or to wait. When the self is stuck in the dark spot, I will usually make it a priority. Sometimes, however, a client may need to remain in the dark spot, as he or she works through a certain part of their healing process.

18

Before Incarnations

Soul Entities

In the Ego-State Protocol, once an ego-state has received Light and information about healing, the next step is to identify it more specifically. Present-life/past-life? Male/female? Adult/adolescent/child? Name? Place? This sequence works most of the time. However, there are other kinds of soul entities that can present in a client's healing process that don't fit a time/space framework. Questions about present life and past life make no sense. In my experience, this doesn't happen often. I have encountered figures, for example, that I call inner guides, created by the soul, and sent forward to assist a person. You might even mistake one for a spirit guide unless you ask whether it is part of the self/soul. I have also encountered soul entities that appear to be from other dimensions within the soul, living an existence I know nothing about. Usually, it's one that has stumbled into my client's inner world or the inner work has taken us to some kind of interface with it.

There is another kind of soul entity that can present during a session that is also outside time and space. These are parts of the soul that answer *yes* when asked whether they existed (were present, or created) even before the soul began its incarnations. I've never known what to call these entities, or how to conceptualize them. They have no identity within a time/space reality. They have never lived a lifetime. Some of them are aware of the soul's subsequent incarnations, and some have played a significant role in one or more of those lifetimes. Others, however, don't know anything about the soul's incarnations until the higher self or a guide communicates information to them or helps them to have a conscious experience in the present.

When these soul entities do present, it is usually later in the healing process. It's rare that I encounter one early in a client's treatment. Most of the time when they present it's because they are connected to the issue or close to the area we are working in. They may come forward because the inner work has triggered their own pain, conflict, or confusion. Other times, the higher self identifies one because it's where the clinical trail leads. Some of these entities are aware of the inner work and, for their own reasons, are attempting to stop it. It's as though they knew we were coming and they had reacted. Many of them have been lost or entangled in darkness, or preyed upon by dark souls. Many of them also will be found outside the soul, having been taken or become lost at the time of their creation. These are ones who will need to be retrieved.

Although they are not ego-states, they are akin to them. They are conscious and intelligent and, like ego-states, often present as autonomous beings. They are not necessarily in human form. Also, like ego-states, they carry some kind of negative experience or distress that keeps them dissociated from the soul/source energy. Most of them are not receiving Light, or their connection to it is dim or distorted.

Most importantly, as part of the soul, they have the capacity to receive Light, just as the ego-states can. Some are afraid of the Light. Some are angry at the Light, and some have no memory of the Light. Sometimes they have names, but often not. Like with ego-states, some will communicate verbally, others only through ideomotor signals.

What I know about these entities comes from my clinical experience and my collaboration with Gerod. Unfortunately, by the time I had gained enough experience to begin exploring this phenomenon more deeply, my collaboration with Gerod was winding down. We did talk about them, though, in about a dozen cases. Since that time, I've encountered many more.

One of the most significant insights Gerod offered about these soul entities goes back to what he called the soul's initial separation from the Light. I discuss this at length in my first book, *Soul-Centered Healing*, which I assume you are familiar with. In brief, Gerod said that the Light created all souls at the same time; and that all souls were perfect in the Light, but not complete. He compared it to a baby that is perfect, but not yet fully conscious and aware. For Gerod, the complete soul is an awakened soul.

He said the darkness reacted to the creation of souls and the Light made an agreement not to create more souls until those already created were given a choice between the darkness and Light. The Light's one condition was that every soul remain absolutely free to choose at any time, no exceptions. A soul could even be in the pits of hell and be free to return to the Light at any instant if it chooses.

The agreement requires that each soul, in order to truly have a choice, must separate from its Oneness with the Light, its Creator. For the soul, the separation is an experience of darkness.

As a creation of Light, it also means a separation from its own Light, a total eclipse, so to speak, at least momentarily. In Gerod's terms, it is the soul's first encounter with "what it is not." He said the soul comes to know what it is by first knowing what it is not. The darkness is at once both a mirror and a complete unknown.

According to Gerod, the soul begins its journey of awakening with this separation, this experience of the opposite. When he first talked about it, I assumed that a soul experienced this separation at the start of its first incarnation. It was only later, when I began to identify these entities as *before incarnation*, that I began to think in terms of other or deeper dimensions of the soul and soul realities. What I learned was that most of these entities were created at or around the moment of this separation from Source and the confrontation with darkness. For some souls, this did involve their first incarnation. For others though, the separation happened in a dimension or at a level that came before the soul began physical incarnations. Either way, the ones that presented in my work with clients were ones where this separation did not go well.

Before Incarnations: The Protocol

The protocol for dealing with soul entities created before incarnation is basically the same as for ego-states. It is adapted, though, for entities existing outside space/time and physical reality. The same steps apply: facilitate contact with the Light; retrieve it if it is outside the soul; have it share its experience if necessary, release, and integrate. I know that, just as with ego-states, once an entity like this experiences the Light, it will want more. It will want to be in the Light. It will also, like an ego-state, become cooperative and willing to move through the healing process. The biggest difference, as with past-life ego-states, is that these soul entities will be integrated at a soul level, and not with the conscious self.

The most difficult part in working with these soul entities, at least from my point of view, is having no experiential or conceptual framework by which to relate to these entities and their reality beyond time and space. With these parts before incarnation, the dialogue cannot presume a human context or experience in physical reality. These parts exist at another level of the soul. What questions can you ask that are going to make sense to a consciousness that may not even know of physical reality or human existence? It gets more complicated when that part itself says no to the Light, or has even become aligned with the souls in darkness.

Most problems with these soul entities in the healing process begin with a refusal to receive the Light. When this happens, it's even more important to stay focused on the point of resistance or blockage and follow it to its source. Often it is the entity's own resistance that stops the Light. It is angry at the Light, or afraid of it, or the Light triggers its pain. In other cases, the soul entity is being controlled by outside forces, usually souls in darkness. These situations can be more complicated. Most likely, it means agreements or deals have been made that will need to be undone.

As usual, the trick in using ideomotor signaling is in knowing the right questions to ask and how to frame the dialogue in a sequence of yes/no questions. In dealing with these entities before incarnation, the right questions depend on the entity's understanding of its situation and its motivation to change, i.e., to reintegrate with the soul. The challenge in working with these soul entities is in communicating to a consciousness that has no common basis in human experience or physical incarnation. It calls for a different language, like in mathematics, switching from a base 10 number system to a base 8.

The protocol uses the language of *Light* and *dark* as the basis for communication. Soul-Centered Healing assumes that a soul entity resonates to its own soul's Light and is drawn to it unless blocked by its own resistance or by others. Once it receives the Light and makes the reconnection, it will almost always say *yes* to the healing process and a return to the soul's Light.

The next step in the protocol is to determine which of these situations you are dealing with in order to decide on what strategy to use. If the entity itself is refusing the Light, the questions will focus on the reasons why it resists. When you know that, you can offer an alternate understanding and what its choices are to resolve any pain, distress, or confusion. If outside forces are involved, there is a different set of questions. The aim, then, is to determine how those forces have accessed the soul, what they put into place, and what parts of the self/soul need to end all ties to separate souls, entities, energies, and/or devices.

Once you have identified the source of the resistance or blocking, the basic protocols are used to obtain a soul entity's agreement to receive the Light. The following are examples of the protocol for identifying soul entities from before incarnation.

Before Incarnation: Example 1

Th. To this one: do you know yourself to be part of this self and soul I'm working with?
__ Yes finger lifts.
Th. Are you one first created in this present life of Jim's?
__ No finger lifts.
Th. Are you one from a past or different lifetime?
__ No finger lifts.
Th. Are you one who has lived in a physical body?
__ No finger lifts.
Th. Are you one who was created as the soul was entering the body or leaving it at death?
__ No finger lifts.
Th. Are you one who was present even before this soul began its incarnations?
__ Yes finger lifts.
Th. Are you receiving Light/Love energy for yourself there?
__ Hand lifts.
Th. Would you be willing to receive Light/Love energy for yourself? You can stop it if you need to, but if you like it you can keep it for yourself. Are you willing to receive that and make your own choice about it?
__ Yes finger lifts.

Th. Higher self, please send this one the Light/Love energy, and to this one, let yourself receive that. If you like it you can bring it inside to whatever level is comfortable. First finger when you have made that decision.

___ Yes finger lifts.

Th. If you needed to stop it, first finger can lift. If you decided to keep it for yourself, the second finger lifting.

___ Second finger lifts.

Th. To this one: does it still seem you were present even before the soul began incarnations?

___ Yes finger lifts.

Th. Do you have a name?

Cl. What I'm hearing in my head is "Lucifer."

Th. To this one: is that your name, Lucifer?

___ Yes finger lifts.

Th. Do you still believe that that is the best name for you?

___ No finger lifts.

Th. Would you like a different name?

___ Yes finger lifts.

Th. I'm asking higher self to send you the name that you know fits. First finger when you have that, second finger if there's a problem.

___ Yes finger lifts.

Th. To this one: did you receive that?

___ First finger lifts.

Th. Do you know now about the healing process we're working with?

___ Yes finger lifts.

Th. Do you wish to have that healing and release for yourself?

___ Yes finger lifts.

At this point, the treatment would continue with the Ego-State Protocol.

Before Incarnation: Example 2

Th. To this one who stepped into block, do you know yourself to be part of this self/soul I'm working with?

___ No finger lifts.

Th. If you believe you are separate from this soul, first finger lifting, if you're just not sure, the second finger lifting.

__ Second finger lifts.

Th. To this one: are you willing to know whether you are, or are not, part of this self/soul?

__ No finger lifts.

Th. Does that scare you?

__ Yes finger lifts.

Th. I want you to know that we are here to help, whether you are part of this soul or separate. Each has a different kind of help. As long as it's safe, are you willing to have this information so we know how to help?

__ Yes finger lifts.

Th. I'm going to ask higher self to communicate this to you. First finger when you've received that, second finger if not.

__ First finger lifts.

Th. To this one: if it seems that you are separate from this self/soul, or you're not sure, first finger; if part of the self/soul, the second finger can lift.

__ Second finger lifts.

Th. To this one: are you one first created in this present life of Helen's? If so, first finger lifting, if not, the second finger can lift.

__ Second finger lifts.

Th. Are you one first created in a past or different lifetime? If so, first finger lifting; if not, second finger.

__ No finger lifts.

Th. Do you know when you first came?

__ Yes finger lifts.

Th. Were you present even before the soul began its incarnations?

__ Yes finger lifts.

Th. Do you know now about the healing process we're working with here?

__ Yes finger lifts.

Th. Would you like to have that healing and release for yourself?

__ Yes finger lifts.

Th. Is there something you need to share in order to have that release?

__ Yes finger lifts.

Th. Are you willing to share now what needs to be shared?

__ Yes finger lifts.

Th. Do you know what needs to be shared?

__ Yes finger lifts.

Th. I'm asking that you share it then, right here to the present, what you need to share about it. First finger when complete, second finger if there's a problem.

__ First finger lifts.

Th. Helen, did you receive that?

He. I just got the impression of being lost and the deepest feeling of … I don't know, sadness and grief…

Th. To this one: Is this your sharing about sadness?

__ Yes finger lifts.

Th. Did you become lost?

__ Yes finger lifts.

Th. Do you feel ready to release that sadness and grief now?

__ Yes finger lifts.

Th. I'm going to ask higher self to help you with that. On three, just release the pain and sadness. Beginning, one, two, three… and just release it, right through the body and out. Higher self helping, feel the support as you release all sadness and grief. And as you release that, you can bring in more of that light/love energy. First finger when that feels complete, second finger if there's a problem.

__ First finger lifts.

Th. Were you able to release that all right?

__ Yes finger lifts.

Th. Higher self, are you in agreement that this one can move their place of integration?

HS Yes finger lifts.

Th. Should they have a conscious experience here in the present before integrating?

HS No finger lifts.

Th. I'm asking then that you help this one move now to their place of Light and integration within the soul. First finger when that move is complete, second finger if there's a problem.

HS First finger lifts.

19

Soul Retrieval

Parts and Pieces

It is not unusual in Soul-Centered Healing to discover that parts of a client's self/soul are missing and need to be retrieved. I learned about this phenomenon early in my work with Gerod when he identified ego-states or soul energy as separated from, or outside, the soul. Instead of dissociation at a psychic level, though, I began to think about this more as dissociation at a soul level. This situation presented itself frequently enough that it became another focus in my sessions with Gerod. Why does it happen? How does it happen? How to recognize it? What is its significance for the healing process?

T.   Can you say anymore about this process of taking a piece of the soul, like the Centurion...?

G.   Well, there are many different ways of taking the soul. It's like... this one possesses a fragment of the soul but it is not separated from the soul. It is like going in and isolating a piece of the soul is perhaps more of a correct term and that the one who has isolated it is actually very close to the soul in many ways but it has just been able to isolate a piece of it is how I would describe it. It's not really in essence removed, separated, severed, or gone... It's like a box of candy. If you received a box of candy for a gift, it is a box of candy but there are pieces of candy isolated by the little tissue paper cup that separates it and keeps it from being, so to say, a whole, but yet it is. And when you have a piece of the soul fragmented, that is more like what it is.

T.   Like a compartment as we've talked about?

G.   Yes.

T.   And this is also the case with the Centurion?

G.   Yes.

T.   But apparently in these compartments then these ones can live in their reality and even make contact with others?

G.   That is correct. (Session #211—January 2, 1992)

The answers to these questions came slowly, on a case-by-case basis, involving many clients. It was a complex picture that emerged over several years. I learned that there were many reasons why different parts of a person's soul might leave, be ejected, or be taken outside the soul.

With Gerod, my understanding from the beginning was that any parts of the soul missing were to be retrieved, if at all possible. It was not the case that Gerod would sometimes advise retrieval and at other times advise against it. The basic assumption seemed to be that whatever is part of the soul's energy belongs with the soul. On the rare occasions when a part of the soul needed to be dissipated or severed, Gerod always treated it as a means of last resort. Retrieval of all soul energy, of course, was consistent with our essential aim in helping a client achieve wholeness and integration.

As I learned more about the different possibilities, I developed a protocol for working with a client's higher self to identify when a part has been separated from the soul and the steps to take to retrieve and reintegrate it. The frequency with which I encountered these situations also led me to develop a more proactive role in determining whether parts of the soul were missing. Instead of waiting for the issue to present on its own, I began to work with clients' higher selves to actively review at certain points whether any parts of the self/soul were missing. This is also when I began asking ego-states, before they moved to integration, whether there were any doors. If there were, then higher self was asked to determine whether any of those doors led outside the soul. My concern was that, unless they were triggered by the inner work directly, many parts outside the soul might not be identified and retrieved.

The Retrieval Protocol

The most common scenario involving retrieval is the one I talked about in the Ego-State Protocol and in dealing with extra-psychic doors. Using the protocol, when a group of ego-states has finished their sharing and release and are ready to move to integration, they are asked to look around and see whether there are any doors or openings. If there are, then the higher self is asked to determine whether any of those doors go outside the soul.

This is where the Retrieval Protocol begins. If any doors go outside the soul, the first or second question to higher self is whether any "parts or pieces of the self/soul have left or been taken out through the opening. If yes, then higher self is asked whether a retrieval needs to be done. Most of the time, if there are missing parts or pieces of the soul, the higher self will communicate *yes*, a retrieval is needed. As I said, though, there are times when higher self will say no. While it doesn't happen very often, it is something that needs to be checked out.

The protocol assumes as its goal the retrieval and reintegration of whatever is missing. There are exceptions. There are times the higher self may signal that retrieval would not be appropriate, as though the parts of soul energy had become too contaminated or compromised. Other times, the higher self may communicate that it would be better to wait, or that retrieval is not possible at that moment. Most of time, though, a retrieval is called for and carried out immediately or soon.

The client's higher self is the one that can determine whether parts of the soul energy are missing, and whether they left or were taken out. It is also the higher self, usually assisted by guides, that carries out the retrieval. This is one point where doors can be dealt with simultaneously. Most of the time, when more than one door goes outside, the retrieval can be for all that is missing through any of those doors. Once initiated, the retrieval usually is completed within seconds. It's as though the higher self sends out a signature beam of Light that locks onto these separated parts and draws them back to the soul. The efficiency in which soul energy is retrieved is based on the soul's absolute freedom to reclaim its own energy. At these levels, where the laws of time and space do not apply, once a soul chooses to retrieve, it usually happens instantaneously.

Once higher self signals that the retrieval is complete, the next question is whether it was able to retrieve all. If not, the question is whether to continue with the retrieval or come back to it later. Usually, the retrieval is repeated until all has been retrieved before addressing who or what was retrieved. Once the retrieval is complete, I will ask higher self to close and seal the openings.

The Retrieved

The final step in the Retrieval Protocol is to identify who or what was retrieved in order to know which protocols to use to complete its reintegration with the soul. At this step, I usually deal with two categories: 1) *beings* (ego-states or parts before incarnation) and 2) *pieces of soul energy*. I will ask higher self whether any ego-states were retrieved, and if so, whether they need to be worked with directly. If not, then higher self can help them release and reintegrate with the self/soul. If they do need to be addressed, then they are worked with just like any other ego-state or one from before incarnations. If no ego-states were retrieved, only pieces of soul energy, then I ask higher self to reintegrate that energy within the soul.

In my communication with the higher self, I use the term "pieces of soul energy" as a general term for whatever belongs to the soul and has been retrieved. Once it is retrieved, I will ask the higher self whether it can reintegrate the soul energy and the response is usually, *yes*. I do not try to define or label this soul energy more specifically unless higher self indicates that there is a problem or that it needs to be addressed more directly in some way. For the client, the reintegration of soul energy at these levels usually doesn't register strongly at a conscious level. Sometimes, though, a client will report a very strong shift or change when a reintegration occurs.

Once the retrieval is complete, the next step is to make sure that everything retrieved is part of the self/soul. When retrieving parts of the soul entangled by darkness, it is not unusual that they will attempt to send entities, energies, or devices back with the retrieval to act as hooks for future access.

Soul Retrieval Protocol

1) When ego-states are ready to integrate, determine whether there are any doors, openings, or windows in their area.
2) If yes, determine whether any go outside the soul.
3) If yes, determine whether any parts of soul left or were taken out through those openings.
4) If yes, determine whether a retrieval should be done.
5) If yes, direct higher self and/or guides to carry out retrieval.
6) Confirm that all has been retrieved.
7) When complete, determine whether any ego-states were retrieved.
8) If yes, determine whether they need to be addressed directly.
9) If not, have them release and reintegrate. If yes, begin the Ego-State Protocol.

The chapter concludes with two examples of the protocol.

Soul Retrieval Protocol: Example 1

Th. 22yo, before you and the others move to your new place of integration, I want to ask that you look around where you are there and see if there are any doors or openings. First finger when that's complete, second finger if there's a problem.

22yo First finger lifts.

Th. 22yo, are there any doors or openings there?

22yo Yes finger lifts.

Th. Are there more than two?

22yo Yes finger lifts.

Th. More than four?

22yo No finger lifts.

Th. Are there four?

22yo No finger lifts.

Th. There are three. Is that correct?

22yo Yes finger lifts.

Th. Higher self, do any of those doors go outside the soul?

HS Yes finger lifts.

Th. Does more than one go outside?

HS Yes finger lifts.

Th. More than two?

HS No finger lifts.

Th. Two go outside the soul, is that correct, higher self?

HS Yes finger lifts.

Th. higher self, I'm asking that you place Light at each of those three doors. First finger when that's complete. Second finger if there's a problem.

HS Yes finger lifts.

Th. Higher self, can 22yo and the others now move to their place of integration, if so first finger. If they need to wait until we address those doors, second finger lifting.

HS First finger lifts.

Th. Should 22yo and the others have a conscious experience first before integrating?

HS Yes finger lifts.

Th. Higher self, please help that group now move here to the conscious mind for that conscious experience and perception, when complete, help each to move to their place of Light and integration. First finger when these moves are complete, second finger if there is a problem.

HS First finger lifts.

Th. Higher self, you said that two of those doors go outside the soul. Are there any parts or pieces of the self/soul that have left or been taken out through those openings?

HS Yes finger lifts.

Th. Would it be best, higher self, to do a retrieval? If so, first finger, if not, second finger.

HS First finger lifts.

Th. higher self, are you and guides ready now to do that retrieval?

HS Yes finger lifts.

Th. I'm going to ask, then, higher self that you begin that retrieval now. Bring back here to the soul all parts and pieces that left or were taken. Make sure they are all cleansed and cleared as they are returned here to the soul. First finger when that's complete, second finger if there is a problem.

HS First finger lifts.

Th. Higher self, do you believe you were able to retrieve all?

HS Yes finger lifts.

Th. Can you close and seal those two doors now?

HS Yes finger lifts.

Th. Please close and seal those openings. First finger when complete, second finger if there is a problem.
HS First finger lifts.
Th. Higher self, in this retrieval, were there any ego-states retrieved?
HS Yes finger lifts.
Th. Are they ones that need to be addressed?
HS Yes finger lifts.
Th. I'm going to ask then higher self that you identify one to come forward here with me. To this one, do you know yourself to be part of this self and soul I'm working with?
Es Yes finger lifts.
Th. Are you receiving Light now for yourself there?
Es Yes finger lifts.
(Continue with Ego-State Protocol)

Soul Retrieval Protocol: Example 2

(Speaking to a group of six ego-states who have just had a release.)

Th. To the group: is anyone still feeling some distress or pain there?
Gap No finger lifts.
Th. Higher self, are you in agreement that those in this group can move to their place of integration?
HS Yes finger lifts.
Th. Should they have a conscious experience here in the present first?
HS Yes finger lifts.
Th. To the group: before you move to your new place of integration, please look around and see if there are any doors or openings. First finger if you see any doors or openings, second finger if not.
Gap First finger lifts.
Th. Is it more than two?
Gp No finger lifts.
Th. Are there two?
Gp Yes finger lifts.
Th. Higher self, are you aware of those doors?
HS Yes finger lifts.
Th. Higher self, please place light around each of those doors. First finger when that's complete. Second finger if there's a problem.

HS First finger lifts.

Th. Higher self, should those in the group have a conscious experience before integrating?

HS No finger lifts.

Th. I'm going to ask, then, higher self that you help move each to their place of integration within the self/soul. First finger when that's complete. Second finger if there is a problem.

HS First finger lifts.

Th. Higher self, we identified two doors. If either of those doors goes outside the soul, the first finger can lift. If none go outside, the second finger lifting.

HS First finger lifts.

Th. If both go outside, the first finger lifting. If only one, then the second finger.

HS Second finger lifts.

Th. Higher self, will both of these doors need to be addressed?

HS Yes finger lifts.

Th. With the door that goes outside, are there any parts or pieces of the soul that left or were taken out through this opening?

HS Yes finger lifts.

Th. Will there need to be a retrieval?

HS Yes finger lifts.

Th. If we should do that now, first finger lifting. If we should address the other door first, then the second finger lifting. If something else, the hand can lift.

HS First finger lifts.

Th. I'm asking, then, higher self that you and the guides carry out that retrieval now. Using the Light and soul vibration make that connection now and retrieve all parts of the soul that left or were taken, bringing all back here to the soul. Make sure all are cleansed and cleared as they are returned. First finger when the retrieval is complete, second finger if there's a problem.

HS First finger lifts.

Th. Higher self, do you believe you were able to retrieve all?

HS Yes finger lifts.

Th. In that procedure, were there any ego-states retrieved.

HS Yes finger lifts.

Th. Are they ones that need to be addressed?

HS Yes finger lifts.
Th. I'm going to ask that you identify one to come forward here with me. And to this one, do you know yourself to be part of the soul that I'm working with?
Es Yes finger lifts.
Th. Are you receiving Light now for yourself?
Es Yes finger lifts.
Th. Does that feel all right to you?
Es Yes finger lifts.
Th. Are you one first created in this present life of Jim's?
Es No finger lifts.
Th. Are you from a past or different lifetime?
Es Yes finger lifts.
Th. Are you a male?
Es No finger lifts.
Th. Are you a female?
Es Yes finger lifts.
Th. Do you know your name?
Es Yes finger lifts.
Th. I'm going to ask that you say your name, right here to the present, on three. One, two, three… Just say the name, nice and loud, right here to the conscious mind. First finger lifting when that's complete. Second finger if there is a problem.
Es First finger lifts.
Th. Jim, did something come to you?
Jm Yes, it's something like Marietta or Marion.
Th. To this one: is your name Marietta?
Es No finger lifts.
Th. If your name is Marion, first finger lifting. If it's something different, the second finger lifting.
Es First finger lifts.
Th. Marion, are there others that came back with you?
Ma Yes finger lifts.
Th. Is everybody receiving Light now?
Ma Yes finger lifts.
(Continue with the Ego-State Protocol.)

Part 6
Body, Mind, and Spirit

Introduction

While the focus of treatment in Soul-Centered Healing is on the psychic and spiritual levels of the self, there are other dimensions and realms that can be significantly involved in a person's healing process. Three of these are: 1) the direct contact with spirit guides, 2) dreams, and 3) the physical body. At one level, these are always involved in a person's healing, even if they do not become a focus. Everyone is a body, everyone dreams, and everyone has at least one spirit guide.

There are certain clients, however, where one or more of these realms become an important factor in the healing process. A client's spirit guide, for example, may intervene and offer guidance or information at a certain point in the healing process. Another client may report powerful and meaningful dreams so frequently that dreams become a regular part of the healing. A client who suffered physical abuse as a child may have body memories that became locked in at a cellular or molecular level. Bringing Light to the physical body at these levels is always an aim in healing, sometimes though, it becomes a focus.

The next three chapters discuss each of these realms from a clinical point of view. They are brief, and not meant to be an in-depth discussion of these realms. The focus is on those situations where I have found the methods of Soul-Centered Healing to be helpful.

20

Spirit Guides and Teachers

Soul-Centered Healing recognizes the existence of a spirit realm of Light, and that many spirits existing there interact with humans at psychic and spiritual levels, sometimes even manifesting physically. Gerod would say that not all spirits in the Light are interacting with humans, but that all humans are interacting with spirits, or have in the past. He said this was the promise made by the Light to all souls incarnating: that each would have at least one spirit guide throughout its incarnation. There may be times or periods when additional spirits interact with a person to offer some special assistance or guidance. There are also people who keep their guide at such a distance that there's barely a whisper. These relationships are unique to the individual and the guides, just as our human relationships are with each other.

Calling on these spirits for assistance during a session is common-place in Soul-Centered Healing. Many people, myself included, call on these spirits for assistance in the course of our everyday lives. In the healing process specifically, though, there are a number of ways in which the guides can assist directly. I've given examples of these in this book and in earlier works. I'll ask for a spirit guide, for example, to come and communicate reassurance to an earthbound spirit who is afraid of being punished in the Light. Sometimes, I'll ask for a spirit guide to come and communicate to an ego-state that is in a particularly bad spot. It's also not unusual for a spirit guide to initiate direct contact with the client and myself during a session. Finally, when dealing with dark souls, I will always call on spirits of Light to be present and assist wherever possible.

The problem in writing about the role of spirits in the healing process is that we don't know what they can do, and what they can't—or won't. We don't know the laws and limitations that govern relations between humans and spirits. We also don't know the specific relationship between a client and his or her guide(s), what agreements were made before incarnating, or the history these souls share. Without knowing any of this, the clinical attitude in Soul-Centered Healing is, *it never hurts to ask*. When a situation arises during a session where I think a spirit guide or teacher could be helpful, I'll ask the higher self whether it's in agreement that we call for assistance.

Early in my work with a client, I will ask higher self if it is in direct connection with the client's "highest level guide." If it's a *yes*, I won't go any further with it at that time. I just want to know that the channels between higher self and the spirit realm are open. I trust that the guides are aware of the client's healing process and will work to support it at an etheric/psychic level. I also trust that they will step in and communicate directly with my client or myself if deemed necessary and permissible.

If the higher self signals that its connection to the guides is blocked, I take that as a sign of trouble. It could be something as simple as the protective part perceiving this other reality as a potential threat, and so blocking contact with these spirit beings. It could be a past-life ego-state whose anger at God has been triggered and is strong enough to keep all guides away, wanting nothing to do with the Light. Quite often, it is an attached or intruding spirit that blocks the guides for fear its presence will be exposed. It is also possible that the block is part of the soul's lesson for that lifetime, and is to be left in place for now. Generally, though, I consider an open connection with the guides to be optimal, and when it's blocked, it usually becomes a focus of treatment, either immediately, or soon. I rely on the higher self to help determine that.

From a clinical point of view, given that the client's connection with the guides is open, the question of whether to call for assistance from spirit guides is always an active one. You can run into a situation at any time where the assistance of guides can be helpful, and sometimes necessary. The following situations are those where I have found it helpful to call on spirit guides, healers, or teachers.

1)   When a client is going to have surgery, I will ask higher self to call for spirit healers who are able to stay with my client before,

during, and after the surgery to assist in the ways they are able. Again, I don't know all of what they can or can't do. Once those guides come forward in the session, I will ask that they make contact or be present with the body at an etheric level. I do this to ensure that blocks are not triggered on the day of surgery. If the healers were to approach the body without forewarning, it can set off the defenses, especially by the protective part or certain ego-states. Making this contact in the session is a trial run, so all parts of the self—including the body-consciousness—know what was happening and welcome the assistance. I do not need to know how the Light does what it does in order to ask for its assistance—in this case, in the form of guides and healers. When a person is going to be under anesthetic, he or she can put their consciousness, so to speak, into the hands of the guides. The spirit healers are also able work with the etheric body, as the surgeons work at a physical level. I would, of course, recommend this practice in every hospital, and by every individual preparing for surgery.

2) Whenever I'm dealing with earthbound, wandering, or dark spirits, I keep in mind that each one has a deep connection to other souls in the Light. I assume that some of these souls are aware of what is happening in the session and are ready to make contact if the spirit consents to it. They also seem to know how best to present themselves, or who to send, so the spirit feels safe and will experience recognition. If I can promise to a spirit direct contact with a loved one or a divine teacher, with no strings attached, it is a powerful inducement for many spirits.

3) Soul retrieval is another situation where I will usually ask spirit guides to assist. Often, the higher self can do the retrieval alone. However, because we are dealing with realities and entities outside the soul, I usually ask guides to be involved. As often as not, when ego-states or soul energy is missing, it's because dark souls are involved. So, I will ask guides to work with the higher self to carry out the retrieval and be ready for resistance.

4) In working with ego-states, I will often suggest direct contact with a spirit guide. If it's a present-life ego-state, it will usually be the client's personal guide that makes contact. It can appear in whatever form is most comfortable for the ego-state. If it's

a past life ego-state, it is often a loved one from that lifetime. Once the contact is made, the ego-state will have what it needs to cooperate with the healing process.

5) In some situations, when the higher self cannot find the source of a block, I will ask that we seek help from guides. The higher self is almost always in agreement with this. Once higher self signals that contact is made, I will ask the guides to review and see if they can locate the source of the block. It doesn't always work, but it does often enough to keep it in mind.

6) I will often ask guides to stay present with a client between sessions as well. I assume that, given permission, the guides can work with the client at etheric and psychic levels. It may be to stay with a child ego-state that is frightened, or stand guard at an opening we found but didn't have time to work with, or to offer companionship until the next session to an ego-state that is desperately lonely.

7) When a client has lost a loved one, they often want reassurance that he or she has made it to the Light. If the higher self is in agreement, we call for a guide who can determine if that soul is in the Light. Sometimes it is the loved one themselves that makes the contact and gives the reassurance.

8) Depending on the client and the treatment situation, I will sometimes ask a guide to communicate to my client directly at a conscious level. This communication can take many forms, ranging from a voice, to intuitions and feelings, to images and symbols. Also some clients come already aware of their guide, and some already have had direct communication.

9) Spirits of Light will not violate another soul. With their soul-level awareness, they are much clearer than we can be about where that line is. A person's spirit guide will not violate his or her free soul choices, whether they are choices being made at a conscious level, or soul-level choices made before the incarnation.

These are situations that come up frequently, each with their own variations. As long as my client is in agreement, I will usually ask for a spirit guide's assistance at certain points in the healing process.

There can be deception at times—spirits claiming to be from the Light, but are not. There can be ignorance—spirits well intentioned, but with a limited perspective. I don't find this kind of interference very often. Making contact with guides through the higher self will usually ensure that they are of the Light. This is why Gerod suggested asking for the person's "highest-level guide."

21

Dream Protocol

Usually, at the start of a session, I ask the client whether he or she has had any significant dreams since we last met. My clients know to expect the question; some even bring printed copies for me. Once I've heard or read the dream, I'll decide whether or not to address it with the client consciously. There are times I spend most of the session talking with a client about a dream because it fits so powerfully with what is happening in their life, or the therapy. Most of the time, however, I wait until the client is in trance and then ask to communicate to the higher self.

The dream protocol is simple. I ask the higher self if it is aware of the dream(s) just discussed. (It almost always is.) Then I ask whether the dream needs to be addressed directly. There are certainly dreams that I think need to be addressed, and the higher self and I are usually in agreement about those. I assume, however, that the client's higher self has a greater knowledge about the dream and its relevance to the healing process, or the client's well-being in general. These are levels or dimensions of a dream that neither my client nor myself would ever be aware of, or know to ask about.

If a dream needs to be addressed, then I will ask higher self to review it and see if there is someone or something I should work with. At that point, the protocols are used to further identify and work with what higher self has found. It may be something simple and straightforward, or it may lead into a complex area requiring more than one session. We can never know where a dream will lead.

The protocol gets a little more complicated when there is more than one significant dream, but it's still just a process of elimination.

I include an example of this below. These are three sample dialogues of the dream protocol:

Dream Protocol: Example 1

Th. Higher self, John and I have talked at a conscious level about the dream with the three children in a boat, and a whirlpool. Higher self, are you aware of this dream?

HS Yes finger lifts.

Th. If this is a dream that needs to be addressed directly, the yes finger can lift. If not, if we don't need to worry about it, the no finger can lift.

HS Yes finger lifts.

Th. If we should address the dream now, the first finger. If we should wait on that, and start with someone or something else, the second finger can lift.

HS First finger lifts.

Th. I'm going to ask then that you review the dream and see if there is someone or something that we should work with. First finger when the review is complete, second finger if there is a problem.

HS First finger lifts.

Th. Did you find someone or something that we should address?

HS Yes finger lifts.

Th. If someone, the first finger lifting. If something, the second finger.

HS First finger lifts.

Th. Higher self, please help that one come forward here with me, and to this one, do you know yourself to be part of this self and soul I'm working with?

__ Yes finger lifts.

Note: The session would continue, using the Ego-State Protocol.

Dream Protocol: Example 2

Th. Higher self, Tammy and I have talked here at a conscious level about this dream with that dark figure. Are you aware of that dream?

HS Yes finger lifts.

Th. Is this a dream that needs to be addressed directly?

HS Yes finger lifts.

Th. Higher self, are you aware of such a dark figure?

HS Yes finger lifts.

Th. If that one is part of the self/soul, the first finger can lift. If it is separate, the second finger. If you're not sure, or it's not the right question, the hand can lift.

HS First finger lifts.

Th. Higher self, are you in agreement that I communicate to that one directly?

HS No finger lifts.

Th. Is there someone else I should communicate with first?

HS Yes finger lifts.

Th. Please identify that one and help them come forward here with me. And to this one, do you know yourself to be part of this self and soul I'm working with?

__ Yes finger lifts.

Th. Are you receiving Light for yourself there now?

__ No finger lifts.

Th. Are you willing to have Light sent to you?

__ No finger lifts.

Th. If you're afraid of the Light or don't want it, the first finger can lift. If someone or something is threatening you there, the second finger can lift. If neither of those fit, the hand can lift.

__ Second finger lifts.

Th. Are you aware of that dark figure we've been talking about?

__ Yes finger lifts.

Th. Is that one threatening you in some way?

__ Yes finger lifts.

Th. Higher self, is that dark figure part of the self/soul?

HS No finger lifts.

Th. If it's one you can remove now, first finger lifting; if not yet, the second finger.

HS First finger lifts.

Th. And to this one I've been communicating with, would you like to have that one removed?

__ Yes finger lifts.

Note: The session would continue, using the appropriate protocols to confirm that the spirit was removed, and then working with the ego-state.

Dream Protocol: Example 3

Th. Higher self, Sandy and I have talked about these three dreams: the one with the car wreck, the one about her mother, and the one with the intense fear. Higher self, are you aware of these dreams?

HS   Yes finger lifts.

Th. Do any of these dreams need to be addressed directly?

HS   Yes finger lifts.

Th. Does more than one need to be addressed?

HS   Yes finger lifts.

Th. More than two?

HS   No finger lifts.

Th. If the one about mother needs to be addressed, the yes finger lifting. If not, the no finger.

HS   Yes finger lifts.

Th. If the dream of the car wreck needs to be addressed, the first finger can lift. If not, the second finger.

HS   Second finger lifts.

Th. Higher self, the dream about mother and the one with the intense fear are the ones that need to be worked with. Is that correct?

HS   Yes finger lifts.

Th. If we should work with one now, the first finger lifting. If we should wait on that, and start with someone or something else, the second finger.

HS   First finger lifts.

Th. If the one with mother, the yes finger. If the *intense fear* dream, the no finger can lift.

HS   No finger lifts.

Th. I'm asking that you review the dream and see if there is someone or something we should address. First finger when the review is complete. Second finger if there's a problem.

HS   First finger lifts.

Th. Higher self, did you find someone or something involved in that dream that we should address?

HS   Yes finger lifts.

Th. If it's someone, first finger. If something or an energy of some kind, the second finger.

HS   First finger lifts.

Th. I'm asking, higher self, that you identify that one and help them come forward here with me. And to this one, do you know yourself to be part of this self and soul?

__ No finger lifts.

Th. If you believe you are separate from this soul that I'm working with, the first finger can lift. If you're just not sure, the second finger lifting.

__ Second finger lifts.

Th. To this one: are you willing to know now whether you are, or are not, part of this self/soul?

__ Yes finger lifts.

Note: The protocols would be used at this point to identify and work with whoever it is, whether part of the soul or separate.

The advantage I see in this approach is that the dream requires no interpretation by my client or myself. We don't have to guess about what something might mean, or whether it has any meaning at all. By using higher self, we can work with the source of the dream, and in the process, the dream will reveal itself.

Most of the time, I find that dream figures are ego-states, spirits, or other external beings presenting either directly or symbolically. I do not want to imply that this is true of all dream figures in everyone's dreams, but I do believe it has some applicability to people's dreams in general. In the healing context, though, this is what I see. I also find that the specific settings, conditions, and interactions occurring in a dream often reflect an inner situation and offer clues as to what to ask or where to focus.

For those hypnotherapists like myself, who already work with dreams in different ways, this dream protocol might be another technique to add to your repertoire. For those who seldom work with dream material, this technique offers a way to address significant dreams when they do present and just cannot be ignored.

22

Body Phenomena

Mind-Body Connection

Whenever a client presented with physical symptoms or complaints, I usually asked Gerod for his reading of the condition. In the beginning, this was only exploratory. One question was whether it was a strictly physically-based condition, or was there psychic, energetic, and/or spiritual forces involved? I began exploring this with Gerod early in our collaboration.

T.   Gerod, in terms of the body and healing—some of which, of course, I see with clients—my question would be whether there is much more potential in working with the higher self to address bodily ails and ills, than I necessarily see here in my practice—and I do see some—but is there a lot more potential there than has been really addressed?

G.   Most definitely there is. How better to determine the point of physical illness within a body than to go within and ask that self within that is able to see and feel and understand what is going on.

T.   That may raise a question of whether for the medical field the use of hypnosis and communication with the higher self might be the best way for diagnosis.

G.   A very helpful way. The higher self may not always be able to give a current term for what is taking place, but the higher self will always be able to pinpoint where the distress is, able to pinpoint whether it is an illness that is emotionally based, whether it is an illness that is most definitely genetically or physical in origin. It is often times important to understand this perimeter around an illness because it does aid in the healing process. Physical ills that are caused by emotions are most definitely physical ills, but they will never be successfully cured, permanently cured, until the emotion upon which it is based is examined and explored and also healed. (Session #59—November 25, 1988)

Continuing on the same topic a few months later.

T.   Another issue we talked about before is the capacity of the higher self and the inner mind to in a sense diagnose physical, emotional, psychological, spiritual issues. You had said that the higher self could do this. Are other parts of the inner mind also able to do this or help with it?

G.   They are able to help with it, but they are not able to discern it as readily. It's almost as if sending out feelers throughout the body to look for a problem area, to discern what may be taking place. The higher self is, in all respects, in charge of that process, so to say. But the ego may assist because of its ability to discern what it is defending against, it may pick up clues as to what is going on in that area, but the higher self is most definitely when attuned, in tune with the physical body and able to pin-point problem areas. (Session #70—February 6, 1989)

It was not unusual for Gerod to identify ego-states, intruding entities, or subtle energies as being involved in the client's body issues. When this was the case, it usually became a focus of treatment, either immediately or soon. It was at least something to check out.

With those clients where the body was a major focus, I would talk to Gerod in depth, exploring for possible connections between mind, body, and spirit. During the course of our collaboration, Gerod identified distinct phenomena affecting different clients, which had to do with the body itself. Further, his description implied that I might find the same kind of phenomena operating within others.

Three phenomena like this that I work with most frequently are 1) the *body-mirror*, 2) the *body-consciousness*, and 3) the *shell*. I consider these to be working concepts. My information and understanding of these phenomena comes from Gerod in response to questions about specific clients. They presented as clinical issues frequently enough in my dialogues with Gerod, and were confirmed by clients' higher selves consistently enough, that I accepted them as valid. My experience with these phenomena, however, is limited. Over the years, I have continued to work with them, but have stayed close to the procedures as first prescribed by Gerod. Once our collaboration ended, I was not in a position to explore these subtle or etheric levels in a methodical way without turning the therapy into research. I believe, however, that the recognition of such body/energy states may prove to be valuable in some people's healing process. I include them here because you may run into situations, especially where physical trauma is involved, where it makes sense to ask about them.

The Body-Mirror

Because they are working concepts, this chapter relies on Gerod's own descriptions of these different phenomena. When asking a client's higher self to review for one of them, the description I use is based on one Gerod gave me.

The first is the *body-mirror*. It came up in my work with a client, K.L., who suffered extreme physical and emotional abuse as a child.

T. Gerod, I worked with K.L. I've been working with Jenny—and what I thought was the body—to share this memory of the body being immersed in a concoction and threatened by birds also. As I worked, it came to the point where it appeared that I'm not talking to the body but I'm talking *almost* to a body state or fragmented state of the body that is frightened about this. But it doesn't seem to be quite an ego-state.

G. It's a body-mirror.

T. A body-mirror?

G. Yes. When the body is sometimes in physical situations, it's almost as if the body can escape the situation. So it's not an ego-state, it's more like a mirror. It reflects the whole body and it seems to be as if it was the body, but it is a fragment of it. Not an ego-state, but more of a mirror.

T. Is there a suggestion you would have about this?

G. Well, you would need to merge the two back together. It's like when you squint your eyes at an object and you can slightly layer the object;

you can squint your eyes and instead of one finger you will have one finger with a slight layering of another one. That's an example of a body-mirror. A slight fragmenting or separating, but I call it a mirror because it's the whole. The whole body skews, not just part of the body.

T.   Do you think the sharing itself will bring merging with it?

G.   You can do it either way. You can have that skewed body—the body-mirror—share, and then you can merge them back together or you can merge them and then ask for sharing. And you could almost, I would say, ask for the preference.

T.   Okay.

G.   The body-mirror, the skewed body, knows there is another body. (Session #210—December 21, 1991)

The Body-Consciousness

A second body phenomenon that Gerod talked about was the *body-consciousness*. Like the body-mirror, it is not easy to conceptualize or quantify. Here's Gerod's description:

G.   It is as if to say the physical body has its own consciousness—the cells, the tissue, the organs. Very much a part of the world of physical matter. It has its consciousness, just as all that exists has its own particular consciousness at different levels, we would say. It is the level at which that consciousness functions that says how well you may communicate with it or how well it may be a contributor to the reality, the physical reality. So as a soul exists within a physical body, there is consciousness, of course, that mind-consciousness, ego-consciousness, soul-consciousness, but there is also a consciousness that is that of the physical organism, of that living entity. (Session #188—March 1, 1991)

The idea that one could communicate directly with a client's *body-consciousness* held profound and far-reaching implications, theoretically and conceptually. The idea also raised clinical questions about the potential benefit and limitations of incorporating the body-consciousness as an element in the healing process. However, it also brought me to the line again where the healing process turns into research. For this reason, my study of the body-consciousness has remained limited.

Depending on the client, I will communicate with the body-consciousness, especially when there has been physical trauma involved. One of the main concerns is whether the client's body-consciousness has separated from the body. This phenomenon was first described by Gerod while discussing a specific client. He said the body-consciousness, normally merged with the body, can separate from the *physical entity*. I think of it as another kind of dissociation, but occurring at a body level.

G.   If there is a separation of the physical body and the body-consciousness, you would communicate with the body-consciousness because it does have awareness of the body and it can give information—but then the physical body, as it functions as a physical entity, does not have its full capability, so to say. It will sometimes not have good health. It will sometimes not have good coordination. Sometimes not have smooth running systems because the consciousness which is more capable of regulating systems and responding to stimuli is not able..., is not there. So, it's as if to say the body-consciousness can give you awareness of something that it is no longer fully engaged with, but the physical body... it's like a ship without a captain. (Session #285—May 8, 1993)

It's as though the body-consciousness has moved operations off-site, analogous maybe to the difference between piloting a plane and operating a drone. Gerod said that a well-functioning higher self should be able to determine whether there has been a separation. If so, the therapeutic aim, then, is to re-merge the body and body-consciousness. I think of it as bringing the body-consciousness back online, the body's return to full sensitivity. At the same time, keep in mind that this re-merging can be threatening to certain ego-states, or the protective part, or to the *physical entity* itself.

Five months later, talking about a different client, Gerod suggested suspending a client's body-consciousness in order to reduce the sensitivity. This is a client who was experiencing acute stomach pains following our sessions. I asked whether particular ego-states were involved in the reaction, but Gerod described it as a generalized reaction.

T. Are there any particular ego-states you see this time that triggered that?

G. No. No one in particular that I would point out. The reaction is so generalized at this point. It's almost as if any—*any* is the key word—any ego-state can trigger it now.

T. Do you see any way to disrupt this generalized pattern?

G. What I would suggest is working with the higher self to, so to say, suspend the body-consciousness. It's a body reaction... okay, it's like there are ego-states. They are triggering reactions. Any of them can do it. The reaction settles into the body, triggering a physical reaction. I would suspend the body-consciousness. It is still in connection to the body and the body-consciousness is holding... well, it's accepting the patterns for pain.

T. Is it merged with the body?

G. Yes, to a great degree. I would describe it this way: it's almost as if the body has no will of its own. The body-consciousness is very much controlled by ego-states. It's almost as if the body-consciousness is reacting and performing spontaneously and in a purely reactionary manner without using its consciousness to pick and choose. Which, of course, the body-consciousness can be selective if it has an awareness that it can be. Which is what doing the shell work does. It allows it to be more aware of its ability to selectively react. But this body-consciousness is not aware of that and so it reacts automatically to impulses and messages from the ego-states. So, by suspending body-consciousness... it's not removing it... well, it is in essence, setting up an artificial separation from the body.

T. Do we need permission from body-consciousness to do this?

G. No. No. Higher self would need to investigate the situation and to support it and give agreement to suspend it and that would involve surrounding it, for example, with energy that will disconnect it from the body and disconnect it from ego-states.

T. Do you think it would be good then for C.A. at a conscious level to have a symbol or something from the higher self to reinforce that or...?

G. I believe that could be very helpful. Yes. It's like putting a wild dog in a cage for the safety of others. Once the dog has been, so to say, removed or isolated from stimulus, it will calm down. It cannot create any problems. So it is a temporary isolation of the body-consciousness to prevent any stimulation of body reactions of pain. And whether this would be helpful? I cannot say with complete accuracy that it will take care of it, but I believe it could be very effective. I believe it is certainly a valuable alternative. (Session #307—October 3, 1993)

The Shell

The *shell* is a third body phenomenon identified by Gerod. He described it as a thin layer of energy formed by the body's experience in childhood and locked into place by twelve or thirteen. Picture a suit of armor projected out from the body, like an invisible shield. Gerod said it varies by individual and can be anywhere from an inch to several feet out from the physical body. He said the shell is made up of pieces, like a patchwork quilt, that hold habit patterns, learned responses, memory fragments, and images.

The shell is a facade; it's a protection; it's survival routines; it's habits—all of these and more, according to Gerod. We might think of it as the body's set interactions in physical reality. At the same time, he said it is a very thin and inflexible layer. It does not have the depth of emotions, mind, and soul. It does not take much to dissolve it once one knows it's there and makes conscious changes.

The issue in healing is whether a person's shell is still present and maintaining habitual patterns that appear to have been resolved at deeper levels. Gerod said this can best be determined later in the healing process when the shell is not being "fed" by ego-states, external reinforcements, psychological defenses, and emotional conflicts. It's as though the clearer the inner world becomes, the more the shell will stand out.

The following are excerpts from two sessions where Gerod talked about the shell at length.

T. Can you talk yourself from your point of view or give some description of this shell or consciousness?

G. Yes. I will see how I can explain it to you. As a soul enters into a physical body and begins its experience, the ego part-selves are created because of the protection that will ensure the survival of the body and ensure the opportunity for the soul to do its work, gain its experience. So, as this body stores and records and compensates for the stresses of the physical life, it also creates a physical memory, a physical shell. It is almost—I see this as a bit strange perhaps but—it is almost like the ice cream cone that is whole in itself but you can dip it into a chocolate substance and it creates a shell. It is thin and not extremely flexible. It will break. And this is the shell that is somewhat created by experiences. It isn't flexible, meaning that once it is there it doesn't change unless you alter it consciously in some way. You change the perception and the understanding of the emotional body, of the ego-states, but that does not necessarily affect the shell because the shell is created once, so to say. And as you then have the healing process and change internally, then it almost becomes a process of melting down that shell. And it is not necessary to repair it or replace it because one can then operate from the internal structure, project from a more adult point of view or a more understood point of view.

T.   You're saying this shell is created, but it sounds like you're saying that it does not itself change or develop. Is that right?

G.   That is correct. Meaning that... it's created over the formative years, the years when a child is born and grows. The years when from birth to approximately twelve to thirteen years of age when a child is having many of those experiences that cement it or develop the behaviors, the patterns, the responses from life. So once it is in place, it does not matter what other subsequent experiences take place because they will not alter the shell.

T.   It's like you're saying that those earlier experiences are accruing, are building up, and at some point the shell, in a sense, crystallizes. Is that accurate?

G.   Yes. Yes. It's as if it is complete, or becomes like a paint drying or a shellac setting, becoming firm. (Session #249—August 29, 1992)

G.   And the way to remove it is, for one thing, to have the knowledge that it is there. It is not easy to remove it in the beginning because it's as if it is not easily separated or is not as easy to discern that it is there. It's almost like when you remove turmoil and move the different ego-states into that place where they are comfortable, co-operative, and very much in harmony with the self, then you look back and see what is there and you may see the shell is still there...

So then it's a matter of removing that or dissolving it, and it can be done by introducing energy. That is definitely a more conscious work because, as we say, it is a shell. It's as if it is on the surface. It is not that deep. The deep work has been done, the moving of the ego-states, moving the sources of distress and pain. That is the fiber that, in essence, that pushed out and held the shell in place. So now without that tension against it, it is more obvious to see it because it's more there and that makes it easier to dissolve because that inner tension that held it in place is gone. (Session #249—August 29, 1992)

G. As a person heals and matures, you know, gains their own aware-ness and understanding, they may begin dissolving that shell. As if you may see the whole body encapsulated, with a shell around it, or you may not. It can all be there but only parts of it active, mean-ing that some of the work that a person has done may have already neutralized part of the shell. But the entire shell is created out of emotion and experience but it's not as if all of it is active. (Session #249—August 29, 1992)

G. You might see it in your mind as a smooth shell like an egg but actually were you to microscope it you would see many things. You would see faces, events, emotions, tools, weapons—it's like all the physical imagery and experiences are all there in the shell. It's all the fragments that are there. Fragments of the anger; fragments of the pain and the patterns. And it's like it's all embedded in that shell. But as I say, it's a fine thin shell. It has no great depth to it. And so once the internal that was totally involved with all the experience is moved and resolved, there's nothing to hold it, there's nothing that keeps it there. As we spoke earlier, an addiction becomes a habit when the need for the addiction is gone. And once it becomes a habit, it is much easier to alter because the addictive emotional need is gone. (Session #249—August 29, 1992)

G. The higher self would not have a strong awareness of the shell. It does not necessarily view any separation there for an individual. It is working from that internal structure, that internal point of view, and so is not readily aware of a shell. Much easier for me from my point of view to see it and be aware that it is there but from the higher self's point of view, not so easy. And not even quite so pertinent to it as the higher self is dealing internally and the internal is still so much of what creates the shell. And it does not need to have awareness of creating it.

T. What do you think—that the protective part would be the more appropriate one to have identify the shell?

G. No. Actually, it would be the body that would have the greater awareness of it. (Session #251—September 11, 1992)

G. Dissolving it or working with it is not always easy to do until you have accomplished a great amount of internal work, so then the shell is much more apparent to all and also then has lost any ongoing internal support, that internal tension that keeps the structure there. You could attempt to do some removing, some dissolving of it concurrent with the healing process but it is not as easy to do because as you move one part you must be certain that the underlying structure is removed and no longer supporting it and you must then be aware of anyone moving in to reinforce it. (Session #251—September 11, 1992)

My experience in working with the shell is limited. I do not address it with every client. When I do, it is usually, as Gerod suggested, after a good deal of inner work has been done. At that point, I have the body-consciousness and the higher self determine whether there is a shell in place, and if so, how many pieces comprise it, and how many of those have to be worked with directly. The aim is to dissolve the shell by dissolving the pieces. If Gerod is correct, it should give the conscious person freer movement in the present. Whether the procedure is to be done immediately or not is also something determined by the body-consciousness and higher self.

I believe this thin energy layer, as Gerod described it, is a real phenomenon and a normal creation of the body. I have no proof of this. My own work with clients appears to confirm it, but this is a very limited database dealing with a very elusive phenomenon. It awaits further confirmation. Meanwhile, I do work with these phenomena, or at least try to check them out with clients if I suspect that such body phenomena are involved.

Part 7

John D. – A Case Study in Soul-Centered Healing

23

The Panic

John first came to see me because of his frequent panic attacks. He was in his early fifties, single, and working as a successful business consultant. He had moved to Western Michigan sixteen years before to become the director of a non-profit organization with a strong religious affiliation. He left family, friends, colleagues, and familiar work, to live in a new city and culture, with a new job, and greater responsibility.

Within five years, however, conflicts began to develop between John and the board about the organizational direction. Some of John's innovative ideas challenged the board leadership and some of the organization's religious traditions. It became political, and it turned ugly. John felt abused by the board. He said he remembers coming to the realization that he had made a serious mistake by staying in the position, that he was "in over his head." He also realized that, in the end, he would be forced to resign or be fired. This dawning realization, he thinks, is what led to increased panic attacks and the need for professional help.

As the attacks grew more intense, John was admitted to a psychiatric facility for treatment. He quickly regained his equilibrium, and within a couple of days, signed himself out. Not long after his discharge, he also discontinued his medications. He did not like how they made him feel. He said he knew that drugs weren't the answer, and that he needed psychotherapy to help him deal with what was happening.

John had worked with seven therapists prior to that initial hospitalization. The most recent therapist, Deborah, whom he felt had been the most helpful, had just moved away from the area when her husband was transferred. John knew about Soul-Centered Healing through a former client. He said that his conscious level-therapy had helped, but he felt it wasn't getting to the core of the problem. He thought hypnosis, and specifically Soul-Centered Healing with its spiritual dimension, might help him to uncover and resolve whatever was causing the panic attacks.

In that initial session, John described feelings of chronic anxiety and depression, with episodes of anger and rage. The latter he kept under tight control, and if he did express it, it was only when alone. He also reported periodic flashbacks of abuse that he had suffered as a child and again as a late adolescent. By the end of the session, we both agreed that this abuse was probably involved in the panic and underlying anxiety. At the end of the session, John made another appointment for his first hypnosis session.

24

Backstory

Starting School

John was the oldest of six children. Born of loving parents, he grew up in one of the old Catholic neighborhoods where church and religion played a dominant role. By all accounts, John had a normal childhood until age five when he started school. It became clear very early that John was performing poorly in school, especially in math and spelling. This was the nineteen-fifties when knowledge and awareness of learning disabilities was just beginning to get serious attention. Neither John's teachers nor parents recognized his disabilities. He was viewed as slow or lazy, with questions about his intelligence.

John's mother, Helen, reacted in an extreme way to these school reports. She lacked the experience to raise a child with learning disabilities. With John as the oldest child, this was Helen's initiation into the social/parish world of school, expectations, and parenthood. For John's sake, and her own, she took it upon herself to make him learn his math tables by quizzing him at home on the school assignments. She would give him basic addition/subtraction problems and he had one to two minutes to give the correct answer to a problem. From the beginning of this regimen, John could not give the correct answers to most of the problems in the allotted time. What for most children was a rote memory task did not work for John. Helen, of course, did not understand this. As she quizzed John, he continued to give the wrong answers. She grew more and more frustrated until, during one of these sessions, she began to beat John physically.

It was during this first physical assault that John dissociated. A five-year-old ego-state was created that was terrified, panicked, and feeling totally helpless to understand or stop what was happening. Correct answers were the only thing that would stop it and no matter how hard he tried, he couldn't find them. For John, there was no way out. More than one five-year-old ego-state would be created, and then came the six-year-olds.

The beatings continued for almost three years. John's father appeared to be a reluctant participant, taking on the task at times of quizzing John and meting out punishment. If he had misgivings, however, he didn't act on them.

Meanwhile, the teachers at school were coming to recognize that John was a bright, intelligent child who also displayed leadership abilities and self-initiative. His problem was not one of intelligence or laziness, but a handicap in particular areas of cognitive functioning.

Whether the teachers suspected the abuse, or were just finally able to offer a diagnosis, they called for a meeting with John's parents. They explained about his learning disabilities, and his strong performance in other areas. I think both Helen and Bill were relieved to know that John was neither lazy nor lacking intelligence. They also had a reason now for John's difficulties, and it wasn't their failure as parents. I also believe that Bill and Helen were relieved at a deep level to be able to stop the beatings. It was as though Helen could now hand over responsibility to the school for knowing the best way to help him. John told me that his mother, more than once, expressed deep remorse and regret over the beatings for the rest of her life.

The result of this meeting with the teachers was that the beatings came to an immediate end. By then, however, the damage had been done. Ego-states had been created that still lived in that terrifying world of beatings, failure, and helplessness. From the child's point of view, there was no way out. He could not physically stop her, and he could not defy his mother without risk of further punishment. He could not find the right answers. He could not go to outside authorities who, he believed, would agree with his parents and blame him for not working hard enough. From a five-year-old's point of view, his world of pain and terror was sanctioned by the school, since they gave out the assignments. It would be many years before John told anyone of the beatings.

The ego-states created during this period tell a story of dissociation as the primary means of protection or escape from what was happening. There were many of these dissociations, just as there were many beatings, and many days in school where his failure was on display. The perceptions of these ego-states ranged through the whole spectrum from being worthless to enraged, from profound confusion to total helplessness. Working with these ego-states, as you will see in Chapter 25, was a major part of John's healing.

With the exception of his grandmother, John was mistrustful and emotionally disconnected from others. His fear and terror of being punished generalized from his parents' abuse to those in the outer world, especially authority figures. Because of his intelligence and intuition, John was able to compensate somewhat for his learning disabilities. It gained him some level of success and acceptance at home, in school, and in the community. His defense against the inner pain, terror, and confusion was to become exquisitely attuned to what others wanted or expected of him. In a positive sense, he learned to play the system. His ego-identity, however, was heavily based on being who and what others wanted him to be. To survive and avoid punishment, he had to have the right answers in whatever situation he found himself. It's how he stayed safe, found acceptance, and experienced some success.

This identity, however, was about to undergo a radical assault and redefinition.

Starting Seminary

A second period of abuse started at age nineteen. John had entered the seminary after one year of college. He had always felt a strong religious devotion and wanted to explore the priesthood as a possible vocation, a desire that was first kindled as an altar boy. When he entered the seminary, he had a girlfriend, Sarah. During these first two years, called the *initial formation*, the seminary rules did not prohibit dating. The idea was that the seminarian would use that time to decide whether he was willing to live a single, celibate life, as a priest. This was a major conflict that John hoped to resolve in these first two years. Did he truly want to commit himself to the priesthood or someday marry and have children?

In the novitiate, each seminarian was assigned a spiritual director. John was assigned to Fr. Carl B. He was in his mid-thirties, younger than most spiritual directors. He appealed to John because he had a strong interest in spirituality. Carl was in tune with the changes happening in the church as a result of Vatican II (1962-65). This was the Church Council meant to modernize the church. John very strongly felt he wanted to be a part of that change too. He was looking to Carl to help guide him to some clear direction on these life decisions.

There were also questions, at least in John's own mind, and maybe some of the teachers, about whether he was "smart enough" to be a priest. Due to his learning difficulties, this doubt had dogged him not only during elementary school, but during his high school years as well. The seminary's scholastic education emphasized academics and basic skills. It was a demanding environment for a young man who struggled with reading, writing, and arithmetic.

Finally, John was still adjusting to this new world of the seminary with its all-male culture, governed by what many would describe as a repressive and authoritarian institution. Leaving home and family, and establishing one's identity and friendships in a new social milieu, is a rite of passage for most college freshmen. For John, it was an extreme challenge. He had built up a strong support network over the years, both at school and in church. He learned to compensate for his learning difficulties. He was a good athlete, active in both school and church.

When John moved to the seminary, he lost this day-to-day support network, at least temporarily, until he could form a new one. He was in an unknown world now and had to learn new rules and how to please a whole new set of people, especially those in charge. From John's conscious point of view, this was the world in which he might spend the rest of his life and he had to figure out a way to fit in and belong.

Early in his second year, at the end of a counseling session, whether by plan or impulse, Carl forcibly kissed John and inserted his tongue into John's mouth. This intimate abuse set off feelings of extreme revulsion, profound confusion, and then John dissociated. A nineteen-year-old ego-state was created that tolerated the kissing and touching by separating completely from the self, including the physical body. Later, in his room, John had no memory of it. He didn't tell Carl to stop, or quit meeting with him, or report the incident to his superiors, because he didn't remember it. Over the next eight months, there were more incidents. John estimates that it happened six to nine times, and each time, he dissociated.

What he does remember clearly is the last incident during which he became angry at what was happening, pushed Carl away, and told him in a menacing voice never to touch him again. As John described it, it was as though he woke up from a different state, knew what was happening, and had to stop it. He said part of him wanted to kill Carl in that moment. He had found his voice, but it was out of desperation and survival.

Carl's abuse ended that night. He never touched John again. John did not report it to his superiors until much later, but he distanced himself from Carl and carried on a perfunctory relationship with him. John left the seminary later that year. He transferred to the nearby Catholic college that was affiliated with the seminary. His relationship with Sarah did not survive the trauma with Carl. After graduation, he continued to work in Catholic schools as a teacher, coach, and later, an administrator. He never married. Several relationships were started and ended. From outward appearance, John was successful. He was well liked in the community, ready to help anyone. He had built a support network of friends and colleagues just as he had in his hometown, before seminary.

The non-profit director's position in Western Michigan was a career opportunity for John. It would be taking his career to the next level. He could put into practice the organizational knowledge and skills he had acquired so far in his career. At the same time, in accepting the position, John was leaving the security of his day-to-day support network, just as he had when he left for seminary. It was a new world, a different culture, with new people, and new rules. He also was in a new role of authority, with both its professional and social demands. John was not very far into establishing a new support network, and finding his place in the community, when conflict with the board began. As the conflict built toward crisis, and the loss of his job, John's panic erupted.

The panic was not about finding another job. It was about the fear of failure and rejection. It was about being wrong, and being punished. It was about self-blame and feeling worthless. He was afraid of how others would judge him. It was about the anger and rage at being misjudged and abused. Deeper still was a terror that John was only dimly aware of. He had been here before. The panic attack raised the alarm and broke through the layers of dissociation, denial, and repression that had become a way of life. As would become clear later, the professional crisis struck at John's most basic defenses and tore open deep wounds and contradictions that had never healed.

At its deepest level, it was about "the enclosure," a dark place where ego-states existed that were fully dissociated from any contact with the outer world or the inner mind, and from the body itself. The image I had at the time, as they shared their reality, was that they stepped into a black hole, turned around, and zipped it up behind them. In retrospect, John's healing process was largely one of working his way to this enclosure, bringing in Light, reconnecting with vital parts of himself, and then working his way back to the present. This reconnection with his soul's Light, I believe, affected John at every level, like waking up dead nerves. John described it as bringing parts of himself back to life again. At the same time, John was waking up to how controlled and stifled his life had been by the fear, rejection, and terror.

25

A Bird's-Eye View

The Diagram

In my first book, I presented a schematic diagram to depict a hypothetical case in Soul-Centered Healing (see figure 25.1). It shows an inner world comprised of ego-states (past-life and present), earthbound spirits, and dark souls. While not obvious, it also depicts the sequence in which the groups were identified, beginning with the earliest at the top and winding its way to the latest at the bottom. The diagram is strictly a visual metaphor. It grew out of my need to somehow conceptualize the connections among and between the different ego-states, spirits, and entities that I was encountering with clients.

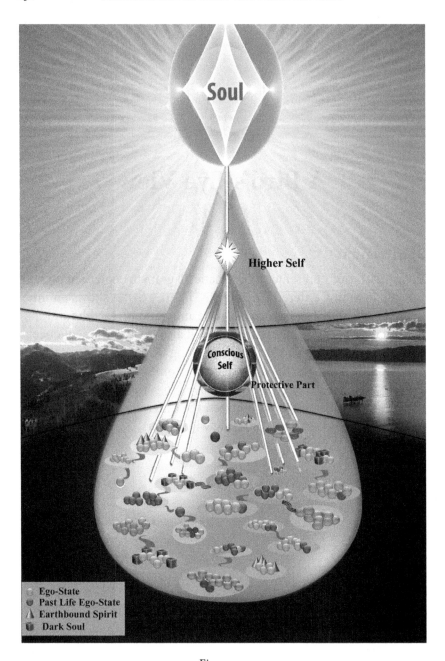

Figure 25.1

In this chapter, I've used that same technique to diagram John D's case. The diagram offers a bird's-eye view of John's healing process over five years (see figure 25.2). In looking at the diagram, you will recognize the mapping elements discussed in Chapter 10, *Mapping the Inner World*. The lighter spheres represent the present-life ego-states that presented in John's sessions. The darker spheres represent past-life ego-states. The dark cones represent attached or intruding spirits. The circled numbers give the sequence in which each group of ego-states and/or spirits were identified during the course of healing. In this numbering scheme, an individual ego-state counts as a group. In general, as in the original diagram, the sequence of sessions runs from the earliest at the top to the latest at the bottom. The rule of thumb is: the higher the number, the later the group was identified. As far as the healing process itself, I visualize it as the Light moving down through the diagram as the different ego-states are integrated and spirits removed.

The diagram is accompanied by a spreadsheet located in the Appendix (see page 273). That table gives a more detailed breakdown of each session in terms of who was identified, who shared, and a brief synopsis of what was shared.

The table runs many pages, and might appear overwhelming at first glance. I include it for purposes of reference, for readers who are interested in more details, or for the purpose of study. However, the reader does not need to refer to it or study it in order to understand the narrative.

The diagram does not depict all the energies and devices that were identified and dealt with in John's sessions. There were quite a few instances of these and they were reintegrated, dissipated, or expelled using the protocols to determine what needed to be done. Some of that information is contained in the table, but it also is incomplete. The diagram also does not identify all the body level phenomena that occurred during the sessions. These body phenomena presented very strongly with John. He frequently reported energy sensations and pathways, blockages, or pain in specific areas of the body, as I worked with different ego-states.

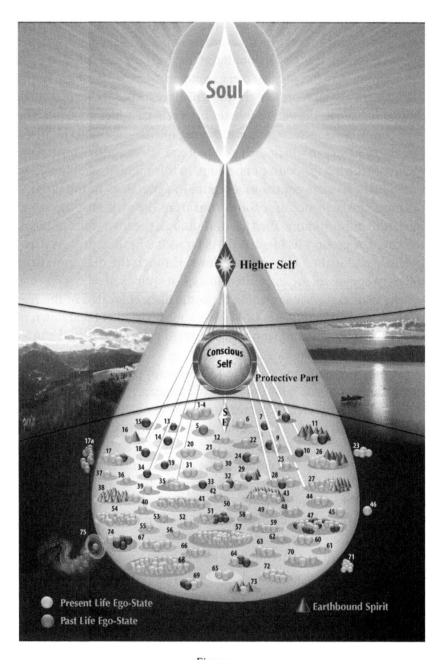

Figure 25.2

26

The Journey Inward

Sessions #1-6: Projection and Introjection

The first ego-state that John's higher self identified was a fifty-two year-old, John's age at the time. He did not have any real depth, or memories to share. He appeared to function as the presenting self, John's public face, to the world. His purpose was to protect the self by adapting to the ever-changing situations and circumstances in the outside world. Rather than a dissociation from the conscious self, he seemed to act as a shield. The closest parallel might be Jung's concept of the *persona*. This ego-state received Light and integrated without much difficulty.

The next ego-state presenting in the first session was named Carl. The higher self confirmed that Carl was created of John's own self/soul energy. He appeared to be what psychologists call an *introject*. To avoid confusion, I'll identify this ego-state as Carl(i), to distinguish it from Carl, the person. Often this type of figure turns out to be an external ego-state (EES) from another soul. In this case, though, Carl(i) was created by the self. His identity was based on the real Carl, and cast in the role of perpetrator and threat. I'm not sure of Carl(i)'s function in the inner world. That specific information was not necessary for its integration. I suspect he was a warning against trusting others and a target for John's repressed anger and rage.

What was even more unusual in John's treatment was that the next three ego-states identified were also *introjects*. Over the next five sessions I worked with Helen(i), John's mother; Bill(i), John's father; and Julie(i), the woman John viewed as instrumental in creating dissension on the board that eventually led to his forced resignation. Helen(i) and Bill(i) were aware that they were part of John's self/soul energy. Initially, Carl(i) thought he was separate. With Julie(i), the question did not come up.

The resolution of these introjects was not difficult. Each shared its perceptions and feelings, and was able to release. However, Carl(i) and Helen(i) could not integrate immediately. They would require further work in later sessions.

Session #7: The Soul and Energy Point

In Session #2, I had asked higher self about the soul and energy point. It said the energy point was free, but the soul was encapsulated. It also said to wait before addressing it. In this session, after the introjects had been resolved and integrated, I came back to the soul's encapsulation. Higher self agreed to address it, and the information was that the soul was encapsulated by an entity separate from the self/soul. This was most unusual. I was concerned that it might be a negative entity. It turned out to be a positive and seemed to have come to give added protection to the soul. I suspect spirit guides were involved.

The entity left without resistance, and the energy point and soul were joined in the heart center without a problem. However, they were separated and rejoined several more times during the course of John's healing process. This happened, I believe, because of what we were dealing with at those particular times.

Sessions #8-9: Exhibitor

When I first began working with John, I had asked Gerod for any information or suggestion he could give. He said it might be helpful to ask higher self to look for *Exhibitor*. When I asked, higher self did find *Exhibitor*. It turned out he was a past life, male, adult (PLMA). When first identified, he did not know if he was part of the self/soul. Higher self helped him to review and become aware of his connection to the soul. He shared an experience of being violated, accompanied by a deep pain in the heart. The experience involved Lisa, a woman in John's present life, whom he had come close to marrying, but then broke it off. As souls, John and Lisa had shared this past life, and *Exhibitor*, who carried the pain of it, appeared to have been triggered in John's present life.

I worked with *Exhibitor* again in the next session. He had a release, but there were two external energies present that had entered the soul and were blocking his integration. Higher self dissipated these, helped Exhibitor to integrate, and then identified a forty-five year-old present life ego-state. This one shared his feeling of disconnection from spirituality. It was the strong sense that something was lost. 45yo was able to release and integrate.

Session #10: Past-Life Abuse

In this session, higher self identified a past-life male, adult (PLMA). His sharing was blocked by a past-life, male, teenager (PLMT). This is the one I worked with. He shared experiences of abuse by a parent. During his sharing, he became frightened of the memory and needed to stop. We would come back to him. Meanwhile, the PLMA shared. John reported twisting sensations in his body as this one shared. After his release and integration, higher self signaled that that was enough for now.

Session #11: Contact with the Original Trauma

I asked higher self about an intense fear that John reported feeling during the week. It found a PLMA named, David, and another forty-five year-old created in the present life. David started sharing first and then stopped it. The Light was distressing him. (John reported a tightness from his throat to his heart). David shared about beatings, being hit, crushed up against a wall, and being alone. Higher self said his release needed to wait for the forty-five year-old.

45yo shared that he first came at five-years-old. He was petrified, literally, and now as we communicate, he's afraid to become animated again. He's afraid to remember what happened, but is willing to answer my questions. He is in his bedroom. His mother is there. He signals that he was hurt emotionally and physically. At that point, John reports that his chest cavity feels like it's being pushed up into his throat. 45yo has a release, but higher self signals that he cannot integrate yet. It says there is a door that needs to be addressed first. It goes outside the soul, and a retrieval should be done. Higher self carried out that retrieval and integrated the soul energy that was returned. There were no ego-states that had left. At that point, past-life David and 45yo were able to release and integrate—David within the soul, and 45yo with the conscious self. Higher self said there would be more to address about fear, but this was enough for now.

Session 12: A Healing Realignment

The Higher self went back to the fear and identifies a past-life, male, child (PLMC). The protective part reacted at this point. The higher self explains to the protective part that John's trauma with mother had reawakened this child, and triggered it forward. He's alone. John reports more weight on the chest and the purple color around his forehead. He reports that a sensation began in his third eye and went through his body "from head to toe." He described it as, "the whole body relaxing, and his chakras being realigned."

Session 13: First Spirits Encountered

We went back to the fear. Higher self identifies a twenty-year-old ego-state. 20yo communicates that there are seven others with him. One is a PLMA, and higher self says the other six are spirits. Higher self was able to remove them without my having to engage them directly. 20yo then shared and John reported a "shift in his chest" that went up to his head. 20yo was able to release and integrate. We went back to the PLMA. He was able to share and John reported a red and purple color around his head, and then a "soft energy." The PLMA released and was integrated.

Sessions #16-23: Nineteen Years-Old

Session #16 was the first appearance of a nineteen-year-old ego-state. There was a spirit present with this one and the higher self removed it. 19yo began sharing feelings of panic, and then it stopped. He's in Carl's room. Higher self cleared him and he shared deep feelings of "self-loathing and self-dying." John reports a pain on the left side of his neck, and his arms are stiff. 19yo is angry at God. The higher self helps him to see that the Light did give him protection. John reported afterwards the sense "that something had died."

In the next session, another 19yo was identified. He was in the dark spot. There were four others with him—two more 19-year-olds, a 26-year-old, and a PLMA. 19yo#1 is profoundly confused. Higher self identifies two openings that go outside the soul. We start a retrieval and it is blocked. 19yo#1 is afraid for these parts to come back into the soul. I ask higher self to create a kind of *quarantine room* within the soul that can safely house whatever is retrieved. 19yo#1 agrees then to the retrieval. Higher self retrieves twenty ego-states, all created at nineteen- and twenty-years-old. 19yo#1 shares again about the confusion. He didn't know where to go. He says the shock of Carl knocked him off his path. He shares that the earlier abuse by his parents became cemented in at nineteen. He said that an impenetrable black shield went up and is still in place. All of the ego-states are aware of it. I called guides to help higher self to dissipate it.

19yo#2 comes forward in the next session. He shares his anger and rage and says most of the retrieved ones carry these feelings also. There is a panic and tightness in the heart area. He shares the tremendous pain of being knocked off his spiritual path. John says this confusion is familiar, and is still strong today. He has shared enough for now. 26yo and the PLMA both share, release, and integrate.

19yo#3 comes forward in the next session. He shares about becoming re-centered and is able to release and integrate. 19yo#1 comes forward again and is feeling safe now and able to release and integrate. During the rest of the session, I work with 19yo#2 for his release. He returns in the next session to continue his sharing. He says there is a ball of dark, negative energy in the abdomen. Higher self helps him to start releasing. 19yo#2 says the abuse by Carl was an extreme shock and it has stayed inside. He also shares that a split was created between his passion and his intellect. He dissociated from his passion. He agrees to let higher self help him gradually begin feeling it again. Finally, 19yo#2 is able to release and integrate.

Sessions #24 and #26: When Darkness First Came

Beginning with the nineteen-year-olds, John's healing work entered a very dark area of the psyche and soul. They were in the dark spot. In this session, we identified a group of five and a group of twenty-four. In the large group, though, fifteen were spirits, and the higher self removed them without resistance. The remaining nine were ego-states. None of them were receiving Light, and when they did, it caused pain and distress. I had to work with many of them individually before they would receive the Light.

In the group of nine, there was a thirty-two-year-old who shared feelings of being violated by Carl. It was the darkness coming at him again. He went on to share that he had been created at the age of three months. He said that he was "conceived in anger," and born into a dark and threatening world. It appeared to be a mixture of both his parent's pain and anger. Helen had witnessed her father's death in a tragic accident, and she still had not recovered from the trauma. Bill, with his memories of combat in World War II, brought the pain and trauma of the war home with him. I'm sure neither one intended that John become a target of the pain, grief, and anger that each felt, but he couldn't be anywhere else.

Two months before John was born, his father had an accident at work and suffered extensive damage to his arm. The impact on this already struggling couple was devastating, like being hit by a tidal wave. John was born of loving parents, but theirs was a dark and painful world at that time. The three-month-old ego-state was created when this darkness came at him. He said it felt "as if it came inside him." Along with it, John said the message was: *repress the pain*. It was the message from the parents, but it seemed to go back generations. At nineteen and at thirty-two, he experienced this darkness again.

Sessions #34-35: Abandoned by Parents

I checked on the energy point and soul. Both were now encapsulated. The higher self communicated that the soul was encapsulated by an energy, and the energy point was inside a metal box. We found a 5yo inside the box, and he was holding the energy point. He had a deep fear of abandonment, and a feeling of never being good enough. He said he first came at three-years-old. John's one-year-old sister had been born with a physical handicap and his parents gave most of their energy and attention to her. He said, "She's always right, and I'm always wrong." When the abuse by mom started, he was triggered again, and the feelings of abandonment were overwhelming. It was the dark energy coming at him, and he shared that he became "lost in a vortex of darkness." He said that with mom, he felt emasculated and wiped out. "Like I never existed."

John said this pattern has been carried on now for decades.

Sessions #36-47: Coming Alive

During this next series of sessions, a significant shift occurred. I would describe it as a *letting go* at a very deep level, followed by an opening up at different levels of John's being. It unfolded over time. It started with the body. As I worked with different ego-states, John began to experience "body releases" in which he reported the release of physical tension and rigidity. At one point, John described it as the "body coming back online." These releases involved the body itself, as well as ego-states that kept the body tense and stiff. One ego-state shared, "When painful energy comes at me, the body freezes. The body shuts down, becomes stiff, and the mind just sort of races. Things become erratic." Another shared that he felt the loss of his core. He said it became blocked, and "now my body wants to loosen up."

The release began to extend to the emotions. John was beginning to experience his emotions more intensely, both in our sessions and in his everyday life. It was new to him, frightening and exhilarating, unpredictable and alive. John knew this was a positive step in healing. His growing capacity to experience the body and emotions also made John aware of how numb he had become and the depth of dissociation and repression that was operating. His ongoing homework was just to tolerate the feelings, stay with them, until he was able to re-center in the present moment and feel. This re-awakening of the body and emotion seemed also to stir up ego-states. Over the months, John reported a number of episodes of intensely painful emotion. Usually, I would ask higher self to review inside and locate the source of that episode.

During this period, John also began to talk of transformation, wanting to develop trust in others outside of him. He had lost this trust at five-years-old, and except for his grandmother, it had cut him off from relationships. This included his relationship with Sarah, but especially relationships after Carl's abuse.

27

The Enclosure

Sessions #63-76: The Island

In Session #63, John told me he had been in a panic for the last several days. He said there was a fear of being alone and fears of dying. He had thought about calling 911. This was the closest John had come to a full blown panic in many months. It was an opportunity to touch into the panic itself, and to see whether there were ego-states involved. When I asked higher self to look for the source, it identified a group of four. There was a six year-old, two five year-olds, and an eight year–old.

I worked with this group over the next three months. It started with a five-year-old sharing his panic after starting school. Each of them shared its own version of being overwhelmed by the outside world and having to retreat inside to a place of isolation and safety. They were all in darkness, and as long as each stayed in isolation, it could be safe. It was a gradual process for these four to share the depths of pain, terror, and confusion that each carried. As the sharing and releasing continued, the Light was approaching closer. One of the four described it like being on an island in a reservoir of Light and it was "feeling stronger and stronger." They finally understood that it was time to let go into that reservoir of Light and they moved to integration.

While we didn't know it at the time, this group was our entrance into what John came to call "the enclosure."

Sessions #76-79: The Cavern

After they integrated, higher self identified two large groups. John's sense was that we were working in a "cavern." I worked with an eight-year-old in one group and a nine-year-old in the other. Like the island, it was another kind of enclosure. The eight-year-old shared about the split between the outer world and the inner. He could not let the outside know his true self, but had to be someone who could please them, while all the time knowing it was a false self. At the end, eight year-old said he could not live in that split any longer.

In the second group, I worked with the nine-year-old. He said he is trapped by his fear of being enclosed, afraid he "won't be able to get out." He says he shut down. He shares deep feelings of loneliness and fear, and so often is overwhelmed by outside situations.

Next, the higher self identified a ten-year-old. He's alone. John says it feels like a core part of himself that was lost. He's aware now that his intellect had become a major defense. It was the intellect that would figure out what others wanted and how he had to act to be safe. John said he was being asked now to "lessen the head," and move more into his feelings and intuition. At the end of the session, John said, "Today is a shift into a whole other space. I don't know how to describe it. I don't have words. The cavern image is gone." John said there is fear of "letting go of the head. It's been in charge for so long."

Sessions #81-85:

30yo first came at three-years-old. Terrified of the darkness and the anger that was coming at him from mom. When Carl came at him—his trusted mentor, counselor, and guide—a decision was made that he would never be that vulnerable again. "I shut off my life energy to the body." At the end of the session, John said, "My whole being is coming back alive."

Sessions #86-91: Keep Quiet

40yo first came during mom's abuse. He came forward at forty to deal with the terror and confusion that had been triggered by the conflicts at work. John felt totally alone and always on guard. He saw the board as having all the power. As the situation grew more tense, John had to do something. He was the director and had to make decisions. Like starting school and then seminary, he was facing a crisis at this new start in his life. Many ego-states were being triggered. Fear of failure. Terrified of being wrong and being punished. Afraid of authorities that had the power to judge and mete out punishment. The pain of being misjudged, mistreated, and rejected, and the anger and rage that wanted to smash them. In this maelstrom of fear and terror, confusion and uncertainty, 40yo brought forward what he had learned: he needed to keep his mouth shut.

A five-year-old and seven-year-old came forward as I worked with 40yo. His fear had triggered them. They carried the same terror he did. "Not to be right was not an option." Yet, the harder they tried to give mom the right answer, the worse it got. "Just keep your mouth shut and take it," or things would go out of control. John says, "The energy around these two is incredible."

Sessions #92-95: The Anatomy of a Kiss

19yo is alone. He first came when John was ten. He was created to deal with the conflict between his passion and desire to learn, on the one hand, and his fear of being wrong and being punished, on the other. It was too risky to speak up and ask questions and expose yourself to punishment, criticism, and humiliation. The fear took precedence, and the passion was suppressed and stifled. Another way to look at it is that the ten year-old protected John's passion from being squelched or extinguished by the beatings at home and the struggles at school. Eventually, this passion was given some expression, but it took a long time.

This 10yo was triggered by the shock and profound confusion caused by Carl's kiss. Because of its sexual nature, and because of his position as John's spiritual authority, the kiss threatened John's two great passions—his devotion to God and Church, and his passion for intimacy with a woman. With his kiss, Carl was forcing his way into those passions, and 10yo came forward to keep him out. His defense, once again, was to dissociate the passions, to bury them, and keep them safe. He said he formed a protective shell around the heart. Feeling his passion for God and the desire for intimacy was no longer safe. To feel them would be to make them vulnerable again.

Sessions #96-105: Six-Year-Olds, One, Two, and Three

These sessions took us deep into the enclosure. Higher self identified three six-year-olds.

6yo#1 – The dark and angry energy from mom and dad knocked him off course. He kept feeling this energy coming at him "like a tsunami." It terrified him, and kept pushing him into this dark space. He said it was so overwhelming, it's like he collapsed in on himself. "Like I went into a dark spot and enclosed myself." He said he is sealed off from the pain. John said it felt like a dark place inside that he could not reach into, and that six-year-old could not get out of. John also received an image. He said, "It's a little boy standing among ruins. He's clueless, and doesn't know what to do or not to do. He's frozen in this spot." John said his "decision-making part became frozen." He says there are two more with him. They are both six-years-old.

6yo#2 – There is pain throughout his being. He developed a frenetic pace, a "speed mode." Always racing the clock to get the right answer. His mantra: "Get it done, get it right, get it over with, so I don't have to get beat up." He says he's "been totally controlled by the outside, that all focus is on the outside world and keeping it happy." John shared later that he's always lived like it was the end of the world. Inside is a rage and he wants to scream, "Just leave me the fuck alone!"

6yo#3 – There is tightness across the abdomen. He says it's "like someone took a bat and kept hitting me in the stomach." He was never able to stop it. He signals that there are many devices in his way. He shares the image of staple-like clamps, with strings attached that can be pulled. He says they go from his throat to his stomach.

The six-year-olds want to leave the enclosure now, but they're afraid of abandonment. They are finally able to start releasing the deep pain of loneliness and fear that had enclosed them.

Sessions #105-110: No Way Forward, No Way Back

After the six-year-olds integrated, the higher self identified an eight-year-old ego-state. There were two others with him, but they were earthbound spirits. 8yo did not want them to leave. However, after contact with a spirit guide, and more reassurance for 8yo about healing, they left without difficulty. 8yo refused any contact with the Light, but he did agree to share.

He was created shortly after mom and dad's abuse ended. The beatings had been such a terrifying and painful ordeal for John that their abrupt cessation left him shell-shocked. It's as though all the attention and energy focused on the beatings was suddenly withdrawn. 8yo shared the picture of a boy who was worn out, depleted, and feeling helpless. It had taken so much energy to cope, "that I had nothing left to keep going." John needed to recuperate. Instead, he was facing an outside world that already had been a source of confusion, struggle, and threat to him. With the end of the physical abuse, the outside world now became the focus of his fear of failure and punishment that had ruled his life for three years. He did not see a place for himself in that world where he could develop his abilities and achieve success. It was a world that had to be survived. The problem was, he had no idea how he would do that. The process of socialization for a child normally begins at five-years-old. John was three years late to the task, and with a view of himself as inferior, success in the outside world felt beyond his reach. There had been no one out there to help him all through the period of abuse, and he saw no one there to help him now.

8yo was created out of this vacuum. It was during that year, when he was preparing to make his First Communion, that John had a mystical experience in which he felt a direct connection to the Divine, and where the idea of the priesthood first took root. It was an integral vision where this young boy saw a place for himself in the world—body, mind, and spirit. 8yo was endowed with this spirit. In the face of a looming and threatening world, he dissociated this spirit to keep it safe and keep it alive.

In our next session, 8yo continued sharing. This time, though, it was about Carl's kiss. That physical contact triggered 8yo and shattered his vision. Carl's actions contradicted his vision at so many levels that it created a profound confusion and threatened to overwhelm him. Instead of coming forward in time to meet the experience, 8yo retreated further into darkness. He said that in that moment he began shutting down, and in the process, shut down his spiritual connection as well. "It's like I put it some place, and now I can't find it." Later in the session, John said it was "like I knew there was a God, but I had no connection to him."

8yo's sharing over these several sessions, involved a whole range of emotion, where the abuse by mom and by Carl overlapped, dovetailed, and sometimes blended. He was able to release, and finally make the reconnection to the Light.

Sessions #111-126: No Way Out

Three twenty-year-olds were identified at the end of the last session. We came back to them here. They were afraid of the Light. They were given a conscious experience in the present, shown the place of integration, and finally moved to a safer place. Still, however, they refused the Light. At the end of this session, though, they agreed to receive a book from higher self about the healing process and how they could be released of all pain and fear. I asked higher self to send them such a book. (This is just one example of a higher self being able to communicate using a particular format. If the situation called for communication only through auditory or only visual, the higher self could do that.)

In the next session, these three did allow some Light to enter and began to share. Over many sessions, they told a story similar to the one told by 8yo. They were all created at six-years-old, very close in time. We discovered later that each had a knife sticking in its right side. They appeared to be the result of a shattering or splitting, so the question would come up later of whether they should merge or not before integrating. They were not in the body. I thought of them as existing in the auric field. (This is not an uncommon occurrence, that ego-states are created outside the physical body, especially when physical trauma or sexual abuse is involved.)

They were created after the beatings began. It wasn't determined how soon after. It was a moment when John could not tolerate the abject terror of what they called the "blackness force" coming at him. One ego-state shared that they were created at a point where each knew another beating was coming, and knew there was nothing it could do to stop it. "No matter what I did, I couldn't figure out a way to get out of it. Even the ones I tried didn't work."

The blackness was more than the threat of physical pain. It was the terror of the vulnerability and total helplessness that came with it. It triggered the feelings of failure and worthlessness. No trust in the outside world, and no hope that anyone would help. The anger and rage had to be suppressed because if it came out, it could only make things worse. They shared that they were created in darkness and their defense was to shut down physically, emotionally, and spiritually. They enclosed themselves. John said their anger and resentment formed a protective shield that built up layer by layer over the years.

Carl's tongue penetrated those layers, striking again at John's core vulnerability and helplessness. Once again, he felt powerless to stop the blackness force coming at him. During the course of Carl's abuse, many ego-states were triggered, and new ones created. These three six-year-olds were triggered in a moment of realization that Carl would come at him again and there was nothing they could do to stop it. There was no way out. This belief and perception, of course, was part of their initial dissociation with mom and now with Carl. These three ego-states were triggered to protect John again. Unlike 8yo, however, they did advance in age to deal with the present circumstances. Now twenty-years-old, their defense was the same—shut down physically, emotionally, and spiritually. This time, though, the shut down took with it John's budding sexuality and his aspirations to the priesthood. Already conflicted, Carl's behavior created such profound confusion for John about his sexual identity and worthiness for the holy priesthood, the only immediate solution was to close them off as well.

As six-year-olds, these ego-states were in a place where no one could hurt them. Carl's abuse proved them wrong. My impression was that, once triggered, they took their extreme defense even further. They said they made a contract with the self at that point that "no one would ever get that close to me again."

Sessions #128-133: Trust No One

After the twenty-year-olds integrated, higher self identified another ego-state to come forward. It was a fifty-year-old. He was in a group of five that included a seven-year-old and three others. What they shared over several sessions was about a total lack of trust in the outside world, or that anyone would help them if they were in trouble. A second issue, following from the first, was the need either to be in control of any situations where such trouble might happen—and have a contingency plan—or avoid them. From their point of view, if trouble did happen, they were on their own. This was how every situation needed to be assessed.

He couldn't take an elevator because it might get stuck and no one would come help him. He couldn't fly in an airplane because all control would be in someone else's hands. He couldn't go through surgery because the anesthesia meant giving up control of the body—his life—to the surgeon and anesthesiologist.

It was true that these were situations where one surrenders control to another or others, and where a mishap can, quite really, result in death. John knew rationally, of course, that these activities and operations occur thousands of times a day around the world without mishap. Yet, at an unconscious level, there was no room for probability. From a strictly logical point of view, there was always a real possibility that something could go wrong. The only way to be guaranteed one hundred percent safe was to never enter the situation.

One way to understand what was happening with these five ego-states is to take the *elevator*, the *airplane*, and the *operating room* as metaphors for the ego-states' reality. These real world situations shared certain criteria that were true about the psychic reality these ego-states lived in—a closed space, no way out, the danger of death, no control, and no one to help. It's as though these outer situations mirror the inner situation in significant enough ways to trigger the ego-states' terror and panic that had led to their own creation. I find that viewing a problem situation in the client's present reality as a metaphor often offers insights into an ego-state's perception, inner situation, and what is being expressed.

This group shared their part in the panic John felt when confronted with these situations. They were all created at five-years-old as the result of a shattering. The moment came not long after the abuse started, when John realized there was no one he could trust to help him; no one he could tell about the beatings. This included grandparents, teachers, and priests. He was terrified that they would side with mom, and that the punishment for telling would be even more severe. It would also be further confirmation by the outside world of his own worthlessness.

Having to keep secret the most intense, painful, and terrifying part of his life forced John into an ever-deeper isolation and loneliness. It also created an emotional disconnect from the outside world. It was a world that carried the same threat as home. For every situation, he had to have the right answers and say the right things, or he could be punished. The abuse by mom, centered as it was on schoolwork, made it easier, I think, for John's terror to generalize from family to community, from parental authority to institutional authority.

At the same time, John still had to achieve in the outside world, meet its demands, and figure out how to survive, and stay safe. The pressure on him to cope with the beatings, keep them secret, and still meet the demands of the outside world finally became intolerable. John's consciousness shattered. This was the moment the group of five shared in common.

The session ended on this note. The plan was to return next time and help them move to a full release. However, as I walked John to the door, and he headed for his car, he slipped on a patch of ice. In a split second, I watched him twist, try to break his fall, and crash to the pavement. His scream of pain and look of agony told me he was badly hurt. When I reached him, I realized that he was in a full-blown panic and had dissociated.

I led him back to the office, and as we sat on the floor, I communicated with an ego-state that had just been triggered in the fall. It was a six-year-old. He was part of a group of four. I communicated that I was there to help them. I reassured them that the body would be all right. I talked to them about present time and current reality. I don't have notes of this interaction, but it was basically geared toward reassuring them that everything would be all right in the present. I also explained to them about the healing process, that they could be free of their pain and terror. With these reassurances, the ego-states were moved to a safer place, and John slowly returned to consciousness.

When he felt steady enough, he gave me his keys and I drove him to the emergency room. I cancelled appointments and waited for him. At one point a nurse came out. John requested that I be present with him in the treatment room. He was close to panic. He felt enclosed. It was one of his nightmare scenarios. He had told the physician about his fear and panic, and so I was invited to work with John consciously as the physician worked on his wrist. While the procedure did not require general anesthesia (that would come at a later date), the fears had all been triggered.

Sessions #134-154: Breaking Through

John and I met the next day, and I came back to the group of four. They were blocked from receiving Light and I quickly learned that there were other ego-states inside each of the four. The term, *inside*, is the one Gerod used when he first described this phenomenon. I think of it as one or more ego-states existing within the stronger or more intense consciousness of another. Like one ego-state being pulled into the orbit of another. It's not a rare phenomenon, and I keep it in mind as a possible source of blocking when working with clients.

I asked higher self to bring all of them out. There were twenty-six altogether. Along with the original four, it was now a group of thirty. Higher self agreed it would be appropriate for them to have a conscious experience in the present. The idea was to reassure them immediately that what happened to them was no longer happening. After this conscious experience (CE), I also asked higher self to move them to a more comfortable place.

I worked first with the six-year-old that presented the day before. He shared that he runs anytime there is trouble. He ran when John broke his wrist. He runs because he knows he is to blame for what's happened, and he knows when others find out, he will be punished. He was created in response to mom's abuse. The premise in that reality was that it was his fault that he didn't have the right answer. There was something wrong with him, and he deserved to be punished.

This was 6yo's enclosure. It's one thing when others blame you; it's something else when you believe it yourself. He was to blame. For 6yo, there was no way to be free of this truth, and so no way to get free of punishment—except to run. The place he ran to is dark, cut off from the self and present reality. Cut off, too, from emotion and feeling. This self-blame was a major issue in John's healing. It led to deeper struggles of self-rejection, feelings of worthlessness, and even self-hatred. John's accident triggered 6yo's self-blame and fear of punishment.

I worked with this group of thirty over a period of six months. Sometimes an individual would share and sometimes as a group. Half of them were curled up in a ball, frozen in position of turning away from mom's punches, and then later, from Carl's caresses. An energy shield had also been created to protect all of them from that world.

Besides self-blame, they shared an intense fear of being wrong and being punished. Getting safe meant having the right answer. With mom, it was an impossible bind, given his disability. This was the first enclosure, no way out but to dissociate it. This fear generalized from mom and dad's abuse to all authorities in the outside world. Having the right answer was still paramount, but became more complex, and in some ways, more threatening, in this larger, social world. It created a constant vigilance, and a never-ending demand to find the right answers and keep everybody happy. This was a second enclosure. The outside world, with all its demands and rules, was always threatening to close in around him. It made him feel even more isolated, lonely, and afraid.

One of the most significant things shared by this group was that a shattering occurred when Carl put his tongue into John's mouth. At a conscious level, John could not comprehend what was happening. It was not a scenario ever conceived of in John's carefully controlled world. With everything at stake, with Carl as his mentor, counselor, and guide, John did not know the "right" answer. It turned his reality upside-down and inside out. He was immobilized.

At an unconscious level, the kiss sent shockwaves down old fault lines and created new ones. John's sexual identity, his struggles about vocation, and his place in the outside world all came into question. What the group shared indicated that, in the shattering, a fundamental dissociation had occurred at the level of the body, the emotions, and spirit. I think of it in terms of energy bodies, each energized and balanced by its own chakra. For John, it appeared that a dissociation or disconnection occurred between these different energy bodies. My impression was that different ego-states were created or triggered forward to deal with specific levels. This impression only grew stronger as John's healing progressed. In the process, we seemed to alternate among levels, as though some balance was being maintained as all moved toward release and integration.

My work with this group was interrupted several times by other groups coming forward. The first was a group of seven. The dominant theme they shared was betrayal—by mom, by dad, by Carl, by Julie, and especially, his betrayal of himself. His hurt, anger, and feelings of worthlessness were all dissociated. In the process, John said later, he lost his voice. He said there was a closing off in the throat, and he could feel the tension in his arms, chest, and throat. He said this is when he went into a very dark place.

These seven joined with the group of thirty. Several sessions later, though, their sharing was being blocked. Higher self said it was by someone from outside the large group. The following week, John had what he called a "meltdown." He had been overcome with feelings of panic and anger. When asked, the higher self identified a group of five. They didn't know they were part of the self/soul, and they had no Light. The one I communicated with was a past-life, male, adult. They, too, formed a protective shield. They said it was "a barrier to moving out in the world." After their release, another group of ten came forward. They didn't have to share, but were able to just release and integrate. Over the course of these sessions, it was like watching groups of figures emerging from the darkness in stages.

Once all the ego-states had integrated, higher self filled the area with Light.

Sessions #155-166: Escape into the Void

In our next session, John reported several episodes of intense fear, verging on panic. One of those incidents involved John's fear of elevators. When asked to identify a source of the fear, higher self identified a thirteen-year-old ego-state. There were five in this group altogether. They shared a terror of being enclosed, where getting free totally depended on the person in control releasing them—or not. First, it was mom. She had all the control. The pain would stop when she said so. With no way to stop it, and the body being pummeled, an ego-state was created that entered a void, outside the body, dissociated from both the inner and outer world that had all control.

Initially this group refused all Light. Over several sessions, they shared about this void. Some of them began to receive small amounts of Light. At the start of one session, however, John reported that the flashbacks of the parental beatings and the abuse by Carl had started again and were intense. The fear of being blamed alternated with feelings of intense anger. He said he felt a darkness around him when he went to bed at night. He was restless; he couldn't sleep. Finally, he had to leave the house.

I asked higher self about the source of the flashbacks and feelings. It identified the thirteen-year-old again. He shared that they had been pulled back into the darkness, and he wasn't sure why. When asked, higher self identified twenty-five energies involved. It said five were part of John's self/soul energy, and the rest were separate. Higher self was asked to dissipate and remove the separate energies and reintegrate the remaining five.

After these procedures, the higher self also communicated that the doors were also involved in pulling the group back into darkness. There were six doors and higher self said four led outside the soul. The higher self retrieved seven ego-states and they joined with the group of five. What they shared was their anger and rage. They "could have killed Carl." They were in a helpless rage at mom. It seemed that these ego-states were exiled from the soul as an extreme move to suppress the rage. Not only dissociate it, but to make it disappear.

My impression at the time was that these seven had been triggered as the group of five began to heal and receive more Light. This is not unusual. I have often found that as an ego-state or a group of ego-states heals, it can trigger others who have connection to them or are close-by. I worked with this group of twelve for several more sessions. Like with other groups, all of them needed to reconnect with the body, and share the terror and rage at a pace that they and John could tolerate. They all wanted to leave the void, yet were frightened of connecting to the conscious self and present reality.

Sessions #167-178: Into Trauma and Back

After this group integrated, higher self identified a seven-year-old ego-state to come forward. He communicated that there were five others with him (later identified as 6yo, 19yo#1, 19yo#2, 20yo, and 32yo). All refused the Light, but were open to the possibility of healing. As with other groups, it was a gradual process of sharing and release, receiving some Light, and then sharing some more.

Like other ego-states that had shared, they were created during a trauma in which John had no way out. The only way was to split off. They became enclosed by the panic and helplessness. "The only thing I knew how to do was get enclosed. I began to wall myself off. Protect the self from anything that might lead to that pain."

What held them together as a group, however, was their panic about what would happen afterwards. The panic was rooted in the fear that others would find out the truth about him and they would abandon him, too. (In the abuse with mom, it was the fear of being judged dumb and worthless. With Carl, it was the fear that others would see him as a homosexual, and he would be expelled by his religious community and abandoned.) Their purpose was to make a stable transition each time from the chaos and terror of the trauma back into John's conscious everyday world, without anyone finding out.

With no one he could tell, and no one to trust, the defense strategy developed to make the transition was one of "keeping still," "becoming invisible." Don't say anything. Act normal. Make it appear that "everything is just fine." This defense signaled a major disconnect between John and other people. John said later that he felt the deepest isolation immediately following an abuse experience. At a core level, it became a "me" against "them" world. This defense grew over time, and came to involve the fear of being wrong and being punished. These six ego-states, however, were only active during the two periods when the abuse was occurring and the transition had to be made in real time. Once the abuse stopped, these ego-states were no longer triggered, except at thirty-two when John's life "took a new direction."

Finally, this group shared a deep anxiety in knowing the trauma would happen again, but not being able to predict when, or to know what the specific situation and circumstances would be. They could never fully prepare. They were like *first responders*—they would have to figure it out on the spot, and quickly. There was always the threat that things could get out of control. This uncertainty created an underlying anxiety that only deepened with the repeated abuse. It led to a state of vigilance. John said later, "This is where the anxiety became an internal state. Always living in a scary and untrustworthy world." He believes that this group is a significant part of the chronic anxiety he feels every day.

As this group moved through the process of sharing and release, it became clear that theirs was a kind of double enclosure. The first was the dissociation from the trauma itself. The second was having the demands and expectations of the outside world always closing in on him. To stay safe, he had to be who they wanted him to be. He felt increasingly isolated and alone.

By the time this group integrated, John reported the start of an inner shift. "Part of me needs to move forward, but I'm not sure what that part is. Something is emerging, but it's not come to its fullness."

Session #179: Escaping the Pain

After this group integrated, John said he still felt like there was "a dome" between him and the Light. Higher self identified this dome-energy and communicated that it was created partly of John's energy and partly of Carl's. It's as though John's inner protection created a shield to stop Carl's penetration and the energies blended on impact to form a shell. The higher self was not able to remove it yet, but identified a twenty-year-old ego-state under the dome. There was also a nineteen-year-old, and four spirits. Higher self removed the spirits without having to address them directly. Higher self then separated out Carl's energy from the dome, and removed it. Finally, higher self reintegrated John's energy and the dome dissolved.

20yo and 19yo shared that they had shut off John's emotional connection to his spirituality to protect it from Carl's assault. "That spiritual lid came down. Carl violated me almost to the core, and at my root."

They said it was like "a dagger went right into me and started cutting out parts of me. I can feel the penetration of the pain." After these two released and integrated, higher self said the four openings needed to be addressed. It said that two doors went outside the soul, and a retrieval was needed. Higher self retrieved eight ego-states who appeared to exist outside the soul in a kind of energy cocoon.

Once returned to the soul, none of the ego-states received Light. A twenty-one-year-old came forward to communicate. He shared that they also were under a dome, and brought into the soul with them. John said later that fear and anxiety cemented this protective shield. "This is when repressing emotions, and then shutting off the spiritual, became intertwined." The image that came to John was someone curled up in a ball. He said, "I got as small as I could in this corner." John said, "he's just a speck and the dome is thousands of times bigger." 21yo said they are afraid to come out from under it.

Sessions #180-189: The Eight Retrieved Ones

I came back to these eight retrieved ones. They were all twenty or twenty-one-years-old, and each had been created, or triggered forward, to deal with the shock of Carl's kisses and molestation. What they shared in common was a fundamental disconnection, a "shutdown," that occurred when John felt Carl's tongue in his mouth.

What they shared in the first two sessions led John to a profound insight into the dissociation that occurred with Carl. He talked about it after that second session. He explained it this way: throughout the abuse by mom, he never felt a severing from the Light, from Love. He said he always knew, at some level, that his mother loved him, that she did what she did—misguided as it was—*because* she loved him. He said there was no Light and no Love in what Carl was doing. His actions were driven by his own needs and desires with absolutely no concern for John—as a person, and certainly not as a soul. John said, "This is when the lights went out. Everything collapsed and spiraled down. It was the first time in my life that darkness was stronger than the Light. Up to this point, there was enough Light to shine on the path."

For John, at a deep level, it was a direct encounter with darkness itself, and it threatened to destroy him. It was coming through Carl, but it was something beyond Carl. It was a primal and overpowering force coming at him, and no way to stop it or get out of the way. In the face of annihilation, it appeared that the conscious self dissociated, and these ego-states dissociated not only from the self, but also from the soul. It's as though each held a vital strand of John's being, took it outside the soul, and all were enclosed in a cocoon. The Catch-22 was that in fleeing the soul to escape darkness, they became enclosed by it. Cut off from their source of Light, each was curled up in its own pain. This is where we found them.

Opening up this pain, and its threat of annihilation, was a terrifying prospect to them. They had to be reassured more than once that they would not be destroyed in the healing process. The depth of their terror was being felt at a conscious level as well. John was becoming acutely aware of how he always stayed far away from any memories of this period, even thinking about it. It was like a "wall had been built around it," and now, John was at the wall. In our third session with them, John said he, too, was feeling resistance to reclaiming these parts of himself. After the session, he said the anxiety he had been feeling since starting with this group was the "fear of dying again." During the sharing, he felt that something inside of him died. He said after that, he became "almost robotic."

Over the next several sessions, these ego-states shared singly, and at times together, about the different levels of disconnection that occurred. There was a disconnection from God. Because of what was happening with Carl, John felt dirty and defiled, blameful and unworthy in the eyes of God. He was sure there was a God, but not for him. Before this connection to God could be snuffed out, it was taken outside and shut down. This was, it seemed, very much a part of the encounter with darkness.

The same was true of his emotions. More than one ego-state shared an intense anger and murderous rage at Carl. They wanted to kill him. These emotions had to be shut down. If they came out, it would not only kill Carl, it could destroy everything, including himself. There was a disconnection also from the body, shutting off sensation so John could not feel Carl's wet tongue and the stroking of his penis. They had to cut off all body sensations, just as they had with mom, only this time the shut off involved the body's sexuality and John's sexual identity. Carl's actions, and all they implied, contradicted John's own sexual identity. It created such profound confusion, fear, and self-doubt, that it had to be shut down. It could not be part of what was happening with Carl. John commented later that it felt like his sexual being had been arrested at this point. He said that he had broken off relationships with several women over the years once they became sexually intimate. He says now, looking back, that these sexual relationships had to end because they led back to Carl and the enclosure, and that whole experience was sealed off.

Finally, the disconnection and mistrust of others that had begun with mom's abuse appeared to become cemented with Carl. The one person he trusted above all to understand and care for him, to guide and look out for him, is the one who ripped him apart. "I trusted my soul to someone and they shredded it for their own needs." If he couldn't trust Carl, then no one could be trusted. This darkness was everywhere.

Sessions #190-198: Mirrored in Darkness

Two months after working with these retrieved ones, the sharing and release became blocked. John said it felt like, "something was holding on; it just wouldn't release." I asked higher self to look inside for the source of the block. It identified a six-year-old ego-state.

He was alone. He was terrified of being enclosed by the outside world. A voice from inside—maybe the higher self's—said he was "the missing piece." 6yo said he was created "when the core began to shatter." It was not clear whether he was one fragment of the shattering, or the one who shattered. Either way, he said he was not ready for higher self to bring those parts back together yet. The suggestion frightened him. Instead, over the next six sessions, he gradually shared about himself. It was like walking him slowly backwards to the shattering where he could become whole.

Looking back now, I think 6yo was a *mirror personality*. Like Natalie, whom Gerod talked about (see Chapter 15), it was 6yo's point of view that was the critical issue in healing, rather than specific experiences he needed to share. He was created, to use Gerod's term, as an *opposite reflection* of a self who was unworthy, always to blame, and deserving of punishment. 6yo was created to *not be* that self. From his point of view, he was somebody else, someone who could survive and stay safe in an unpredictable world. He did this by becoming who others wanted him to be. He did it by keeping quiet, doing what he was told, pleasing others, and keeping everybody happy.

6yo said it started out as protection, a way to shield the self from further pain, rejection, and punishment, but he was soon overwhelmed. He could not keep up with all the demands and expectations of all the different people and situations. "Everybody wanted me to be someone else." This is where he began to feel the outside world closing in. Everyday he lived in the anxiety of what was coming and who he had to be. It began to suffocate him and he finally closed up. This is where we found 6yo.

When we first communicated, he did not know that he was created from inside the enclosure, and that he carried within him the pain and terror of John's abuse. As a separate identity, he also was not aware of his dissociation from vital parts of the self that included John's spirit, his desire to learn, and the power of his voice. As 6yo shared his fears of the outside world, he began to wake up to this level of his pain and terror. He also, however, began reconnecting with these vital parts of the self.

The next six sessions were like watching the conversion of 6yo's identity as an *opposite self*, one anchored in the outside world, to an identity of self who felt worthy, powerful, and safe. John had reconnected with what he called the "core self" months before when he broke his wrist. 6yo was making that reconnection now. As with all mirror personalities, stepping back through the mirror is an all-or-none proposition. In reclaiming his pain and terror, 6yo was reclaiming his true identity.

In our seventh session, John reported feeling overwhelmed in the past few weeks. He said it was becoming more difficult to deal with both the inner world and outer world at the same time. He said he was beginning to see the ripple effects throughout his life of the abuse he had suffered, including at times his own rejecting or abusive treatment of others. I asked higher self to review what was happening. It identified eight openings where 6yo was, all going outside the soul. It retrieved six ego-states, and they formed a group with 6yo. It seemed he had reached a point where it was safe to bring them together. They did not have to be identified or worked with individually, but shared along with 6yo. There wasn't a great deal. It's as though this was the final step in 6yo's conversion. In the next session, the group had a full release and they were able to integrate.

Sessions #199-234: Backtracking

After 6yo and his group integrated, we came back to the eight retrieved ones. The encounter with darkness and the shutdown that occurred with Carl's kiss was still the focus. In many ways, working with these ego-states echoed the process with 6yo, only more encompassing. Reconnecting with the self meant opening back up the pain of the disconnection from God, himself, and others. Looking at it now, I would describe it again in terms of chakras and energy bodies. It appeared that a disconnect occurred at each chakra and had to be reopened and reconnected within that level, from the crown chakra to the root chakra—body, mind, and soul. It's as though each energy body had to be brought into balance, and then all energy bodies brought into harmony. From a clinical point of view, over many sessions, we seemed to work back and forth at these different levels of trauma. Sometimes one level or issue was emphasized in a session, at other times it would be several. There was no way to always keep track of who was sharing, or how many. It all seemed to be happening by its own rules and reckoning. By the time they integrated, though, it was clear that John was exhibiting and reporting significant changes at these different levels as well.

28

Redemption

Living in the Real World

John is still in treatment today, though our sessions are less frequent. The emphasis has shifted from trance work to conscious-level integration. The inner work has shifted as well, from the identification of new ego-states and uncovering pain to an integration of all that has been opened up and shared. I have worked with several groups of ego-states since those eight retrieved ones integrated. Over time, some in these groups have integrated and the others have coalesced into one group. It appears to be a process involving a higher-level integration of the energy bodies—emotion, body, mind, and spirit—with the conscious self in the present. Right now, John and I are discussing whether some type of bodywork might be helpful in this integration process.

John is quite aware that he has changed, and his life has changed. They have been good changes, and evident to me as well. On a symptomatic level, John has not had a panic attack in nearly three years. He has been on the verge a few times and was able to quell it each time on his own. At this same level, there has been an overall alleviation of the chronic anxiety, fear, and dread in his everyday life. He does not have to be constantly on guard against an outside world threatening to overwhelm him. He doesn't need to prepare his defenses and escape routes today for what may happen tomorrow.

What is also evident today, and has been for some time, is John's capacity to feel and be present in the moment. He can tolerate feelings of fear, anger, guilt, and confusion without it triggering a shutdown or a lashing out. In his consulting business, for example, working with organizations where internal conflicts, power struggles, and bruised egos can get emotions running high, he says he is able to remain centered and confident as he guides his clients through difficult negotiations. He says even when one of his own issues is triggered, he's aware of it almost immediately and is able to put it aside until later, or just let it go. John is aware of how quickly he would dissociate in the past when these feelings were triggered. He says he can still feel the pull sometimes, but he doesn't go. It's the pull of the enclosure.

The dissociation and suppression of emotion did not limit itself only to the painful and negative emotions, but to the suppression of John's emotional life as a whole. In working with the ego-states, John began to experience emotions and feelings that had long been dissociated. It taught him and the inner world that it was safe to express these painful emotions in the present, and on a deeper level, that it was safe to feel. This opening up of the emotions was a major step in John's healing. While painful, it was also exhilarating. John began to experience the whole range of positive emotion and feeling, and it felt good. In his everyday life, he also became increasingly aware of when his feelings were being shut down. This reconnection with his emotions began before we found the enclosure. In a real sense, it was his preparation for it.

Another significant change is John's feeling of being at home in his apartment. When not traveling for business, he always had reasons to leave—to eat, visit friends, go to the gym, volunteer his services, or take in a movie. He knows it's an old pattern. He hasn't felt at home since before the beatings began. *Home* was a place to stay away from as much as he could. Then, it happened again in his new home, the seminary. After Carl's abuse started, John made himself busy, and stayed away from his room as long as possible each day.

He says now that he enjoys being home. He's preparing meals there now instead of always eating out. He has been re-arranging and decorating rooms so they "fit" and feel good to him. He's not afraid to go to bed at night. He has begun to spend some holidays at home, instead of always traveling out-of-town to family. He values his time alone now. In short, his home has become a safe harbor.

Another change that has been evident for some time is that John has found his voice. We did a lot of inner work involving the throat chakra, and the shut down of his voice. Over the months, I've listened to it become stronger and clearer. He is speaking up in situations, where before he would not have taken the risk. He is speaking up for himself, and for others, when called for. He is confident in stating his opinions, and will challenge or confront others when necessary. It reflects a newfound trust and confidence in himself, and in others.

Besides speaking up, John has also begun speaking out. In the eighteen months, he has written several papers, and given talks to colleagues, on innovative ideas and practices developed in his own work with organizations over twenty years. They are ideas that will challenge the dominant paradigm in his field. He is willing to take the risk and put them to the test. He is incorporating also what he has learned in his own healing about how the inner world operates, and the powerful ways it can effect a person. It has given John added perspective on the dynamics at play within organizations and its individual members.

John is also speaking out by giving me permission to publish his story. When I first asked him to consider it, his immediate response was a yes. He said if it could help even one other person, then he wanted to do it. The risk of exposure and vulnerability, which before would have set off all kinds of triggers, didn't seem to faze him.

Conversion

John still looks back to his accident as a turning point in his therapy, and in his life. I see it the same way. When John broke his wrist, it broke open the enclosure. He suffered what psychologists would term a *psychotic break*. It had happened a few years before when his panic and decompensation led to his hospitalization. This time, though, there was the opportunity for an immediate intervention that identified the ego-states that had been triggered. Once reassured that they were safe, and that the body was safe in the present, and after they were given information about healing, they became calm and agreed to communicate in our next session.

At the same time, this made it safe for John to return consciously to present reality, sitting in my hallway, aware of his pain and predicament. Like waking from a dream and reorienting, John came back to the present with the conscious awareness of the dissociative episode. He had touched into very deep parts of himself, which up to that point had been sealed off from the self and conscious awareness. It's as though he had caught himself in the act of dissociating, and now had a foot in both worlds. He knew himself in the present, and simultaneously knew the dissociative reality he had lived for so many years. It's not that he knew all that was being held at this level—that would come in the many sessions ahead—but that he knew the dissociative reality was there. In that experience, I believe, John knew himself as a whole person. It was a conversion experience. It altered his conscious identity and his place in the world. He described it later as reconnecting with his *core self.*

Another element in this conversion was John's experience of being loved and cared for in the hours immediately following the accident. Friends came to the hospital, and other friends began arranging for the help he would need in the coming month. A week after the accident, John talked about it in our session. The following are his statements taken from my notes:

- Last Wednesday, there were people advocating for me.
- For the first time I could feel the love and connection.
- I wasn't all alone.
- There were people there for me.
- I knew what steps I had to take.
- I was never able to connect with it before.
- I know this isn't the first time people have been there for me.
- It's just that this time I felt it.

John's experience of love, I believe, awakened within him the knowledge of himself as a soul, a being of Light. In this knowledge, he also knew he was loveable. This knowledge nullified the self-blame, guilt, and shame as an essential part of him. He said later it was the first time he had loved himself enough to overrule the terror and panic and do what was best for himself—in this case, to have surgery. Knowing he was loveable also altered John's identity and place in the world.

Finally, in his experience of love, John also felt a reconnection to his spirituality, and to God. It was an inner knowing. The knowledge took him beyond his fear of God's rejection, and his anger at what he felt was God's abandonment and betrayal. Again, these feelings and conflicts about God were not all resolved and healed in John's experience of love. It's just that he knew, at the deepest level, that they would be. This knowledge has also freed him from his love/hate relationship with the Church. In his reconnection to God, he knew it was, and always had been, independent of the Church. While still involved socially in the Church community, he has turned to the mystical traditions for guidance and understanding.

I don't know whether John's reconnection to his core self, and his experience of being loved were simultaneous, part of the same experience, or whether one led to the other, or some other possibility. Conversions are always a mystery—so many factors, conscious and unconscious, external and internal, coming together in a moment to alter one's consciousness of self and reality. This was true of John's conversion as well. In the weeks immediately following the accident, however, it was clear to both John and me that a significant change had occurred in his perception of himself, of others, and the world. He talked of feeling connected and centered in his everyday life in a way he hadn't felt for a very long time, if ever. The connection brought with it a sense of his own power, inherent self-worth, and freedom to choose in the present.

Without being able to explain it, I believe that John's breaking bones was an important, if not necessary, part of the conversion—not just a sprain, a twist, or bruising, but a break. It's as though the break had to happen right down to the physical level in order to break through to this enclosure. It may have been found as the healing process continued, but I don't know. The broken bones took things totally outside John's control. There was nothing he could do to fix it. He had to give up control to the surgeon and anesthesia if he wanted to have a fully functioning hand and wrist. But it was his worst nightmare—becoming enclosed. John was making a conscious choice to override the inner terror, in order to take care of himself in present reality.

It was after this conversion that the terms, "being in current reality," and "being pulled out of current reality," became a part of our therapeutic dialogue. As we worked our way through the enclosure, and all that was being shared, John's conscious-level awareness, insight, and understanding seemed to grow exponentially. He saw how deeply the effects of the abuse and dissociation had rippled through his life, crippling him more severely than the learning disabilities had. The latter he was able to adapt to and compensate for over time. The enclosure, however, was sealed tight. When it broke open, it's as though the *core self* was free to come into the present, become anchored, and then start bringing the ego-states into present integration.

The Healing Journey

One of my favorite metaphors for Soul-Centered Healing is the symphony orchestra, where every instrument is out of tune. The music is divinely inspired, and the conductor aspires to it by bringing every instrument into tune. One by one, it still doesn't sound good at the start, but gradually, musical strains can be heard, until the music resounds in full concert.

In this metaphor, every ego-state is out of tune in its own way. As each receives the Light, shares, and moves to integration, it comes into tune with the self and soul. I cannot count the number of ego-states I've worked with whose initial resistance or fear about healing was instantly changed when they made contact with the Light. I cannot explain this change, except to say that the ego-state seems to instantly know its oneness with the Light and its place within self and soul.

On one level, the aim of Soul-Centered Healing is to identify each of these parts of the self and bring them into attunement with the self and soul. At its deepest level, the aim of Soul-Centered Healing is to help a client know he or she is a soul, a being of Light. This is not an intellectual knowing, though it can inform the intellect. It's a deeper knowing that has no words. Many clients who seek healing already have this inner knowing. This is usually a plus, though it doesn't mean the healing will be easy. For others, like John, there has been a disconnect from the soul at very deep levels.

The higher self plays an essential role in this process. It is a person's direct connection to the Light and inner knowing. The higher self knows it is a soul creation. It knows it is the Light. It also knows what is part of the soul and what is not. In terms of the metaphor, the higher self is the one that knows the music, and when asked, can help find and attune those parts in discord with the self and soul. At the same time, I believe that working directly with the higher self helps a client develop a greater awareness and intuitive relationship with this part that Gerod called, "the active part of the soul." It's not something that can be given to a person, but must be found and come from within, like osmosis. The aim of Soul-Centered Healing is to help facilitate this for each client.

Afterward

The practice of Soul-Centered Healing presumes a trust in the Light—in the Divine Light, in the client's Light as a soul incarnate, in his or her higher self, and in those spirit guides that offer different kinds of assistance. The presumption is that the Light is always present to the client—within and without—but the Light will not violate those defenses and blocks created within the self and soul that refuse the Light, restrict it, or actively oppose it. The major aim in Soul-Centered Healing is to identify those blocks and defenses and bring Light into each situation. It may involve ego-states (past-life and present), intruding spirits or other external entities, or energetic damage to one or more of the chakras.

Soul-Centered Healing presumes the power of the Light will heal these situations, once it is received. From a clinical point of view, this healing power of Light is most evident in working with ego-states and spirits. I've seen the pattern repeated hundreds of times, if not thousands. There is an initial refusal to receive the Light, then a negotiation, followed by an agreement to just try it, then contact, immediate acceptance of the Light, and full cooperation in the healing process. We cannot explain, or see into, what happens in that contact with the Light to instantly change a *no* to a *yes*. It's as though the Light already knows exactly where the individual ego-state or discarnate soul fits into the greater Light and instantly transmits this knowledge on contact. While we cannot explain it, what is clear is that the change occurred as a direct result of that contact with the Light.

Soul-Centered Healing presumes that the Light operates in this same way at other levels of a person, both physical and energetic. Blocks and obstructions can be created at these levels, as well as the psychic and spiritual. Dramatic and instant change can also occur—the instant relief from a headache, for example, or a sudden, pleasant sensation of warmth spreading through the body. More often, though, the changes at these levels are subtle, or take longer to manifest, and so causal connections are much more difficult to demonstrate. From this point of view, bringing Light directly to the site of a broken bone will promote and further its healing. The bone may not fully mend overnight, but that doesn't mean the Light isn't working with the body at those subtle levels.

In bringing Light to the inner world and the conscious self, we never know where a client's healing journey will lead. We don't know from one session to the next who or what might interrupt or block the process. Most often, it is a circuitous path, with its twists, turns, and surprises. We won't always understand the sequence by which ego-states or external entities are presenting, or how they are related to what has come before. In this sense, we are along for the ride. We are troubleshooters and negotiators. We have to be ready for whatever presents. Only in retrospect can we have some map of a client's journey, as I've presented with John (see Figure 25.2, page 216). If I backtracked ten other cases, you would be reading ten unique journeys and looking at ten very different maps, each one a personal story and a soul story.

My purpose in this book, and in Volume I, is to provide tools and procedures to help facilitate a client's healing process. This includes especially the protocols for identifying and resolving the blocks that are bound to present on this journey with a client. Secondly, I've tried to provide a rudimentary map of the inner terrain to help navigate through the many phenomena, conditions, and situations you might encounter at these psychic and spirit levels. This map is not complete. If you work at these levels, I have little doubt that you will encounter entities and phenomena new to me. Finally, I've shared the methods I use to chart a client's progress through the inner labyrinth, keeping track of where we are, and where we've been. Charting the course plays an important part in the practice of Soul-Centered Healing—for back-tracking, identifying patterns and themes, and gaining new insight and perspective. The methods I share here for notetaking and mapmaking are ones I have found effective and economical. It's not the only way to do it, I'm sure, but they may at least be useful as a model.

I want to end this book with a favorite Sufi teaching: *There are as many paths to God as there are souls.* It doesn't take long in the practice of Soul-Centered Healing to have a clear sense of this. When I meet a new client, I know we are meeting soul-to-soul, and that soul is on its own path to God. The aim in Soul-Centered Healing is to help a client know he or she is in accord with the soul and on a clear path back home.

Appendix

The following table presents the chronological course of John's healing process. The first column gives the session number, beginning with the first hypnosis session. The second column gives the group number, signifying the order in which that group was identified in the healing process. For these purposes, a group can be comprised of a single ego-state or external spirit or entity. The rule is: the higher the group number, the later they were identified in the healing process.

The third column gives the number of the group(s) worked with during the session. It is not unusual for a group to be identified in one session, but requiring several sessions to work with and resolve. Sometimes, a group identified several sessions before is brought forward again once another group has finally been resolved. In John's healing you will see a number of instances where one group was worked with over many sessions.

The fourth column tells the specific ego-state(s) or entity which I communicated with directly in that session. If you read, *13yo & 12 others*, for example, it means I communicated directly with the thirteen-year-old ego-state, but worked with the group of thirteen as a whole. Also, if you see an ego-state followed by a different age in parenthesis, it means that the ego-state was originally created at that earlier age. This kind of data is spotty because not every ego-state is identified and asked how old the body was when it first came. This information is usually not necessary for the healing process. Sometimes, however, that information is given in the sharing, or becomes an issue for an ego-state that is having great difficulty remembering or sharing. I included the information when available.

The fifth column gives a brief synopsis of what occurred during the session. It's meant to give the reader a sense of what is shared and the flow from one session to the next.

Most sessions were some combination of inner work and conscious level processing. The sessions where we did no hypnosis are also noted.

Session #	Group #	# in Group	Group Worked With	Part identified	What was shared
					Mother died two weeks ago.
#1					Woke up last night feeling angry and nauseous, finally throwing up. Flashbacks of mom and Carl. Start hypnosis. PP & HS both in agreement with healing. In identifying part to work with, HS is blocked. Identifies Carl, and then Helen.
	1	1	1	Carl(i) - an introject	An ego-state with identity of Carl. Created in weeks after first abuse. Function seems to be a constant reminder of threat.
	2	1	2	Helen(i) - an introject	An ego-state with identity of mom. Created when Helen was 30yo. Knew from the beginning she was part of John. These two introjects involved with blocking John's spirituality and sexuality.
#2	3	1	1	Julie(i) - an introject	An ego-state with identity of Julie, John's nemesis in the conflict at work.
			2 & 3	Carl(i) & Helen(i)	Energy point is free and in heart center, but the soul is encapsulated.
#3			1, 2, & 3	Carl(i), Helen(i) & Julie(i)	Work with all 3 together. Great Darkness around Carl(i). Cannot reconnect to John. Carl(i) in the dark spot. Cannot move out yet.
#4			1	Carl(i)	Still in darkness. John's spirituality is shattered. For first time, John becomes consciously aware of Carl's attraction to him. Carl was dissociated, living in his own world. John feels completely objectified, used.
#5			1 & 2	Carl(i), Helen(i),	Carl releasing. Address soul encapsulation. Helen involved, and an energy block. Tension between Helen and sister carries over to comparing their oldest sons (about the same age). Helen refuses review.
#6	4	1	2 &4	Bill(i) - an introject	Goes into panic because mom would get angry and then beat him. Identifies 74yo Bob (dad). Bob shares about amputation of his leg 2 months before John is born. This is trauma Bill(i) holds in John's inner world.
#7				Soul & energy point	Entity is encapsulating soul. Has great sympathy for John. (May have been created with help from guides.) HS removes entity and rejoins energy point and soul. John aware of "being himself."
#8	5	1	5	Exhibitor (PLMA)	John reports panic while driving, feeling closed in. Exhibitor, feeling alone and abandoned. Broken relationship. He was violated; pain in his heart.
#9			5	Exhibitor	Exhibitor released. John feels strong energy in body. 2 external energies blocking Exhibitor's integration. Removed. Exhibitor integrates. 45yo identified. Says Carl experience fractured his spirituality.

Session #	Group #	# in Group	Group Worked With	Part identified	What was shared
	6	1	6	45yo	Alone. Shares about reclaiming spirituality.
#10	7	1		PLMA	Identify PLMA, shares wisdom. Releases.
	8	1		PLMT	Identify PLMT, shares about abusive relationship.
#11	9	2	Joseph (PLM 45yo#2 (5yo)	Joseph (PLMA), 45yo#2(5yo)	Joseph (PLMA) shares about being hit, crushed up against a wall, alone. Much tightness in throat to heart. Feels like solid weight. Releases. 45yo first came at 5yo. Shares beating by mom. Fear of abuse cemented. Chest cavity is being pushed into throat. There is 1 door. HS does a retrieval and reintegrates soul energy. Now both release and integrate.
#12	10	1		PLMC	HS expels 2 energies. PLMC shares. Involved with John's fear of anesthesia. John feels deep relaxation flow through body. PLMC integrates.
#13	11	8	20yo, PLMA, 6 EBS's	20yo, PLMA, 6 EBS's	HS removes separate ones. 20yo & PLMA both share. Lots of energy moving. They release and integrate.
#14	12	1		52yo	52yo Shares. Tightness in throat moves to heart. 52yo integrates. Jack shares panic from more than one lifetime. Was violently beat up. Involves head injury. Jack releases and Integrates. Second PMLT shares. More body realigning. Releases and integrates.
	13	1		PLMT	
	14	1		Jack (PLMT)	
#15	15	1		Joan (PLFA)	Light is being blocked to body. HS identifies Joan. Head feels so heavy. Integrates. Head feels like concrete. HS identifies device, a crown of thorns, created by self. HS dissipates it.
#16	16	2		19yo, EBS	John has been close to panic lately. Crown of thorns has been dissipated. HS identifies 19yo and spirit. HS removes EBS. 19yo shares one incident with Carl. Feels self loathing & "self-dying." Help 19yo to realize he had God's protection. Feels part of him died. (fear of anesthesia & dying on surgery table).
#17	17	23	17	three 19yo's, 26yo, PLMA, 20 present life ego-states retrieved.	John had experience of "losing it." HS identifies 2 doors, both go outside soul. 19yo#1 stops retrieval. HS communicates to him. HS carries out retrieval. Profound confusion over Carl's sexual kiss. John recognizes confusion. Has lived with it. "Like I went into this dark spot. Knocked off my path." Discover this whole group is in dark spot. The self is presently stuck in it. 19yo#2 says early abuse by parents became "locked in here." Says a black shield was created and is impenetrable. HS says it is created of external energy. Call on guides to help deal with this between sessions. Self starts moving through dark spot again.

Session #	Group #	# in Group	Group Worked With	Part identified	What was shared
#18			17	three 19yo's, 26yo, PLMA + 20 present life ego-states retrieved.	Back to confusion. 19yo#2 - sick from stomach to throat. Also many in group angry and enraged. Tremendous pain. There's been some kind of spiritual disconnect. Same issue shared by 26yo and PLMA. These two release and integrate.
#19			17	three 19yo's, 26yo, PLMA, +20	Has lived life in darkness. Process of receiving Light and releasing.
#20			17	19yo#2	Pain was a shock to the system and stayed in there. 19yo dissociated from his passion. HS helps him step into it briefly. He moves into it.
#21	18	1	18	PLFA, Carl(i) & Helen(i)	Start with group #14. More sharing about reclaiming his voice, but then a block to throat. The block is Carl, Helen, & a PLFA. Some kind of encasement here. HS dissipates it. There are 8 doors here.
			1 & 2	Carl(i) & Helen(i)	
#22			1, 2, & 15	Carl, Helen	Back to 8 doors. HS and guides do retrieval. Jose releases and integrates. Carl has a full release and integrates. Helen releases and integrates. Both 16yo's receive Light and it causes distress.
	19	1		Jose (PLMA)	
	20	2		Two 16yo's	
#23			16	19yo	Has left integration. Deep sadness & tears. Still releasing about disconnect from spirit.
#24	21	3	21	36yo & 37yo	In a dark hole. 14 openings, 7 go outside soul. HS does retrieval. 4 ego-states retrieved (Group #17). Moved to a safe place. Joins group #16 and #17. HS removing energies and devices, finds 5yo. Joins him with group
	22	1	22	38yo	Joins with Group #21 (36yo & 37yo)
	23	4		4 retrieved ego-states.	
	24	2	24	38yo#2 & PLMA (Bob)	
	25		25	5yo	The external ego-states removed.
#25				No Hypnosis	
#26			25	Back to 5yo	Intense anger and rage.
	26	25	26	Group with 27yo, 32yo, & 23 others. Separate ones removed. Now a group of 9.	Blocked by 27yo (group of 25, 16 are EBS). HS removes spirits. All 9 sharing. 32yo first came at 3 months when a darkness descended on him (Mom and dad's own experience of darkness. Message was "repress the pain." This is where John begins to allow himself to feel the pain. This will continue in the therapy.

Session #	Group #	# in Group	Group Worked With	Part identified	What was shared
#27			25	Back to 5yo. Discover There is 7yo & PLFA also	Loss of innocence. Darkness got stronger and stronger. Body begins shaking. A discharge of energy.
#28			25	Back to 5yo, 7yo, & PLFA	John made move to Michigan at 40. 5yo shares rage and anger and now deeper pain. Body feels rigid.
#29			25	Back to 5yo, 7yo, & PLFA.	Pain left side of abdomen. Remove device (locket). Group of 9 sharing and release.
			26	Back to group of 9	
#30			26	Back to group of 9	One is 16yo-never good enough. "I would go it alone."
#31	27	25	27	Group of 25.10 are EBS	EBS leave. (They were a voice of opposition.) Feels clear now. PLFC, PLFA, & 27yo (female) are worked with directly. All integrate.
#32	28	5	28	1yo, PLFA, & 3 others	Fear & trepidation. There are 16 doors.
#33			28	Back to 1yo & group, PLFA.	sharing intense pain. PLFA comes through a door. All share, release, and integrate. 8 openings go outside. HS retrieves and reintegrates soul energy. Next door. 25yo in group of 5, 2 are separate. Separate ones removed, group shares and releases.
	29	5	29	25yo & group of five.	2 in this group are separate. 1 is EBS and 1 is EES. 3 ego-states integrate.
#34	30		30	5yo(3yo)	Energy point and soul each encapsulated. The soul is surrounded by an energy, and the energy point is in a metal box created of separate energy. Someone inside the box holds the energy point. 5yo. Deep feelings of inadequacy. Never measuring up. First came at 3 years-old. Younger brother had special needs and got all the attention. Feelings of abandonment begin. Brother could do no wrong, John could do no right. Cannot rejoin energy point and soul yet.
#35	31	2	31	Next door. Two 3yo's.	Share about the darkness. Back to 5yo. Flashback to mom yelling and his "whole body going nuts." This dark energy was coming at him; overwhelming. Panic started. Became lost in a vortex. Couldn't find my way out. There is no Light. Isolated and alone. With mom felt like a non-entity. Like I didn't exist. This feeling became compounded over the years. My way of dealing was to close off. Cannot rejoin energy point and soul yet. Both 3yo's integrate.

Session #	Group #	# in Group	Group Worked With	Part identified	What was shared
#36	32	3	31	7yo & 2 others.	7yo has noose around neck. PLMT releasing feeling and sensations of Carl's tongue in his mouth. Body is beginning to "thaw."
	33	1		PLMT	Issues of trust and sexuality.
#37			32	Back to PLMT.	Growing sense that Carl's abuse "arrested" John's development. Seems to be past life connection here involving betrayal. John hungered for love and connection, and Carl gave that, then torn away. PLMT Integrates. Body release.
	34	1	33	PLMA	Involved in body distress. Integrates
#38	35	6	34	25yo & 5 others.	Still doing major release. Letting go, making transition. "Feels like a whole new place." John becoming more settled and comfortable in the present. All 6 integrate.
	36	1		30yo(15yo)	Find energy point now with 30yo. Much body release. The body is waking up. "The body froze up and the mind raced."
#39			36	Back to 30yo.	Feeling ugly and defiled. Knocked from my spiritual path. Body became like concrete. "It's like he got inside my body. The spiritual path is how he got in." 30yo says there are two energetic boulders, one near right side of throat, the other in the 2nd chakra. Sense of dissociation at the throat level. Separation of body and head systems.
#40	37	1	36	26yo	Ready for final vows, but doesn't feel the spiritual connection. His convictions were shattered. 30yo and 26yo group together. Energy point released. John feels a shift. 26yo and 30yo integrate.
#41	38	15	38	25yo(6yo) & 30yo(7yo) & 13 EBS	Spirits removed. 25yo now carries the soul. Feels in a cocoon. Time to break out. Wants to let go, be free. Anxiety and uncertainty about future. 25yo first came at 6 and 30yo came at age 7.
#42			38	Back to 25yo & 30yo	Feels a split from spiritual. "Mom and Carl's energy dwarfed me and shriveled me up." Got lost. Helpless.
#43			38	Back to 25yo & 30yo	Emotions are beginning to surface. It's okay to cry. Always punished for showing emotion. Both integrate.
#44	39	1	39	24yo	Start to rejoin energy point and soul. Block. It's a 24yo, alone.
#45			39	Back to 24yo.	"Spirituality is being resurrected." Seeks a trust in his deeper knowing. There is a sword in front of 24yo. HS removes it and John feels vibration through the body. 24yo integrates. 12yo identified. Caught behind protective shield. HS identifies group that keeps the shield in place. 4yo & 24 others. 12yo releases.

Session #	Group #	# in Group	Group Worked With	Part identified	What was shared
	40	1	40	12yo	Has energy inside. HS removes it. 12yo beginning to trust self and future. Involves reclaiming voice. Releases after next group is identified.
	41	25	41	4yo & 24 others	This group forms a shield. Was in place before 12yo.
#46			41	Back to 4yo & 24 others.	Deep confusion. Began to learn how to anticipate and protect self when dark energy was coming. Grandfather was part of that energy. 4yo & 24 others integrate. Identifies 54yo.
	42	1	42	54yo	Was present before conception and entered body at 3rd trimester. There's a connection between dad's struggle with his father and John's struggle with Carl.
#47	43	30	43	Group of 12 ego-states & 18 separate ones. Group includes 3yo, 6yo, 12yo, 22yo, & 33yo.	HS removes the 18 spirits. John has been in dark funk for several days. Feels attacked. There is 3yo, 5yo, 22yo, 6yo,12yo female, 33yo and 7 more. 3yo & 6yo were attacking. They say a needle runs through the throat. Created by 12yo(2yo) female. She created 3 of them. 33yo (5yo) first created at 5yo, then at12yo and split from female. He has needle through the chest and says his voice was cut off. He put the clamp on himself. Speaking out only led to more trouble.
#48			43	33yo (5yo), 12yo female	John is beginning to recognize how anxiety and fear has controlled his life. 33yo is angry and wants revenge on Carl.
#49			43	Back to 33yo (5yo), 12yo, 22yo	The weight of holding everything in all these years. Releases and integrates. 12yo-Link to 33yo is reclaiming their voice. Time to rebuild foundation. 22yo-I gave away my power. I created what I thought others wanted.
#50	44	2	44	During Birth #1 & #2	John is feeling fear and cannot re-center. HS identifies two. Born into a world already of mom and dad's distress, anxiety, and pain. John wonders if it's a life pattern.
#51					No Hypnosis
#52			44	Back to During Birth #1 & #2	Anxiety at birth created a disposition to live in an anxious world.
			43	Back to 33yo (5yo), 12yo, 22yo	Back to group #43. 25yo-created a split between fear and anger like I did between head and heart (feelings). Reclaiming emotional and spiritual self. Feels its strength. Group releases
#53	45	1	45	13yo (6yo),	Alone. Pain and anger in 2nd chakra. 3 openings. Has mental model that separates spirituality and relationships.

Session #	Group #	# in Group	Group Worked With	Part identified	What was shared
#54			45	Back to 13yo (6yo),	Feeling alienated from family, community, and church. Feels disloyal but must do it for survival. 25yo (5yo) retrieved - gave so much energy to keep others happy. Sees one door to outside.
	46	1	46	25yo (5yo)	This one is retrieved. 25yo says it's "time to leave the tribe."
#55					No Hypnosis
#56			46	Back to 25yo (5yo).	Blocked from Light. An energy is identified and expelled. Identifies group that carries family pattern of not being loved for who you are. It's a group of 35. Identify PLMA
	47	35	47	PLMA & 34 others	All are part of self/soul. Feeling abandoned by God, Feels they will never overcome darkness.
#57	48	2	48	30yo & 20yo	30yo is carrying the soul. Had to do everything himself and it was never good enough.
#58			48	Back to 30yo & 20yo,	It's okay to feel the pain, sadness, and grief. Energy is moving up the spine, re-connecting. 30yo releases soul. Is rejoined with energy point. Back to group of 35, PLMA. Opening up the heart, Taking down a wall.
			47	Back to PLMA & 34 others	Regaining purpose in life. Feels new energy wrong heart. Call to break down wall built around the heart. This group is the wall/
#59	49	1	49	15yo	Alone. Always trying to find someone to help him. Mom & dad never there for him. Feeling abandoned and on my own. Scary. The fear is still deep today. Overwhelming. No one will be there for me. 5 devices.
#60			49	Back to 15yo..	"Overused my gut instinct to survive. I've located my entire being in this." As the gut heals, other parts can have freer reign. This has been a wall. Felt "I lived a bi-polar life. I've lived in confusion." Struggle about moving into Light.
	50	1	50	19yo	19yo keeps 5 devices in place. Says a whole part of him died. Stomach problems started at 19yo. A whole part of me just died. Huge set back. A whole shift of energy. (Stomach problems started at 19.
#61			50	Back to 19yo	Still distressed. Belief that people are against me or want to hurt me. Time to break this mental model. Let go of fear. 19yo integrates.
#62					No hypnosis.
#63	51	9	51	Group of 9, 4 ego-states, 5 are EES's from Mom and Dad.	John feeling intense anger lately. HS identifies a 6yo. Believes mom and dad are still alive. Ego-states believe mom and dad are still alive.

Session #	Group #	# in Group	Group Worked With	Part identified	What was shared
#64					No hypnosis.
#65			51	Back to group of 4. 5yo	The panic begins. Feels futility. Only safe place is outside by myself. Lost my home and center. Body became rigid from being yelled at. No trust for outside world. Went into shell and never came out. Lost my true self.
#66			51	Back to 5yo & 3 others.	Tremendous fear of giving voice to what is inside. Body tight from neck to knees. Deep abandonment.
#67			51	Back to 5yo & 3 others.	Body wants to cry. Walls began to go up. Stopped the feelings. A whole part of me started shutting down.
#68			51	Back to 5yo & 3 others.	Flashbacks of being hit. Hold in stomach. Want to disappear. Fear energy was so overwhelming. Came right at me. Don't know what to do. These 4 are angry.
#69			51	Back to 5yo & 3 others.	More anger and rage and ties in with Carl abuse also. Despair. Helpless
#70			51	Back to 5yo & 3 others.	"I'm being asked to trust a part of me I buried." Fear to embrace the spiritual. It always brings up anger at authorities
#71	52		52	New 5yo identified	Deep feelings of failure and worthlessness. Frequently triggered.
#72			52	Back to last 5yo.	Needs to let go. Releases and integrates.
			51	Back to 5yo & 3 others.	Back to Group #43-5yo & 3 others. Control was protective device. The more control, the safer. Shame, hurt. Choice was not to be vulnerable.
#73			51	Back to 5yo & 3 others.	Knocked off bearings, emotionally. Lost his anchor. "Been trying to find it that home base all my life. Always put myself second." Deep pain of fear began to take hold. "Like my whole system in the solar plexus tightened. Emotional knot I'm gut, layered over the years.
#74			51	Back to 5yo & 3 others.	"How powerless I've been. Lost my power." As much as he could, stayed away from family/ home and from school. Built an island for himself. Becoming aware of deep reservoir of strength. Need to tap into it. Fear is blocking. Still angry. Island is not to be the center. Now 8yo. A lot trauma. Pain in abdomen. They brought the island inside. "I became like a zombie and the island became home. Year of helplessness. Couldn't do anything right. Went into a psychological/emotional darkness. They've been on island in middle of reservoir. This was the only safe space they had.

Session #	Group #	# in Group	Group Worked With	Part identified	What was shared
	53	1	53	8yo	Has had a lot of trauma. Pain in abdomen also. Couldn't do anything right. All coming to a head. Darkness around me. I became like a zombie. 8yo can't move out of darkness yet. The island was the only place where there was hope.
#75	54	35	54	8yo & 34 others,	A different 8yo is identified. It is a group of 35. They are moved to a safe place. HS says to work with 8yo from last time.
			53	8yo from last time	"Repression of feelings began here." When we moved the island back inside it scrambled everything. Could no longer live in a dual world. This also triggered fear and anger. Terrified of going into emotions. Anger and rage. "When I brought the island inside in, the depth of anger, rage, and shame began to trigger. 8yo integrates.
#76			54	Back to 8yo from group #54	"I've lived in 2 worlds. Keep outside world happy. Never let the inner me surface." May be point where everything shut down.
#77	55	1	55	9yo identified, alone	Feeling negated. Angry at self for allowing it. Feeling enclosed. Afraid I can't get out.
#78			55	Back to 9yo	Overwhelmed. Not know how to deal with outside world. Stunned. Deep fear about speaking up. Bewildered. Life still had to go on. Lived life of avoidance. Affected self-esteem. Anxiety started to ripple out. This was foundation of living a fearful life. Sense of new level opening up in the healing.
#79			55	Back to 9yo.	Wants to move out of this. Growing desire to let the Light him. 9yo integrates.
	56	1	56	10yo alone.	10yo - lost connection to my core. Depth of fear releasing. Shift away from head. Feels shift happening. Protective part is reacting to letting go. Give reassurance. 10yo integrates.
#80	57	40	57	32yo (5yo) & 39 others	Pain & anger that dad was never there to intervene, and church was never there to intervene about Carl. At the mercy of mom, then Carl. Anger. Always blamed self. A vicious bind. That's beginning to change.
#81	58	1	58	30yo (3yo)	Blocking emotions. Need to let the feelings out. "Overwhelming how much I kept inside." Always on guard for the negative. Block in throat. "My being closed up on itself to form a safe cocoon. I tried to shrivel up."

Session #	Group #	# in Group	Group Worked With	Part identified	What was shared
#82			58	Back to 30yo (3yo)	Vigilant. Spent so much energy preventing hurt. 30yo is in throat. Says what others want him to say. HS—"we're moving into delicate area." There are others connected to 30yo.
#83			58	Back to 30yo (3yo)	Was frozen in time. Couldn't rescue himself. Feel pain throughout the body. Anger, bitterness & rage. With Carl experience, system was short-circuiting. With mom and Carl, tried not to exist. Thirteen years (since Carl) living in chaos. He was always the one who was wrong.
#84			58	Back to 30yo (3yo)	Opening up feelings. Couldn't protect myself from anything. Shut off life energy to the body. Pain in the abdomen. They had all the power. I was their slave. Developed strong bitterness.
#85			58	Back to 30yo (3yo).	Leaving priesthood. Body is beginning to wake up. As emotions awaken, the body awakens. "My whole being is coming back to life." Like coming out of a coma incrementally, slowly coming into the present. Needing to forgive self. Integrates.
	59	5	59	40yo (3yo), 19yo, & 3 others	40yo – panics about closed situations—elevator, surgery, airplanes, etc. All receive Light except 19yo. He is angry at the Light and blames it for what happened.
#86			59	40yo (3yo), 19yo, & 3 others	Left everything to come to West Michigan. Felt lost personally & professionally. Became more insulated. Realizes how much he has lived in confusion.
#87			59	40yo (3yo), 19yo, & 3 others	At 40 years-old. Everything came to a head. Panic & fear. "Losing myself." No outside security. Please everyone to stay safe. Can't trust myself.
					Join energy-point and soul in heart-center.
#88			59	40yo (3yo), 19yo, & 3 others	Isolated from everyone & everything. "Keep your mouth shut and keep going. I didn't exist in it. It was surreal. I was in it and wasn't in it." The pain is excruciating. "I lived in terror, completely shut down." No one there for him.
#89			59	40yo (3yo), 19yo, & 3 others.	Allowing the emotions to come. Afraid of them. Others beneath them. HS identifies a 7yo and 5yo.
	60	2	60	5yo & 7yo	7yo shares. Fear, helplessness deepens. Things got out of control. Deep pain on right side of abdomen.
#90			60	Back to 5yo & 7yo	Pushed harder and harder to get right answers. Didn't want to be hit or yelled at anymore. "Not to be right is no an option. The energy around these two is incredible." Feeling energy flowing through arms and legs.

Session #	Group #	# in Group	Group Worked With	Part identified	What was shared
#91			60	Back to 5yo & 7yo.	5yo & 7yo share. Always trying to stay ahead and avoid punishment. Always trying to please others and stay out of double bind. 5yo & 7yo integrate.
			59	Back to 40yo & 4others	40yo - became aware of disconnect at work, but couldn't get a handle on it. Then the panic began, the fear of closed places all started. Knew there was disconnect with board of directors. Things starting to fall apart. All in this group integrate.
#92	61		61	19yo(10yo) alone	Confusion around sexuality and spirituality. Buried spirituality to protect against Carl and what was happening. Need to connect with heart and passion. Might be a shattering here. Energy shell around heart.
#93			61	Back to 19yo	First came at 10yo. "Caged my feelings about Sarah, as I chose religious life. These feelings never re-connected later after leaving." Pain of loss. John feels guilt over people he hurt out of his protective anger and fear.
#94			61	Back to 19yo	When I told superiors they acted like I was in the wrong. Church abandoned me. "Feel stupid and I'm angry." Shut down from here until 40yo. "Only in the last 6 months I've started to become centered."
#95			61	Back to 19yo.	19yo shares more, releases and integrates.
	62	2	62	7yo's #1 & 2	7yo's - Trouble in spelling & reading. Felt split between anxiety and fear of beatings and wanting to learn. Wanted to learn but nobody to help.
#96	63	1	63	6yo	Angry. This is when conflict in school began. Get started in school and then mom and dad's energy is coming at me. Could not get back on my feet. Collapsed in on himself. "Went into a dark place where I became anonymous, where I could find a protective spot. I enclosed myself. Weird sensation that there's place I'm in, a dark spot that I can't reach into it, and I can't get back. It is like sealed from pain. I went into space and didn't know how to get back out. Even now I'm not sure how to get back out of it. I made concrete judgment that no where was going to be safe for me, so I would never come out again except just enough for survival. Nothing could penetrate. Like the energy petrified me. I was so scared and overwhelmed, it was encapsulating the whole person." 6yo releasing. This raw energy pushing me back into this dark space. Couldn't handle it. Like a tsunami. I'm standing alone in the ruins. A little boy, clueless of what to do or not to do." Stunned look. "I was paralyzed. I was just there, everything's gone and I'm frozen in this spot. Didn't know where to step next."

Session #	Group #	# in Group	Group Worked With	Part identified	What was shared
#97			63	Back to 6yo. 2 others with him.	Two other 6yo's are discovered with him. "I've always been battling the outside."
#98			63	Back to 6yo. 2 others with him.	Became frenetic. Internalized model: get it done, get it right, get it over with, so you don't get beat. Had to do everything fast. Grew up making the outside happy. Totally controlled by the outside. So much was buried just to survive.
#99			63	Back to 6yo. 2 others with him.	Still in dark place. Lost voice; no power. If I always said yes, chance I wouldn't get beat. Can't move out of dark yet.
#100			63	Back to 6yo. 2 others with him.	Dream of concentration camp. 6yo - like someone took a bat to my stomach. They see 20 devices. They want to leave their cocoon.
#101			63	Back to 6yo. 2 others with him.	This is where enclosure began. Went into fetal position. Only safe place. Didn't want to leave it. No one to trust. Closing in on himself, psychologically, emotionally, and socially.
#102			63	Back to 6yo. 2 others with him.	Says a cord at neck that is tied to stomach. Has taken on so much responsibility in order to gain control. Grew more enclosed. Doesn't trust the inside or outside.
#103			63	Back to 6yo. 2 others with him.	"Image of myself in a cave with huge boulder blocking opening. You'll have to dynamite to get through." Stuck in this space of darkness and negative energy. Still not ready to feel emotions. Afraid of his rage.
#104			63	Back to 6yo. 2 others with him.	Showing feelings only led to trouble. Living afraid of being hurt or punished. Fear and dread inside have controlled him. This is pattern: when afraid, withdraw, close up.
#105			63	Back to 6yo. 2 others with him.	From 6yo on, tried to force things to make it work. Disconnect began. The 6yo's release and integrate.
	64	3	64	8yo & 2 EBS's	8yo & 2 EBS identified in dark area. Spirits go to the Light. 8yo did not want them to leave.
#106			64	Back to 8yo	Like I hit a wall. Wasn't connecting. Barely surviving. Worn out. I entered darkness. No way forward and I couldn't go back. Became more and more frustrated, angry and started storing it inside. "I was one pissed off little kid that didn't know where to go. Couldn't be centered in the moment. Always trying to get ahead to get a handle on things."
#107					No Hypnosis.

Session #	Group #	# in Group	Group Worked With	Part identified	What was shared
#108			64	Back to 8yo	Trying to protect myself spiritually. Why is this happening to me? Where is God? Very aware of the Carl experience. When Carl became physical, 8yo shut down the spirituality. "Like I put it someplace and now can't find it—what was most important to me." Felt violated at spiritual level.
#109			64	Back to 8yo	8yo still not ready to receive Light. Blames the Light for what happened. Feels isolated. Living life of total helplessness. Everybody else has the power.
#110			64	Back to 8yo,	Intense anger throughout system. First communion and thoughts of priesthood. Spiritual connection. 8yo integrates.
	65	3	65	Three 20yo's	20yo is when the enclosure became permanent. "By the end of Carl's abuse, I had shut down. I cracked at some level."
#111			65	Back to 20yo's.	Soul/energy point separated again. "When Carl kissed me, the whole reality of my life was shattered." The Light went out. Deep shame and guilt and fear of others' judgment.
#112			65	Back to 20yo's.	Self stuck in dark spot. 20yo's created very close together. Take steps to merge them. Not yet. receiving tiny piece of Light.
#113			65	Back to 20yo's	Work situation setting off fear, tapping into vulnerability and helplessness he felt with Carl. If I make a mistake, I'll be punished. Made a contract with self. I'll never let anyone get that close to me again. There is a knife in his side.
					Rejoins energy-point and soul.
#114			65	Back to 20yo's.	Fear and anxiety. After abuse incident he wanted some control. With mom and Carl, felt defenseless at a deep level, and frozen in space. "A blackness force was hitting me." Suppressed the anger and hopelessness as it got stronger. Withdrew even more from others. "For most of my life I never developed a safe place. It was safer outside my homes than inside."
#115			65	Back to 20yo's.	What started out as protection from the outside turned into a prison. Resents himself. By protecting Carl, he avoids having to face abuse himself. Feels controlled. John trusted Carl with the most precious thing he had - his spirituality.

Session #	Group #	# in Group	Group Worked With	Part identified	What was shared
#116			65	Back to 20yo's.	Almost like two worlds - the world of light and this world of repression, blocking, and protection. When I was young there was so much darkness coming at me; it was scary, petrifying. Terrified of becoming that afraid and helpless again. Used anger and resentment as protective shield. The Light was overwhelmed. It's beginning to come back. John feels the enclosure has lost some of its energy today.
#117			65	Back to 20yo's.	Pain was so powerful, he just wanted to shut down and go to a spot where he would never be touched again. Resignation. At 20yo, cemented my life in dark and started a downward spiral until mental breakdown.
#118			65	Back to 20yo's (6yo).	20yo's all came at 6yo. Moving into blackness, felt abandoned by God. Felt he didn't deserve any better. "Part of me gave up." Became immobilized.
#119			65	Back to 20yo's.	Angry now that Carl steered him away from Sarah and women and then violated him after he ad made vows. They are quite fragmented and disconnected from heart. The message is hat there are more than these 20yo's involved.
#120			65	Back to 20yo's.	"I spent so much time in my head trying to control, that I cut off from my emotions." And body was anxious. Living life in defensive posture. Allows energy shield to be dissipated.
#121			65	Back to 20yo's.	Enclosure has become normal. Moving out is unknown territory. Vulnerable. Not going back. John says the 20yo's will have a full release as he untangles the mental scripts developed in the "enclosed life."
#122					No Hypnosis.
#123			65	Back to 20yo's.	Aware of how much dread and anxiety he has lived with. Feels body is disconnected. Work with body consciousness. 20yo's can't feel body. Shut down bodily. "Body is coming back online. To this point it's been frozen… There's an awakening going on inside me."
#124			65	Back to 20yo's.	So much shame and guilt. Taking on responsibility for what happened. Feeling unworthy. Can't do anything right. It is never okay to feel. Block feelings with Sarah. Also, fear of my anger. Shame and deep feeling of being defiled from Carl experience. Not wanting anyone close again.
#125			65	Back to 20yo's.	Profound confusion around Carl experience. Confusion was sexual, academic, and vocational.

Session #	Group #	# in Group	Group Worked With	Part identified	What was shared
#126			65	Back to 20yo's.	"Body and emotions are beginning to thaw. It's like softening my whole system. First time I feel like I can move forward, like I have the capacity now and not all the old baggage. It's like jumping from 20 years-old to 40 years-old." 20yo's integrate.
	66		66	three 40yo's(7yo)	All came around 7yo. Struggles about spirituality. A split. A disconnect. Like a corner of my being I've not been able to tap into. There's a block somewhere. Sense of darkness.
#127					No Hypnosis.
#128			66	Back to 40yo's	Tried to reclaim spiritual dreams I had. New job, like outside authority saying I'm not smart enough. (Constant theme.) Implied question: Was I worthy in the eyes of God? 40yo's Integrate
	67	5	67	50yo(5yo) & 4 others	Whole dream of spiritual life vanished. Disoriented. Can't find it. Move group to safer place.
#129			67	back to 50yo(5yo) & 4 others	Lost fundamental trust in outside world; it's profound. If going to move forward must have more trust in outside world. Becoming aware of depth of fear and pain and its impact. Always try to have the right answer to avoid punishment.
#130			67	back to 50yo(5yo) & 4 others	After last session, John had first flashback with emotion. Intense pain across stomach. 50yo sharing: Fear of being with mom, then Carl. Moved from one darkness to another. Petrified with Carl, body stiff. Stored all energy in abdomen. Angry at Carl. Want to beat him. Feels helpless. Began trying to control everything. "Hate myself for not doing anything." Feels defiled.
#131			67	back to 50yo(5yo) & 4 others	Darkness from outside kept dwarfing the Light inside. Deep fear about uncovering the Light. "It's like foreign territory for me." Negative energy was overwhelming. "Spiritual life has been squelched."
#132			67	back to 50yo(5yo) & 4 others	Flashbacks. Inner message: "Slow down." Find proper physical pace. Hard to slow down. I'll be punished. 7yo is youngest in the group. The faster I go, the more anxiety. Felt outside world wouldn't help with mom or Carl.
#133			67	back to 50yo(5yo) & 4 others	Feel responsible for all of it. Couldn't get control. Overwhelmed and confused. Feels shattered and defeated. John breaks wrist after session.
	68	30	68	19yo, 6yo, & 2 others	These four identified immediately after John breaks his wrist. All four have others inside them.

Session #	Group #	# in Group	Group Worked With	Part identified	What was shared
#134			68	Back 19yo, 6yo, & 2 others. 26 more inside. Now 30 altogether	Inside these 4 are 26 more. HS brings out 26 others from these 4. 6yo shares: wants to run from everything.
#135			68	Back to all 30.	Always to blame for everything. "I dissociated the Carl experience. It made me sick." So tired of living this way. Had to plan every move for safety. Exhausting.
#136			68	19yo, group of 30.	19yo sharing. Flashbacks of Carl. Deep feelings for Sarah and now so confused. Carl energy was pressuring me to stay in religious life. Wanted to be with Sarah. When he touched my penis I was ready to kill him. Gave power to Carl. Lost my chance for marriage and children.
#137			68	back to 19yo & 29.	Try to control everything. Pattern is so old of controlling everything (or try). It's 2nd nature.
#138			68	back to 19yo & 29.	Learning how to trust. Head has always controlled. First time he starts to balance head with emotions and body. Give group experience of body. At 19yo began to open myself to spiritual and was slammed shut with Carl. John aware of shattering.
#139			68	back to 19yo & 29.	19yo still separated from body. 7yo feels disconnected. 13yo feels disconnected. "the body disconnect kept growing over 12 years. All 30 sharing. Hunger to have spirituality and body reconnected.
#140			68	back to 19yo, 7yo, 13yo & 27 others.	Depth of control starting at 7yo dealing with mom's abuse. At 13yo: starting high school. At 19yo: shattering of spirituality. These three ages, knocked off center. After Carl, like living in desert. No trust.
#141			68	back to 19yo, 7yo, 13yo & 27.	More sharing. Move entire group to safer place.
#142			68	back to 19yo, 7yo, 13yo & 27.	7yo keeps blaming self. Cannot meet outside world's expectations. Blaming pattern solidified at 19yo. Try to make sure outside world accepted me. "Outer world became driver within me. Had to keep outer world happy. Outer world became dominant controller of me. In order to meet demands of outer world, had to close off so much of me. If I didn't get it right, world was going to come down on me. With broken wrist, first time I didn't run. For first time, I'm moving forward, truly moving into the Light. For first time, past is not as strong as present."

Session #	Group #	# in Group	Group Worked With	Part identified	What was shared
#143			68	Back to group of 30. 65yo(3yo)	First came at 3yo. Part of group of 30. In a dark place. No life. A few dilapidated houses. Not dark, but no sunlight.
#144			68	Back to group of 30.	Lives with negative expectations. "Living in enclosure, I have no control." Vigilance and avoidance.
#145			68	Back to group of 30.	"I've been looking so deep inward, but am beginning to look out." Like frozen in position. Created wall (shield) from mom. The wall grew stronger and stronger. All alone. Escape from world became pattern. The shielding created the darkness inside. "I have to unfreeze this so more Light can come in."
#146			68	Back to group of 30.	Helplessness is very deep.19yo shielded Light. Entire group now receiving some Light. Energy-point/soul still joined, but in abdomen. Awareness Light is always there.
#147			68	Back to group of 30.	7 are part of group of 30 and are given Light and join with the 30. These 7 carry feelings of betrayal by mom, Jim, board, and even myself. Almost like a dome was placed over everything. "It squelched my creativity, confidence, and talents. Mom's abuse, and then Carl's, closed my throat. Anxiety in my arms, throat, & chest, tension at speaking my voice.
				21yo. Another 7 in dark area of this group.	
#148			68	Back to group, now 37. 19yo	Self-blame. He's turned into "I'm not worthy."
#149			68	Back to group, now 37. 19yo	19yo-image of dark door (60ft high) holding lots of sludge behind it (probably emotion). HS identifies door. Someone behind it. Feels it is ominous, overwhelming, it will blow him away. Face to face with next level of darkness. Holds the energy in throat and chest.
#150			68	Back to group, now 37.	Letting go of fear, dread, anxiety. After Carl experience, didn't know what to do, where to go. I went into a cocoon. Holding it all inside. Protecting myself from the outside. Feelings are beginning to surface.

Session #	Group #	# in Group	Group Worked With	Part identified	What was shared
#151			68	Back to group, now 37. 19yo	19yo: Deep sadness and grief about freedom lost. "Lost my center. All I could do with mom and Carl was to take it." Image of curled up 19yo in corner. 22 of this group are still curled up. Whole body went into a dark space. Like it is atrophied. Something or someone outside this group is influencing it.
#152	69	15	69	PLMA & 4 others	John had emotional meltdown. HS finds 5 ego-states that are involved and hidden. This group is like a protective shield from going out into the world. They integrate. Still 10 more hidden.
			69	10 hidden ones.	10yo in this group. They also release and integrate.
#153			68	Back to group, now 37.	Not worthy of anything. Outside world became like a guessing game and I hardly ever guessed right. Abandoned and alone. Image of knife in his right side and starts cutting. 7yo is one who feels it.
#154			68	Back to group, now 37.	7yo, PLMT, & 1 other are sharing. Sharing of mom's beatings more intense now. Helpless and defeated. No way out, no matter what I did. Internalized "I'm no good." This is when Light dissipated and dark came in. Darker and darker. Flashbacks of mom. Group of 37 now integrates.
#155	70	5	70	13yo & 4 others	John reports intense fear. Intense fear of being enclosed and never getting out. HS finds 13yo. Removes energies. They are enclosed and 6 openings. 5 go outside. An inner scream. "With Carl and mom I was enclosed. They had all the control and I could only be released by them. Carl was kissing a mannequin, I had dissociated."
#156			70	Back to 13yo & 4 others	Fear of being helpless. Starts the panic. "Cannot get in touch with my anger." Wants revenge. I wanted them to feel what they made me feel. Kept building darkness over darkness. Still not trustful of the Light.
#157			70	Back to 13yo & 4 others	Flashbacks becoming more intense and frequent. Fear and anger are building. Can't sleep. HS identifies 13yo involved. These five were pulled into dark area since session two days ago. 25 energies involved. Some removed. Some reintegrated. 6 doors, 4 go outside. Doors involved in pulling group back into darkness.
	71	7	71	12yo & 6 others	7 ego-states retrieved. They join Group #70. Grief and anger.

Session #	Group #	# in Group	Group Worked With	Part identified	What was shared
#158			70/71	Back to 13yo. Now a group of 12.	Terror, fear and dread in these situations. Neither inner world or outside world is safe. Only safety is to be completely removed. Only way to survive was meet others' needs. I lost myself. Depth of emotion and energy feels scary.
#159			70/71	Back to 13yo. Now a group of 12.	One in this group is outside the body. Not sure of age. This part has Light. Is pushed out of body by others. "I've lived life trying to be somebody I'm not."
#160			70/71	Back to 13yo. Now a group of 12.	"Suppressed anger so I could keep what I did have." This covering was quite limiting. It's time to let go of the institutional Church. Felt like a non-entity to them. Depth of pain in stomach is tremendous.
#161			70/71	Back to 13yo. Now a group of 12.	In leaving church, I'm leaving my "tribe." After abuse, parts "lived in a void." Still feels the void. Always the question, "Will I be safe?" Always feeling to blame.
#162			70/71	Back to 13yo. Now a group of 12.	As I move into current reality realize how focused I always was on future. Always in protective mode. Constant anxiety. Beginning to realize in current reality I feel strong, when look to future, anxiety starts. When feeling to blame, move to the future to prevent it. Blame creates mass confusion. Became more isolated.
#163			70/71	Back to 13yo. Now a group of 12.	Felt panic last night. HS identifies 13yo & group. Energies were triggered, now reintegrated. Overwhelming feelings of anxiety and blame. Whole personhood was shattered. May have affected all chakras. John becoming aware of how often he is "outside of body." Strong emotion as group reconnects with body.
#164			70/71	Back to 13yo. Now a group of 12.	Always anxiety and fear. Backing away instead of stepping into risk. Couldn't trust that others would be there for me. Always had to have right answer or there would be trouble. When feeling double bind, body wants to curl up.
#165			70/71	Back to 13yo(5yo). Now a group of 12.	13yo first came at 5yo. Fear is feeding on fear. When fear, leave the body. Afraid I'll be trapped. By the time of Carl experience, I was numb. No fight left. They agree to enter body.
#166			70/71	Back to 13yo. Now a group of 12.	2 in group still having trouble. One is PLMA. Sense of divide. When someone says everything is wonderful, there is a shadow side. Didn't know how to deal with the shadow side. Group releases and integrates.

Session #	Group #	# in Group	Group Worked With	Part identified	What was shared
#167	72	6	72	7yo,19yo#1, 19yo#2, 6yo, 20yo, & 32yo.	These ego-states are bound together. They are in a cave. Afraid to separate. Shares panic carried at these ages. From 6 to 7, from 19 to 20, & at 32yo went in new direction. John was deeply alone in all of it. "My real body is trying to become nothing." Feeling part of him emasculated. It was this way with Carl and mom. With Carl, it was like I lost my heterosexual identity.
#168			72	7yo,19yo#1, 19yo#2, 6yo, 20yo, & 32yo.	At 7yo couldn't trust my own knowing. At 19yo, couldn't trust my emotions and sexuality. Fear and anxiety went inside. Recognize I need others, but can't trust. Fear of being enclosed. Aware of rigid tension in whole body. This is when they stepped out of the body. Depth of isolation after Carl experience was terrifying.
#169			72	7yo,19yo#1, 19yo#2, 6yo, 20yo, & 32yo.	Fear and anxiety blocking the voice. Kept everything in. Feels energy in arms, chest, & throat. John feels strong desire to move out of the cave. Upper part of the body feels frozen. Feels helplessness and vulnerability. "By tensing my body, it was a buffer against what was happening." Had been aware of the tightness below, but this is a new awareness. The fear stored at these levels is immense.
#170			72	7yo,19yo#1, 19yo#2, 6yo, 20yo, & 32yo.	"Have to allow myself to slow down. As a child, everything had to be fast. "The stuckness in my throat is from trying to react fast. The fear of not having it right is a strong threat to me." This slowing down is critical." Tension, pain and sadness in upper arms is so real. Depth of fear of not being good enough. The ego-states now step away from each other.
#171			72	7yo,19yo#1, 19yo#2, 6yo, 20yo, & 32yo.	Frustrated by the deep helplessness and vulnerability. With mom and Carl did not know how to get safe. Paralyzed. Chose to do nothing. I couldn't risk. Wanted to be invisible. Began to act as if everything was fine. Releasing. "There's a huge shift happening here."
#172			72	7yo,19yo#1, 19yo#2, 6yo, 20yo, & 32yo.	Moving into space where fear of mom and Carl is terrifying. "The depth of emotion here is scary. I had created a buffer around it. My whole body begins to feel it when I get close to that." Totally helpless and vulnerable with no way out. This group says there is a deeper place of helplessness.

Session #	Group #	# in Group	Group Worked With	Part identified	What was shared
#173			72	7yo,19yo#1, 19yo#2, 6yo, 20yo, & 32yo.	Feels terror in the body. Flashbacks of mom. No place to turn for protection. No way out. Not knowing who to trust to help. They would side with mom or Carl. "The beatings and kiss were like an avalanche coming at me. Seems the only thing I could do was enclose myself. Began to isolate myself from anything that could cause that level of pain." Avoidance patter enclosed him more and more.
#174			72	7yo,19yo#1, 19yo#2, 6yo, 20yo, & 32yo.	Terror of being betrayed. "If I don't do it right, they can leave me. Blamed myself for not solving it." Waves of emotion coming up. Terror, blame, and not being worth enmeshed together. "If I don't come up with the right answer, I'll be blasted."
#175			72	7yo,19yo#1, 19yo#2, 6yo, 20yo, & 32yo.	Abandonment after being traumatized. No one to turn to. Went deeper inside and more anxiety. Anxiety became underlying state. Feeling like a loser. No way to change it. "It's like I lived in a shocked state." Couldn't breathe. Became stiff and rigid.
#176			72	7yo,19yo#1, 19yo#2, 6yo, 20yo, & 32yo.	Tightness in jaw. Need to connect heart and voice (throat). Always preparing to meet external world and afraid of being punished. Have to learn to be patient; let the healing unfold.
#177			72	7yo,19yo#1, 19yo#2, 6yo, 20yo, & 32yo.	Releasing. Trusting the moment and the process. Sense of deep healing going on.
#178	73	4	73	5yo & 3 spirits	Spirits removed. 5yo releases and integrates.
			72	Back to 7yo & 5 others. 19yo, 19yo#2, 6yo, 20yo, & 32yo.	During beating. In a closed place. Can't get out. Bubble of energy comes and surrounds him. Impenetrable. 2nd bubble around the Carl experience. HS dissolves bubbles and reintegrates the energy. All six integrate.
#179	74	6	74	20yo, 19yo, & 4 spirits	John aware of a "dome of energy" covering. HS can't remove yet. Dome created of John and Carl's energy. Identifies a group under the dome. HS removes spirits. Dome was created in reaction to Carl. Afraid to let the spiritual force come out. There are 4 doors, 2 go outside soul. "Carl violated me almost to the core. Like a dagger went into me and starting cutting out parts." 20yo and 19yo release and integrate.

Session #	Group #	# in Group	Group Worked With	Part identified	What was shared
	75	8	75	21yo & 7others	HS retrieves 8 ego-states through 2 doors going outside. They are all curled up. One is 21yo. The fear and anxiety cemented this protective dome (shell). Repressing emotions and then shutting off spiritual too. He is just a speck and the dome is a thousand times bigger. These 8 are afraid to leave dome.
#180			75	21yo & 7others	When abuse started with Carl, everything collapsed and started to spiral down. "I was blossoming and then boom, it was all shut down. I became lost." More anxiety and isolation. Just trying to survive. Became a way of life. Robotic. (Tremendous energy in torso moves to throat.) "I'm integrating my whole person for the first time." HS pulls back the dome.
#181			75	21yo & 7others	"With Carl, part of my heart was shut off. I shut off the passion within me." Spirituality ran deep but never came back to the surface. "Knocked me completely off my bearings. First time in my life that darkness became stronger than the Light. Up to this point there was enough Light to show the path. My voice was shut down." Intense anger. Felt a "split" happen at this time. Became super vigilant. All in this group are 20 or 21 years-old. Lot of darkness still here. Weight put around heart area.
#182			75	21yo & 7others	Resistance to reclaiming these Carl experience. Fear of dying again. The darkness is so strong. It's not yet time to feel body. Energy in throat and pain in abdomen. "My whole being is pulled into abdomen to protect heart and soul." Immense anger. Wanting revenge. Church protected Carl. No longer feel safe as part of faith community. "Broken wrist took me into this dark place."
#183			75	21yo & 7others	Began to spend time out of building until bed time. Kept all the anger, pain, and hurt inside, but did start having outbursts. More afraid and enclosed. 2 of these first came at 12yo. Couldn't believe it was happening. "I trusted someone with my soul and they took it and shredded it for their own needs." Couldn't make sense of it. Felt defiled. Never wanted to go back to the Carl experience. Put all in a bottle and on a shelf. Hard today even to believe it happened.
#184			75	21yo & 7others	Short fuse this week. Afraid of the intense anger, of opening up this space. A protective seal has kept it shut. All carry memory of the kiss. With Carl, the lights went out. A dim light has now appeared.

Session #	Group #	# in Group	Group Worked With	Part identified	What was shared
#185		75	21yo & 7others	After Carl, lost purpose in life. Felt Like Carl's whore. Afraid to go into emotions. HS finds energy devices blocking. Reintegrates them. Feels unworthy, dirty. Deep confusion.
#186		75	21yo & 7others	Doesn't want to go into 'Carl space.' "His tongue in my mouth was sickening." Anger, emotions coming up. Tears. Got lost in the insecurity of mom and Car's abuse. "Whole body is shaking." From childhood to adulthood, had no one to turn to. "Body has been frozen. Got disconnected."
#187		75	21yo & 7others	HS shows group place of integration. Carl's kiss & all feelings for women got scrambled. Didn't know what the truth was. Caught up in dual reality. It was agony to be at his mercy. Always vigilant. Feeling attracted to women but it leads back to Carl memories.
#188		75	21yo & 7others	More anger. Dance between enclosure and dissociation. Felt energy & growth as a sexual being was arrested. "Enclosure kept me from embracing the emotion, spirit, intellect." Kept them disconnected from outside world. Body and emotions froze. Dissociation turned off so many switches. Enclosure was way of holding in the pain, fear, & confusion. "I lived in outer world, but no root to center." Never felt at home. For first time, beginning to feel at home in own apartment.
#189		75	21yo & 7others	Blames self for not being able to control all and have good outcome. "I was totally to blame. Mom, dad, Carl had no responsibility. I started down a path of negation. Moved inward and downward." Now the 8 retrieved ones are blocked.
#190	76	1	76	6yo alone	Aware of block. HS finds 6yo. This is when the enclosure began. Paradox—I don't want to be enclosed but I enclose myself. There's a protective shield in stomach. Conscious and unconscious world begin to separate. Panic, fear, and dread began to grow. Could no longer be me. Overwhelmed. Had to be someone else for outer world. Lost my identity. Core began to shatter. HS confirms there was a shattering.
#191		76	6yo alone	Never feels safe. Outside people have the power. Started to mistrust the Light, lost it in midst of pain and horror. "I should be able to control everything and when I can't I should be punished." Began to run away from home as much as possible. In healing, beginning to move back to the fear.
#192		76	6yo alone	Overwhelming fear of being enclosed. Going into feelings of fear and defilement. Depth of feeling vulnerable and no control.

Session #	Group #	# in Group	Group Worked With	Part identified	What was shared
#193			76	6yo alone	"I could get out of it if I took the punishment. I lost all trust in me, my voice, & how to connect to outside world." Became more and more enclosed. Always figuring it was his fault. After Carl, the door was sealed and did not know how to open it again.
#194			76	6yo alone	Anxiety grew over time. "The more I couldn't get the right answer, the more my system revved up with anxiety." Becoming aware of the magnitude of anxiety that controlled his life.
#195			76	6yo alone	Fear of coming back to outer world after beating. Feels terror located in abdomen, heart, and throat. 6yo knows the terror. "I learned to swallow it all the way down." Feels trapped in corner.
#196			76	6yo alone	Overwhelming emotions last 3 weeks. Aware of the ripple effects of abuse. There are 8 openings. All go outside. HS retrieves six ego-states. Call a guide to stay with them. "As I move out of enclosure, I see more ripples. Things are opening up for me now."
#197					
#198			76	6yo alone	Enclosure, betrayal, and abandonment have become intertwined. Release. 6yo integrates.
			75	Back to 21yo & 7others	Energy knot in throat. "Lost my voice and kept going inward."
#199			75	21yo & 7others	Realizing how abuse has rippled through generations—mom and two uncles. It's a collective unconscious story. Developed repression in family. It allows for continued abuse. Realizing how grandfather's accidental death affected mom. My choice was to be come more enclosed and withdrawn.
#200			75	21yo & 7others	Lots of anger. HS says John has entered dark spot. Blocking energies are present. Energy blocks in left side of jaw. With Carl, it's like my mouth became wired shut. All 10 energies reintegrated.
#201			75	21yo & 7others	Buried the rage and anger. Feeling the enclosure. Terror of being in that space again. Now always vigilant. "Depth of terror still pervades my life." Stuck, frozen, immobilized. Felt so ugly and defiled. Never felt so unloved and unworthy. Like someone had taken the life out of me. HS takes his dirty clothes and brings him new ones from the Light. There's a reservoir of emotion and energy here.
#202			75	21yo & 7others	Realize I've focused on external to survive. Frustration trying to match up to demands of outer world. "Anxiety and panic has been norm for me. Intense energy pulls me inward and bends me over." Denied himself in order to survive and not get beat. "If I deny myself, I'll be okay" or "if I know the terrain, then I know what dance to do."

Session #	Group #	# in Group	Group Worked With	Part identified	What was shared
#203			75	21yo & 7others	Scared of moving into this space. The energy is so strong. When mom was screaming at me, I internalized the unworthiness. Total helplessness. I learned never to let my guard down.
#204			75	21yo & 7others	"When I move into enclosed space, overwhelming terror and fear. A tsunami of energy comes at me." Shock of the unexpected—mom and Carl. John always surprised by the beatings and Carl's approach. In this space, I am totally lost. I was responsible for everything. Had to get it right. If I can't solve it myself, then other people have control.
#205	77	3	77	Group of 3 - 19yo, 10yo, 8yo	John reports intense anxiety. HS identifies three ego-states. They receive Light. Move to more comfortable place. There are 50 doors, 10 go outside.
			75	Back to 21yo & 7others	Begins to feel the helplessness. Tension in arms. Overwhelming sense of energy I couldn't deal with. Deep fear of having no control. "Like it's embedded and hard to release." Body is stiff and paralyzed. Only head can move. "Even now I feel the depth of terror in body."
#206			77	Back to Group of 3 - 19yo, 10yo, 8yo	HS retrieves ego-states through 10 doors. They join group #70. Now 35 altogether. Sharing huge amount of blame and shame. All integrate.
			75	Back to 21yo & 7others	4 of group do not believe what happened. HS helps them to review. One is 7yo. Now they believe. An energy wall keeps them separate from the others. HS dissipates wall.
#207					No Hypnosis.
#208			75	Back to 21yo & 7others	20yo(6yo). Light has been drained from him. Shares a disconnect from body. Can't "unfreeze" body. A reflexive, automatic protection. So traumatized, no longer believe in God. This 20yo(6yo) not aware of the others. Blame & shame—not deserving of Light. 6yo rejoins with body.
#209			75	Back to 21yo & 7others & 20yo	20yo(6yo) again. 20yo inside him. As authorities, nothing 20yo(6yo) could do to stop mom or Carl. Totally helpless. Sense of being in shock. Wanting to lash out. Where is God? Darkness comes. 20yo is given Conscious Experience.

Session #	Group #	# in Group	Group Worked With	Part identified	What was shared
#210			75	Back to 21yo & 7others & 20yo	Back to 20yo(6yo) and 20yo. Stepping back into body. Wants to lash out at Carl. Afraid. All emotions dissociated. Was just integrating his own sexuality when Carl's kiss hit him like a tsunami. Profound confusion. "Just shut me down."
#211			75	Back to 21yo & 7others & 20yo	Back to 20yo(6yo) and 20yo. Anger & rage energy inside. Depth of aloneness and confusion in all this. "In both cases, I had to be someone I wasn't." Releasing.
#212			75	Back to 21yo & 7others & 20yo	Back to 20yo. 5 energies inside. Keeps self stuck in dark spot. Now all in group sharing. Fear of letting go of anger and rage. Still a block. 10 energies inside. HS removes them.
#213			75	Back to 21yo & 7others & 20yo	Angry at how much was shut down; how much energy went into protecting. Depth of pain and unworthiness has blocked him. "If I give voice, I could get hurt/beat up." Act as if everything is OK. "The Great Pretender."
#214			75	Back to 21yo & 7others & 20yo	Still great anger at Carl and Church. 4 still do not want to release it. HS shows them place of integration.
#215			75	Back to 21yo & 7others & 20yo	Anger has been more intense. Felt he was at fault for what happened with Carl. Felt he was wrong when he didn't want Carl's touch. Now feeling used.
#216			75	Back to 21yo & 7others & 20yo	More anger. Feels raped, used like a whore. There's energy from penis to throat. Energy block at throat. HS removes it. "Anger masks the terror I felt with Carl."
#217			75	Back to 21yo & 7others & 20yo	Feelings and emotions now coming up strongly. Feeling of always being punished. Could not be me. Felt like non-entity.
#218	78		78	8yo & 9 others	Past week, flashbacks of mom & Carl. Feels like it's happening in real time. HS moves them to safer place. They have release.
#219			75	Back to 21yo & 7others & 20yo	Anger & rage that Carl got away with it. Memories of being hit and kissed. "Had to go inside to protect myself." Terror of moving inward to enclosure. "When I went inward, I was denying the depth of terror, fear, and pain. Energy went so deep, right down to my feet." Only head was not protected.
#220			75	Back to 21yo & 7others & 20yo	Never realized how much life was lived in fear and protection. Beginning to move out of the enclosure and embrace Light. This is a new path I've never allowed before. Afraid whether he'll be safe.

Session #	Group #	# in Group	Group Worked With	Part identified	What was shared
#221			75	Back to 21yo & 7others & 20yo	Deep terror. Lots of energy in jaw, throat, and back.
			78	8yo & 9 others & 20 retrieved ones.	19yo in group #70. Light was taken from him by a spirit. HS removes it. 5 openings. HS does retrieval. 20 retrieved. Moves all to safer place.
			75	Back to 21yo & 7others & 20yo	Put on protective shield from Carl, but it cut me off from others too. Total shut down.
			Check on energy point and soul	Rejoin them.
#222			78	Back to 8yo & 9 others & 20 retrieved ones.	5 energies. HS dissipates and removes them.
#223					No Hypnosis
#224	79	12	79	Group of 8. 6 doors. 4 retrieved. Now 12 altogether.	Claustrophobic reaction. 4 retrieved. These 12 are in three areas of body—groin, heart, & throat. From throat down, became frozen. Head tried to control things. Only way to survive was to keep everything stuffed down. From 19 to 32, I was "blanked out." Give them Conscious Experience so they see Carl is no longer in John's life.
					Had dream of being buried alive by Nazis.
#225			79	Back to group of 12 again.	HS identifies 20 energies blocking. HS reintegrates them. Aware of protection from throat to groin. Fear and terror moved him more and more within. Constant vigilance. Huge part of me stuck in protective state. Release. Moves them to Integration.
	80		80	PLMT - Michael & 5 others	Connected to dream of Nazis. All 6 are past life. 5 doors to outside. Retrieves and reintegrates soul energy.
#226			80	Back to LMT(Michael) & 5 others	Overwhelmed by pervasive abuse in these past life ego-states. Same vulnerability felt with Carl. Release & integrate.
#227			75	21yo & 7 others	20yo sharing: when I go into Carl space, pain in groin to right side. Anger that all sexuality was severed. I trusted him at time when very vulnerable. Spirituality and sexuality were awakening. Releases.
#228			75	21yo & 7others	Sensation of Carl "still inside me." Tension in arms. Fear in heart. Fear then goes to throat. Feels vile and defiled.
#229			75	21yo & 7others	Protective shield in place. "Keeps me locked in." Scary loneliness.

Session #	Group #	# in Group	Group Worked With	Part identified	What was shared
#230					No Hypnosis. Remaining more centered. Seldom feel any panic now.
#231			75	21yo & 7others	Sharing focused on John's self blame. "Unless I was perfect, no one wanted to be around me." Depth of fear in situations where I don't have control. Like a knife pushed inside. Want to crawl into enclosure. Depth of helplessness. This is where protective shield developed. The body froze.
#232			75	21yo & 7others	3 ego-states not receiving Light. Involves enclosure. Fear & trauma has been held in abdomen and heart. Paralyzing fear became protective shield. The enclosure got smaller and tighter. These 3 have release.
#233					No Hypnosis
#234			75	21yo & 7others	Swallowed the pain, "I ate it like food." Becoming more and more inward. Moving out of it is such a new experience. "I'll create an illness if I don't let this move out." This group finally released & integrated.
The case study narrative stops with the integration of this group. The following two groups were the last identified					
#235	81	7	81	20yo & 6 others	20yo sharing. The terror at Carl's touch. I just checked out. Terror became the norm. Felt ugly, defiled, shame, and worthless. All the life sucked out of me. Knocked off center. Massive confusion. Terror also of being completely alone. Put on armor against the world. I move away from the outer world unless 100% safe. Something snapped inside. Created a shield.
#236			81	20yo & 6 others	Shield created in 3 parts to protect head, heart, and body. Body is slowly coming back online. Beginning to relax. Head & heart more integrated than lower body. 2 haven't had conscious experience (CE) yet. With Carl, an out of body experience.
#237			81	20yo & 6 others	Rough week since taking shield down. Feels he was set up (groomed) by Carl. Disconnected from real world. Feels surreal. Just the thought of Carl brings feeling of enclosure.
#238			81	20yo & 6 others	Body still racing. Can feel the powerlessness right now. Agitation but can't define it. Like I lived in 2 worlds. Feels like fear-based personality in any situation. Created a hyper-vigilance.
#239			81	20yo & 6 others	Fear I'm going to get hurt. Being at home in my own skin is foreign to me. I clamp down on my voice, and the muscles in my arms, and probably clamped down my heart. "Like I've lived in an Iron Man suit." "Sense of body and feelings coming online is so different than what I've ever experienced before. Some excitement about it."

Session #	Group #	# in Group	Group Worked With	Part identified	What was shared
#240					No Hypnosis
#241			81	20yo & 6 others	20yo sharing. Betrayal is strong. Put it in a box as though it never happened. Only way to survive. Had to enclose it even more. John feels overwhelmed by feelings. Thoughts of vocation just knocked off track. Desire for wife and family were winning out. How to deal with Carl's pushback.
#242					No Hypnosis
#243			81	20yo & 6 others	20yo & John: Heart is coming back online. I was violated in heart and shut down feelings for a "higher calling." Encounters with Carl's shut down spiritual side of me. Like it was a message from God not to go down spiritual path. Light shut off and went underground. Moved me into "controlling state: all was dependent on me. Became island unto myself."
#244					No Hypnosis
#245			81	20yo & 6 others	Moving out of head-world. Trusting feelings more. "New me is maturing and coming forward. So counter to the way I've been. Before, emotions just mean more abuse." Feeling more and more Light in daily experience. Protective shell has come off. Moving into vulnerability. I'm on truer journey. Each step, my voice is getting stronger.
#246			81	20yo & 6 others	Feeling ugly with Carl, his tongue in my mouth. Like part of me died. Body became disconnected. Beatings and kissings so terrifying, body shriveled up. No protected space with mom or Carl. Broken and defeated.
#247	82	20	82	8yo & 19 others	Body became frozen. Rigid in its protection. HS says body consciousness and body are separated. Fear of body revitalizing. Moved in a paralyzed state. Carl's tongue in mouth made me sick.
#248			82	8yo & 19 others	20yo sharing. 5 not receiving Light. Body releasing sick feeling and defilement. By not taking blame, it's a whole new shift in perspective. Self-Blame led always to looking for solution. Vicious circles. As John deals with emotion, body needs to know it's safe. Body wants everyone at a distance. Shield from right shoulder over heart. The more I got hit, the more panic. Left body when kissed. No place is safe.
#249			82	8yo & 19 others	Depths of emotion still inside. Emotions so strong, I went into shell. Carl's energy and mom's are present here. HS clears it. I was wide open. No safe place. When that energy comes at me, I lose my center.
#250			82	8yo & 19 others	Time to walk through the terror. Watching self be beat. Overwhelming emotions. With mom, still some sense of Light. With Carl, descended into darkness.

Session #	Group #	# in Group	Group Worked With	Part identified	What was shared
#251			82	8yo & 19 others	Deep sense of fear and anger. Wants revenge against Carl. Sees Carl was all about Carl. Mom wanted to help, but Carl wanted for himself. Trust I put in him used against me. Can't forgive him.
#252			82	8yo & 19 others	Still pushing back Carl memories. Shattered my spiritual space. Still putting pieces back together. Body/spirit split occurred with Carl abuse. When violated, the Light went out. The Darkness is vast.
#253			82	8yo & 19 others	Deep anger, fear, & terror. Feeling powerless. Lived in a dissociated state. Images of being shattered. Final loss of voice happened with Carl. Spent life keeping everyone away. Deep sadness and grief.
#254			82	8yo & 19 others	20yo: Wants rational answer for something not rational. Carl had his reasons for what was happening, John didn't. Feeling sick. Carl's abuse spiraled into sexuality and relationship with Sarah.
#255			82	8yo & 19 others	Depths of powerlessness and vulnerability. Just want to go away. Still much buried emotion. Need release. Inner message: "Don't feel." Don't show emotion. Got lost. Spiraling deeper into darkness. So lonely. Trapped the darkness inside myself and then lived in it.
#256			82	8yo & 19 others	Block in throat. John feeling his intelligence and personality "coming out." Throat held all he couldn't say. Terror and self-blame are habitual reactions. Perpetual helplessness. Emotionally paralyzed.
#257					No Hypnosis
#258			82	8yo & 19 others	Realizing I developed an anxious, guarded personality. Habitual state: Something is always going to go wrong. Tie to that the self-blame and unworthiness. More body integration.
#259			82	8yo & 19 others	Carried blame a long time. Modus operandi. If I could just get it right, I would be okay. Went more inward. Knife pain on right side. I've lived so I would never be at fault. Felt I didn't deserve God's love. 2 can't connect to the Light.
#260			82	8yo & 19 others	2 from last time. 6yo & 7yo. Afraid of the Light. Afraid it will lead to beating. Afraid to make any move. Holding so much terror they are immobilized. Was shocked into another dimension. Can't connect with rest of the group. Now coming out of that dimensions. It was safe. Something torn apart or ripped. HS find 5 outside the soul. Retrieves them.
#261		Now 25	82	8yo & 24 others	Back to 6yo, 7yo, & 5 retrieved ones. Emotional shutdown. Too intense. Overwhelmed by fear and terror. Internal and external worlds got scrambled at same time. Psyche is splitting all over. More I couldn't find answer, more the terror grew. Better to be enclosed. At least there was quiet. Alone is only safe place.

Session #	Group #	# in Group	Group Worked With	Part identified	What was shared
#262			82	8yo & 24 others	Back to 6yo, 7yo, & 5 retrieved ones. Afraid to feel the terror. Do it slowly. Always tried to run away, but abuse still always happened.
#263			82	8yo & 24 others	John sprained ankle. Back to 6yo, 7yo, & 5 retrieved ones reacted. Confuse accident with violation. Panic and darkness are linked.
#264					No Hypnosis
#265					No Hypnosis
#266			82	8yo & 24 others	HS identifies 3 vortexes. Partly external energy. Keeps emotions spinning. If I can't do something, I get angry at me. Angry at mom, but can't allow it.
#267					No Hypnosis
#268			82	8yo & 24 others	Back to 6yo, 7yo, & 5 retrieved ones. 6yo shares. Having right answer would have given him some control. Obsession now to do everything correctly. 3 of the 7 do not feel safe.
#269					No Hypnosis. Discuss Bishop Tutu's book on forgiveness.
#270			82	8yo & 24 others	Back to 6yo, 7yo, & 5 retrieved ones. Anticipatory anxiety became entrenched. Body became split between head, heart, and intuition. These parts starting to feel in harmony. Feeling more comfortable in body.
#271					No Hypnosis
#272			82	8yo & 24 others	Back to 6yo, 7yo, & 5 retrieved ones. It's a pivotal time. There's a shift happening. Internalized—If I don't know something, then I'm wrong. Forced to come up with something I couldn't come up with. No amount of beating would produce it. Queasiness as it all becomes conscious. Always before, buried it.
#273					No Hypnosis
#274			82	8yo & 24 others	Back to 6yo, 7yo, & 5 retrieved ones. Enclosed in darkness. Not ready to move out. Started with Carl. Touching and kissing drove them inward. Frozen in shock. No frame of reference for this experience. Like body went into dark spot.
#275			82	8yo & 24 others	Back to 6yo, 7yo, & 5 retrieved ones. Intense anger at Carl. Light went out with mom. It became extinct with Carl. Wonders if he was set up. Angry at self for keeping silent.
#276					No Hypnosis
#277			82	8yo & 24 others	Back to 6yo, 7yo, & 5 retrieved ones. An 8yo shares. Healing has moved me from enclosed to conscious and aware. Group has release and integrates.

Acknowledgements

I want to thank the many friends, colleagues, and supporters of Soul-Centered Healing who have given their support and encouragement over so many years. While too many to name individually, there are those who helped directly in bringing this book to print. For their proofreading, editing, or feedback, I want to thank Alan Sanderson, Mary Kay O'Neil, Katharine Mackey, Michael Kivinen, Christopher Bache, Michael Jamail, and Gary Breen. Because of their help, and sharp eyes, this is a better book.

I want to thank "John D." for granting permission to publish his own healing journey as a case study in Soul-Centered Healing. He does this in the hope that it may benefit others—those who have been traumatized by abuse, and those who treat them.

I want to give special thanks again to Katharine Mackey, Gerod's clear channel, for her essential role in the development of Soul-Centered Healing over so many years. I am grateful also for her continued support.

I reserve my deepest gratitude for my wife, Jane. As well as a life partner of thirty-six years, she has truly been a partner in the development of Soul-Centered Healing as well. From managing the household, to typing transcripts, to proofreading manuscripts, she has supported and helped me in more ways than I can count.

Finally, I am grateful to the spirit guides and teachers who work with us in ways mostly unseen. When called upon, they are present during the healing process, and I frequently ask for their support or intervention.

About the Author

Thomas Zinser, Ed.D., is a hypnotherapist, author, and international speaker with a private practice in Grand Rapids, MI. He holds degrees from the University of Notre Dame (B.A.), Xavier University (M.Ed), and received his doctorate in Counseling Psychology from Texas A&M University: Commerce in 1977.

After serving as a staff psychologist at a local psychiatric hospital, Dr. Zinser started in private practice in 1980. In 1987, he was specializing in hypnosis and the treatment of dissociative disorders when he met Katharine Mackey who channeled a spirit entity named Gerod.

Through Katharine, Gerod offered information about specific clients that was helpful in their treatment. He also offered information about spiritual and metaphysical realities in general. After several sessions with Gerod, Dr. Zinser established a clinical collaboration with him that continued for fifteen years.

In addition to helping clients, this collaboration led to an unprecedented mapping of psychic and spirit dimensions of the self. The result was an approach to healing which he called Soul-Centered Healing. Dr. Zinser tells the story of this collaboration, and the healing methods that emerged from it, in his book, *Soul-Centered Healing: A Psychologist's Extraordinary Journey into the Realms of Sub-Personalities, Spirits, and Past Lives.*

A second book, *The Practice of Soul-Centered Healing,* Vol. I, was published in 2013. This book is written for hypnotherapists who wish to incorporate methods of SCH into their own work. It is an instructional manual describing the protocols and procedures and the different phenomena one can encounter. For the non-professional, but interested reader, the book presents a great deal more information on a number of phenomena.

Dr. Zinser offers spiritual counseling and hypnotherapy to individuals who wish to address these psychic and spiritual dimensions in their own healing process. Soul-Centered Healing accepts the validity and importance of what we currently know about the physical, emotional, and psychological levels of an individual. However, Soul-Centered Healing expands this framework and vision to include the psychic and spirit dimensions of a person as well.

You can learn more about Soul-Centered Healing at the website: http://www.soulcenteredhealing.net.

9 780983 429432